Advance Praise for

DANCING WITH THE TIGER

Business is the economic engine of our global society and empowers construction as well as destruction. It is a myth that companies are either entirely good or bad. There are only people, and in ALL companies there are bold change agents who take risks by dancing with the power in order to change its direction. *Dancing With the Tiger* is the deeply meaningful story of these people and the undeniable dynamics of change they are leading towards greater corporate responsibility and sustainability. We are all dependent on their success and there is no other way but to learn from them. I highly recommend this book for its many lessons, insights, and wisdom.

— **Dr. Karl-Henrik Robèrt**, Founder and Chair, The Natural Step

Dancing With the Tiger accurately captures some of the complexity and challenge faced by Nike as a global brand in our attempts to 'do the right thing' in the interests of all our stakeholders. Nattrass and Altomare have had inside seats at Nike as we move ahead step by step on our own path of corporate responsibility. This book is filled with valuable advice from the corporate players themselves who are daily in the global high-stakes game called sustainability. I highly recommend it.

— **Maria Eitel**, Vice President and Senior Advisor for Corporate Responsibility, Nike Inc.

Here, finally, are the personal stories of change agents in the sustainability movement — people inventing more restorative and equitable ways of making a living in place. The oral tradition captured so deftly in *Dancing With the Tiger* gives sustainability a human face, one in which we can recognize ourselves and the difference that we might make. These wayfinders give us the greatest gift, of making the path seem possible. Cultural shifts begin with a buzz, and a buzz always begins with a good story. Pass this one on.

— **Janine M. Benyus**, author of *Biomimicry*

At this point the sustainability movement is just emerging. So as a community, to read andhear about others trying to find their way to becoming more sustainable is both inspiringand educational. One can only hope that *Dancing With the Tiger* will spread the work of the organizations written about so others will pick up the torch and follow.

— **Mayor Hugh O'Reilly**, Resort Municipality of Whistler

Something profound is happening in the world, as society awakens
to a new mind-set and gradually discards an old mind-set. As acceptance
of the reality of a finite Earth displaces the deep-rooted, but flawed, view of
an infinite source and sink, to be taken for granted, humankind is gathering
itself to move into a sustainable future. Brian Nattrass and Mary Altomare
have again chronicled early corporate movers, in this most instructive
and encouraging account.Read it for knowledge and inspiration.

— **Ray C. Anderson**, Founder and Chair, Interface, Inc.

Imagine you're trying to learn the Tango, and Fred Astaire and
Ginger Rogers are your teachers. Reading *Dancing with the Tiger*
will give you an equal level of grace and expertise if you're on the journey
of sustainability. Brian Nattrass and Mary Altomare have written a common
sense yet inspiring book that is based on true stories of real people and
competitive corporations trying to master a new way of operating.
Like the Tango, the steps and movements are not easy for new
students, but the passionate beauty of the dance is worth the effort.
CH2M HILL is proud to be part of this important book. We hope
our story, as well as those of Nike, Starbucks and Whistler Resort,
will help other companies and individuals.
After all, if we are to survive, we must learn from each other.

— **Michael D. Kennedy**, President, Regional Operations, CH2M HILL

Once again, while dancing on the edge, the wings of angels bring us a voice
of something reasonable. The change agents and visionaries of the real work
are deservedly honored here. It is like Dancing with a Tiger. The practicality
of making it real amidst the riotous scramble to stay the same is just the pre-
scription for the next wave of making it up as we go along. They have
perfected the art of storytelling as a metric. Whenever it appears dark on the
edge of the next step, Brian and Mary graciously deliver another thought
provoking, and more importantly practical, set of answers to light the way.

— **Anita M. Burke**, Senior Advisor – Sustainable Development and
Climate Change, Shell Canada Limited

This book provides important detail on how innovative firms create change
that moves them toward the integration of social, environmental, and economic performance. As the book shows, through the lens of The Natural Step
framework, executives and employees can understand the larger context for
corporate action and craft practices appropriate to a company's products and
operations inside and throughout the supplier network. The accounts are

valuable in their rich detail about the entrepreneurial individuals and their strategies within firms. Most importantly, the issues raised are important to the future of all companies. The innovations documented represent a wave of change in the business landscape as forward-thinking firms incorporate the new realities of global society and natural systems into operations and strategy. There is a paucity of information from inside the organization about these changes, thus the authors make an important contribution to our knowledge.

— **Andrea Larson**, Associate Professor of Business Administration, Darden Graduate School of Business Administration, University of Virginia

Read these most significant dance instructions for the 21st century — and then practice. Packed with insights, how-to advice, and captivating stories, they may well spark the sustainability giant in you. Listen to the rhythms of the future and join the dance floor.

— **Mathis Wackernagel**, Ph.D., co-author of *Our Ecological Footprint* and program director at Redefining Progress in California

As the need for responsible global action becomes painfully evident, and while governments are struggling to provide meaningful, concerted direction, it is hopeful that the business sector is demonstrating true leadership. Altomare and Nattrass have provided valuable case studies that should keep us all on task.

— **John R. Emrick**, Chairman & CEO, Norm Thompson Outfitters

Brian Nattrass and Mary Altomare have a unique talent for describing the dire, global consequences of our unsustainable ways in a manner that spurs urgency, understanding and action rather than guilt, denial, and inertia. In *Dancing with the Tiger*, Nattrass and Altomare shine a bright but gentle light on some of the world's leading examples of large, complex organizations experimenting with new, more sustainable ways of doing business. By extracting from these pioneering initiatives the most important lessons learned, the authors have made their own invaluable contribution to our journey toward sustainability. These crisply told stories of corporate courage are an invaluable source of ideas and insights for those of us already out here on the dance floor — and a rousing call to action for those still watching from the bleachers. Above all, *Dancing with the Tiger* is a gift of inspiration. When I finished reading this book, I had a powerful urge to rush to my office and get back to work— even though it was well after 10 p.m. on a Saturday night!

— **Steve Nicholas**, Director, City of Seattle Office of Sustainability & Environment

Brian Nattrass and Mary Altomare mix music with poetry,
and all in the framework of the power of rewriting the stories
of those uniquely human engines — corporations. But not any
corporations. These are corporations peopled by otherwise ordinary
people who also happen to have the vision to perceive that the ultimate
success of what they are trying to do is directly related to their success
in helping to maintain the integrity of the Earth's ecological systems.
The authors don't gloss over the difficulties or failures,
nor do they pretend that their examples are models of sustainable
perfection. Rather, they emphasize that the Earth has limits,
and demonstrate through the stories in this book that learning to
understand and then to live and function within those limits provides
insurance against external ecological and resource instabilities — which
translates to better business. Just as life is not an end, but rather a
journey, so do the authors note that the joy in the dance for
businesses is in the steps toward sustainability — the writing
of the new stories to replace the outmoded old ones.
And finally, what rings throughout this book is the power
of the individual, translated to the power of the particular
collections of individuals in the corporate examples they give,
to make a difference through leading by example, with the
wondrous natural physical and ecological systems of the Earth
serving as the teachers. The reader of this book will come away
better equipped to participate on this beautiful journey
— and to be more successful in the process.
— **Donald W. Aitken**, Ph.D., Former Senior Staff Scientist,
the Union of Concerned Scientists, Former Scientific Coordinator,
the Natural Step USA

Dancing
with the
TIGER

Learning Sustainability
Step by Natural Step

BRIAN NATTRASS & MARY ALTOMARE

Foreword by Nicholas C. Sonntag

NEW SOCIETY PUBLISHERS

To further the dialogue about sustainable business practices and corporate responsibility, you can contact Brian Nattrass and Mary Altomare via e-mail at: innostrat@aol.com

Cataloguing in Publication Data:
A catalog record for this publication is available from the National Library of Canada.

Cover design by Dianne McIntosh. Tiger image ©Corbis.
Illustrations by Z-point Graphics.

Printed in Canada on acid-free, partially recycled (20 percent post-consumer) paper using soy-based inks by Transcontinental/Best Book Manufacturers.

New Society Publishers acknowledges the support of the Government of Canada through the Book Publishing Industry Development Program (BPIDP) for our publishing activities, and the assistance of the Province of British Columbia through the British Columbia Arts Council.

BRITISH
COLUMBIA
ARTS COUNCIL
Supported by the Province of British Columbia

Hardcover ISBN: 0-86571-455-X

Inquiries regarding requests to reprint all or part of *Dancing with the Tiger* should be addressed to New Society Publishers at the address below.

To order directly from the publishers, please add $4.50 shipping to the price of the first copy, and $1.00 for each additional copy (plus GST in Canada). Send check or money order to:

New Society Publishers
P.O. Box 189, Gabriola Island, BC V0R 1X0, Canada
1-800-567-6772

New Society Publishers' mission is to publish books that contribute in funda-mental ways to building an ecologically sustainable and just society, and to do so with the least possible impact on the environment, in a manner that models this vision. We are committed to doing this not just through education, but through action. We are acting on our commitment to the world's remaining ancient forests by phasing out our paper supply from ancient forests worldwide. This book is one step towards ending global deforestation and climate change. It is printed on acid-free paper that is **100% old growth forest-free** (100% post-consumer recycled), processed chlorine free, and printed with vegetable based, low VOC inks. For further information, or to browse our full list of books and purchase securely, visit our website at: www.newsociety.com

NEW SOCIETY PUBLISHERS   www.newsociety.com

Dedication

To my daughter Sarah,
whose life, and those of the children of tomorrow,
is my inspiration for engaging in this work;
and to my father and mother with gratitude for
providing me with the many opportunities and insights
that helped make this path possible.
BN

To those I hold most precious, Staci, Kristen, and Mingo,
and especially Kylee and Sydney, tomorrow's children,
who will inherit the world we are creating;
and to my parents, brother and sisters
for teaching me to love, question, and dream.
MA

Finally, to each other
for the deepening courage, commitment,
and love that is emerging
through our shared lives and work.
BN & MA

Contents

List of Figures

Acknowledgements

THE WORK OF ADVANCING corporate responsibility and sustainability within organizations is not easy work, while at the same time it is deeply satisfying. The men and women we write about in this book, many named and quoted, have truly become our heroes. Without exception we admire them enormously. For them, sustainability has become a symbol and a rallying point for creating a better world, healthier organizations, and a brighter future for their own and all the world's children.

As you read about the sustainability pioneers in this book, remember that in almost all cases they are bucking the system in one way or another to help create a path to a better world. In fact, each of them is walking the path less traveled, and we only know that there is a path by following in their footsteps. Sometimes we see those footsteps leading down blind alleys, or making sharp turns to the left or right, or signs that the person has stumbled, yet in all cases the only way forward to a more sustainable world is to reorient oneself, and begin the journey anew. A healthier, more vital, secure, equitable and prosperous world for all is the vision they pursue. We who follow are all in their debt.

To each of the organizations that entrusted us with their story, we are deeply grateful. To the sustainability pioneers named, and to their colleagues who were not, you have both our gratitude and our admiration.

We give special thanks to our colleagues around the world at The Natural Step International — particularly in the United States and Canada — including Karl-Henrik Robèrt for his ground-breaking contributions to sustainability research and education, Catherine Gray, Executive Director of The Natural Step in the USA, Dru Palliser-Teed for her ongoing support in our work, and Jamie MacDonald for his recommendations on the manuscript. Special thanks also to Judith Brand for her meticulous editing and indexing, and to Eckhard Zeidler of Z-point Graphics for taking our ideas and developing them into clear figures and illustrations.

Our publishers at New Society, Christopher and Judith Plant, have themselves been sustainability pioneers for well over a quarter of a century. They have provided a forum for the voices of many of the most original and innovative writers of our time in the critical domain of creating a sustainable future. On behalf of all the readers of this book, as well as ourselves, we thank Christopher and Judith for providing a forum for the insights and views expressed here.

Preface

WHEN WE WROTE *The Natural Step for Business* three years ago, it represented the culmination of five years of doctoral studies and research on learning and change in human systems as applied to sustainable development. Our interest then was finding and testing a framework for sustainability that could be used effectively by organizations of all kinds, including businesses, governments at every level, and non-profit organizations. *The Natural Step for Business* details the results of that search by documenting the background of The Natural Step, an international, non-profit sustainability research, education and consulting organization, and the development of The Natural Step framework for sustainability. We studied and documented the experience of how four companies, innovative leaders in their industries, applied the framework: IKEA, Scandic Hotels, The Collins Companies, and Interface, Inc. We concluded then, and have confirmed through subsequent experience, that The Natural Step framework provides companies with an excellent framework for understanding sustainability and how it relates to their strategic planning and operations.

Dancing with the Tiger focuses on the actual experience of four icon organizations, internationally known in their fields — Nike, Starbucks, CH2M HILL, and the resort community of Whistler — and explores both the theory and practice of personal and organizational learning and change, leadership, and innovation in the areas of corporate responsibility and sustainable development. It tells the stories of how individuals, groups, and organizations in corporate, government, and non-profit sectors are working toward greater social and environmental responsibility while they are dancing with the demands of continuing financial performance and other stakeholder expectations. We explore some of the dynamics of this process in the business realities of both strategy and day-to-day operations, and elicit specific advice to the reader based on the actual corporate and government experience of these pathfinders. It is our hope, as you read these accounts, that you will find inspiration, ideas, and practical ways to begin or strengthen your own journey toward greater organizational responsibility, sustainability, and long-term prosperity.

Brian Nattrass and Mary Altomare
Whistler, British Columbia
March, 2002

Foreword

Nicholas C. Sonntag

IN JANUARY, 1996 while visiting Stockholm, Sweden, I had the good fortune to share a private lunch with oncologist and scientist Dr. Karl-Henrik Robèrt, founder of The Natural Step (TNS), at the TNS headquarters then located on Skeppsholmen in beautiful Stockholm harbor. Little did I realize how significant this meeting would be for my eventual stay in Sweden as the Executive Director of the Stockholm Environment Institute (SEI) from 1996 to 2000, and since then as President of CH2M HILL Canada Limited.

The lunch with Karl-Henrik had been suggested to me by my colleagues and close friends, Brian Nattrass and Mary Altomare, who thought there was a high likelihood that Karl-Henrik and I would find common ground in our respective paths to sustainable development. Fifteen minutes into our lunch, we did indeed discover a world of exciting parallels in our passion around sustainability, and the basic concepts and principles for providing a 'road map' to take sustainable development from concept to action. Although we had come from very different backgrounds — mine in engineering and operations research, and his in cancer research — we had arrived at a very similar place: a total commitment to the urgent need for action; a belief that when people and organizations understand the need for urgency, they will want to do the 'right thing' to sustain the future of the planet; and, for these people and organizations to do the 'right thing,' they need easily comprehended frameworks, tools, and processes to guide their action — just the sort that are described in detail in this book.

Since that time, Brian and Mary have become internationally respected leaders in corporate responsibility and sustainability. They are the North American practice leaders in The Natural Step framework for sustainability and work with some of the most progressive corporations, municipalities, and governments in the U.S. and Canada. *Dancing with the Tiger* makes an invaluable and immense contribution by sharing, and analyzing, the rich experience of four leading organizations — three large global corporations and one famous mountain resort community: Nike, Starbucks, CH2M HILL and the Resort Municipality of Whistler — in their quest for sustainability. To accomplish this, Brian and Mary worked tirelessly, in some cases over a number of years, to establish an open environment of trust within each of the organizations described.

This trust allowed them to work intimately with key executives in each organization and extract invaluable insights — warts and all — leading to a rich synthesis of common themes and dynamics, which are essential to organizations wanting to become part of the solution. As both an engineer and a senior executive with one of the case corporations in this book, I can personally attest to the value of their work to our organization, and to the sustainability insights accurately captured on the pages to follow.

The need for a focus on sustainability arises because our global society is on a perilously unsustainable course. Our planet and humanity are under great stress. No one can credibly deny the evidence that mankind is severely impacting the ecological, and undermining the social and economic, dimensions of our world. Not a day passes without us hearing an increasing chorus of concern from all sectors of society witnessing a frightening range of pressing issues. For example: the loss of species biodiversity in all of the world's major ecosystems; the pollution of our air, water and soils through totally inadequate management of man-made wastes; the increasing urban sprawl and traffic congestion found in our major cities; the increasing disparity between the rich and the poor in both the developed and developing world; the lack of any basic health care or education in so many communities in developing countries; the desperate situation of the more than one billion people who live in abject poverty; the rapid decline in cultural and spiritual diversity as more and more cultural groups are absorbed into the global commercial community; and so on. As depressing and overwhelming as many of these issues are, we cannot let ourselves become pessimistic, for pessimism can quickly become a self-fulfilling prophecy. Rather we must maintain hope and work in new and creative ways to find solutions to these issues, and most importantly, support and encourage implementation of these solutions no matter how daunting the challenge. We must build new and innovative partnerships among people, governments, corporations, and non-profit organizations that actively look for the synergies, which can generate awesome, not just adequate, outcomes.

We must also find new and engaging models that communicate and support a systemic view of our world, a view that explicitly captures the dynamic — and uncertain — interactions among our ecological, social and economic systems at all scales, from our local communities and cities, to the whole planet. Finally, and arguably most important-ly, we must actively share our experiences and help each other (e.g., within and between individuals, communities, countries and corpora-tions, etc.) to learn, create, and adapt as quickly as possible. History has shown that through open sharing and collective learning, societies are able to change more quickly. Clearly the speed with which we are able to make the transition to sustainability is paramount and thus sharing and learning are key to our success. This new work by Brian and Mary, *Dancing with the Tiger*, makes a unique and extraordinari-ly valuable contribution to this need by describing the internal dynamics of change of four leading organizations and extracting the lessons learned directly from the executives, engineers, and imple-menters of change within the organizations. We learn first-hand the steps taken, challenges encountered, and strategies employed by these organizations as they embrace corporate responsibility on their jour-ney to sustainability.

Since the report of the Bruntland Commission in 1987, and the resulting 1992 Rio Earth Summit, society has taken many significant steps — and in some cases great steps — to implement actions sup-portive of sustainable development. Although each of the organizations described in *Dancing with the Tiger* must be praised and supported for their commitment to the goal of a sustainable future, their actions alone are not enough, nor have they gone far enough. However, their successes — and failures — provide rich experience and insights into how to move from inaction to commitment to action.

We are an experience-based species. As with most other living crea-tures, we learn through experience — by doing. Ideally, we build on our successes and learn from our mistakes, although one might seri-ously doubt our consistency and commitment to learning given the continuing decline of the planet's ecosystems. What is critical, howev-er, is to survive our planetary mistakes. We must learn from them, communicate the lessons to others, and then provide the necessary leadership to take us to a better outcome. This approach has often been called *adaptive management* and truly serves as the underpinning of the case studies provided in this book.

Dancing with the Tiger is no ordinary collection of case studies. Rather, each chapter is written with a specific sequence in mind to provide full expression of the insights the authors have gleaned from these pathfinding organizations. As a result, the case studies integrate into a history of sustainability lessons and insights, where the impact of the *whole* story exceeds that of its individual parts and each chapter depends on what has come before. Throughout this book, and all the work behind its creation, Brian and Mary have truly provided us with a wonderful gift. They have shared their passion and intellect, and challenged us to join them in the *dance* of change. As they so clearly point out, dancing requires knowledge, experience, communications, coordination, and focus. The dance of sustainability is rife with uncertainty, surprise, accomplishment, and disappointment. What they seek is a deep commitment not to tame the *tiger* — for that is impossible, and ultimately disastrous — but rather to understand it, and learn to dance (e.g., adapt) in a way that is *safe to fail* rather than *fail-safe*. We must strive to survive the experiment and seek continual improvement through learning. Failure to do so will be our ultimate demise. Thus success is paramount to humanity's long-term survival.

In *Dancing with the Tiger*, Brian and Mary have added a critically important chapter to the sustainability literature. The insights and wisdom described will be invaluable to readers seeking guidance to the challenges of corporate responsibility and sustainable development. Further, the questions and challenges posed will provide a basis for future work in this very urgent area of enquiry. Without a doubt, humankind is dramatically shaping its planetary future in unprecedented ways. We are now at a time of reckoning and all of us are challenged to take action. I sincerely hope that each of you who takes the time to read *Dancing with the Tiger* will personally take on this challenge and work aggressively within your family, community, and place of work to challenge others to take on this *dance* of change. Our common future depends upon it.

Nicholas C. Sonntag,
President, CH2M HILL Canada Limited
Former Executive-Director, Stockholm Environment Institute

CHAPTER 1

THE DANCE OF SUSTAINABILITY

And when you get the choice to sit it out or dance
I hope you dance. — Sanders and Sillers[1]

THERE IS A QUIET REVOLUTION occurring in boardrooms, design studios, factories, and government agencies across North America and around the industrial world. This revolution has the promise and potential of eclipsing any industrial or commercial revolution before it. It comes with many names, such as sustainable development, sustainability, The Natural Step, biomimicry, natural capitalism, ecological footprint, Factor 10, ecological design, corporate social responsibility, and many others. The promise is that humankind will finally attain that long-dreamed state of global prosperity, creativity, harmony with nature, freedom, security, and peace that is our highest aspiration. The danger is that this benign revolution is not emerging rapidly enough to forestall the needless tragedies of want and destitution, poverty, starvation, and warfare that result around the world from an unconsciously "take-make-waste" socio-economic system. So while the trajectory of the sustainability revolution is filled with promise, the velocity and eventual outcome of this revolution is uncertain.

Now is the time, perhaps more than any other in all of human history, when people from every corner of the globe and from every walk of life are being called to take a stand for a bountiful future of opportunity for all humanity. It is not sufficient that revolutionaries emerge from the destitution of impoverished third-world countries. This time in history calls for sustainability revolutionaries in pinstripe suits on Wall Street, for sustainability revolutionaries with computers and periodic tables in laboratories and classrooms, for sustainability revolutionaries in sales, marketing, advertising, and public relations.

1

It calls for the ordinary person who believes in the possibility of creating an extraordinary world.

Lance Armstrong, three-time winner of the world's most grueling athletic event — the Tour de France — has become one of our heroes. Lance is an outstanding athlete, yet more than this, he is a man whose life story inspires hope and reminds us to value what is most precious and irreplaceable: life. In his book, *It's Not About the Bike: My Journey Back to Life,*[2] Lance tells the story of defeating his most formidable opponent — cancer — and, in the process, his discovery of who he really is and can be. At the age of 25, Lance learned that he had testicular cancer and that it had spread throughout his body. One day he was invulnerable, a world-class athlete training for the Tour de France, rationalizing away his symptoms until one day they became undeniable. At that point, all of Lance's focus and energy turned to running the only race that really matters: the race for his life.

At the outset of his book, Lance writes:

> Death is not exactly cocktail party conversation, I know, and neither is cancer, or brain surgery, or matters below the waist. But I'm not here to make a lot of conversation. I want to tell the truth.[3]

The truth he tells is about an ordinary man — by his own admission, by no means a saint — who performs the extraordinary in his struggle for life itself.

Like Lance, in our book and work, we strive to tell the truth — in our case the truth about the body corporate and finding pathways to a healthy and prosperous future. We find that sustainability is not exactly cocktail party conversation either; but the truth is, our global society is heading in an unsustainable direction ultimately leading to the impoverishment of us all — every one of us is involved and affected, none of us can escape the corruption of the global biosphere. The evidence for this statement is accumulating rapidly and is widely available, some of which we'll discuss in the second part of chapter 2. Yet for a variety of reasons, perhaps out of ignorance or the false comfort of denial, collectively we are not heeding the warning signs.

So why do we feel hope? For one important reason: we have had the privilege of working with and witnessing ordinary folks accomplishing extraordinary feats. They work in corporations, government agencies, and non-profit organizations that are striving to "do the right thing" in the fast-paced, demanding, and often confusing and contradictory world of the early 21st century. We do not pretend, nor do they, that these organizations are perfect, that they have all or even the best of answers, or even that they always know all the right questions to ask when it comes to sustainability. But we know firsthand that these individuals, and the organizations in which they work, are applying their best creative and managerial thinking to the challenge and task of sustainable development. It is a daunting task. We liken their experience to the challenge of dancing with a tiger.

Why dancing with the tiger? The tiger is truly the lord of its realm. A deadly predator of exquisite beauty, it is cunning, stealthy, and capable of instantaneous and lethal response when threatened or when hunting for prey. The tiger is at the top of its food chain. Yet despite its ferocity and success as a predator, the future of the tiger is in serious jeopardy. Extinction looms, as the global population of these magnificent creatures has fallen from an estimated 100,000 tigers in the wild at the beginning of the 20th century to approximately 5,000 remaining at the beginning of the 21st century. The tiger is fierce, tough, and competitive, yet completely unaware, and at the mercy, of the complex human-made forces that are cumulatively and persistently contributing to its extinction: degradation and loss of its habitat and cruel death at the hands of poachers harvesting its body for human use.

The modern industrial system is like the tiger. This capitalist, market-based, industrial economy has become the most powerful, innovative, and formidable force ever unleashed by the mind of man — it has become the dominant system in the complex web of global societies, cultures and economies. Today's multinational corporations are the leading players in this realm. Yet the real foundation for this entire web, the Earth's natural capital, is everywhere, and often invisibly, under attack: not at the hands of another species, but at our own hands. Natural capital — those resources, living systems and ecosystem services that provide such essentials of life as rich topsoil, pure air and water that are ultimately the source of all wealth — is being rapidly and seriously eroded by the very means of success that have brought the modern industrial system to its current position of global dominance.

Like those of the tiger, our systems of survival are under siege, and frighteningly few of our modern institutions seem aware of this fact or acknowledge the role they play, and the responsibility they hold, in creating this reality or in finding solutions. The organizations that are becoming more aware are also becoming the leaders in the movement toward sustainable development and corporate social and environmental responsibility. We believe these organizations are not only the competitors that will be best positioned for their own long-term survival, but they can also be a source of innovation and solutions for the future we so urgently need to create.

The business strategies being utilized by most corporate tigers today are like those characterized by the ill-fated Maginot Line created by the French prior to World War II. This was a line of massive, heavily armed fortresses built by the French between 1929 and 1940 along their borders with Germany and Italy. Intended to prevent the Nazi military forces from making a land assault on the French Republic, this massive undertaking, like a modern day Great Wall of China, lulled the French people into a false sense of security — one that helped lead to their easy defeat when new circumstances presented themselves. The Maginot Line was designed perfectly for the previous war, but failed utterly to be effective in securing the French against the new tactics and technology of mobile armored warfare and attack-aircraft employed by the Nazis at the beginning of World War II. Similarly, from the perspective of sustainability, most corporations and governments today are focused on a relationship with the natural world and global society that is outdated and obsolete.

Just as the French failed to perceive a new kind of threat to their security that was surreptitiously taking shape against them, and as Lance failed to give attention to the warning signs that threatened his health, so the vast majority of modern corporations, governments, and municipalities fundamentally fail to perceive the threat inherent in carrying on business in the current paradigm, the mode of business characterized by author Paul Hawken as the "take-make-waste" system of commerce. We live with false security born of a lack of awareness or of denial, believing that the strategies that have served us thus far will continue to ensure our success simply because they have worked in the past. But as Einstein's dictum warns us: we cannot solve our problems with the same level of thinking that created them. We need to shift paradigms, and we need individuals, teams and organizations that are willing to engage in the dance that such a shift entails.

The truth is, if we continue along our current course — the contamination of our global food and water supplies, the chemical transformation of the very air that we breathe through the release of pollutants and greenhouse gases, the rising levels of cancer and other immune system-related diseases through the release of toxic synthetic chemicals into the biosphere — we will sow, albeit unconsciously, the seeds of our own destruction. Yet there is another truth we need to face: while this is happening on a wider ecological scale, our organizations, and the individuals within them, are caught in their own complex survival game.

Obsessed by the tyranny of the financial markets, driven to relentlessly increase sales and profits quarter by quarter, forced to match every competitor's advance with an equal or greater advance of their own, determined to seize market share from adversaries like a tiger snatching prey from the jaws of another, today's corporations leave the actions needed to ensure long-term survival to someone else. The problems are once again deferred to someone else's watch. It is as though our leading institutions, both commercial and governmental, are afflicted with a kind of myopia, a tyranny of today's urgencies, that prevents them from taking a long-term view of their own best interests and those of the society that they serve and in which they are so intrinsically intertwined.

Fortunately, there are exceptions to this unconscious and ultimately self-destructive behavior, and it is often the lone individual, or a small teams of individuals, who are stirring the beast from within. Often working deep within the corporation or government organization under the radar, these agents of change are striving to raise the consciousness of their organizations and to pioneer a new and fundamentally more sustainable way of doing business. They are choosing to dance with the tigers of the global industrial system, of the industry in which they are located, and often of the very organizations that employ them.

This book is about the creative and groundbreaking work being performed by some of these individuals and teams. Their stories exemplify the innovative steps of pathfinders, those individuals who take one step after another through a demanding, sometimes dangerous, and often exciting jungle in order to develop better products, processes and practices that are more compatible with the living systems on which we utterly depend.

Just as Lance Armstrong made the decision to choose life, so must each of us. This book contains stories of people who have made that choice and who are working to influence the long-term sustainability of their institutions — both commercial and governmental — and of our society. In our previous book, *The Natural Step for Business*,[4] we describe the innovation and organizational learning of four very progressive corporations, two of them publicly traded, which are pioneers in the growing movement toward corporate responsibility and sustainable development. In the present volume, we focus on the transformative work of individuals and teams in four leading entities — two well-known multinational corporations, one global consulting firm, and one internationally renowned resort community — each an icon in its respective domain.

These four organizations are very different from each other, yet each is respected worldwide as the leader in its field: Nike, one of the most recognized brands and the leading sports and fitness company; Starbucks, the leading specialty coffee retailer that has revolutionized its industry; CH2M HILL, a great leading professional services firm with a substantial environmental engineering practice; and the resort municipality of Whistler, British Columbia, internationally acclaimed as the premier mountain resort community in North America.

As advisors on sustainable business practices and corporate responsibility working directly with the sustainability innovators and pathfinders within these organizations, we were able to share their triumphs and frustrations, come to understand their motivations, observe their behavior, and witness the challenges of their roles as internal change agents for sustainable development and greater corporate responsibility. It was through this experience that the metaphor "dancing with the tiger" arose. How does one dance with the tiger? You do it carefully, skillfully, courageously, in tune to the same music, and advancing step by natural step.

While dance comes in many forms, the dance of moving sustainability forward in organizations and communities requires both clever choreography and deft footwork. You need to synchronize your planning and performance with your partner in such a way that you move sustainability forward without getting attacked or devoured. Sometimes you need to take one step back in order to take two steps forward. As a choreographer, you need to lead others by being a few beats ahead of them, but not so far ahead that they cannot see where you are going. You need to understand the capabilities and limitations of those individuals and systems you work with in this dance. In other words, the dance of sustainability is not a solo performance. It is a dance you do in relationship with the tiger whether that tiger is your company, community, or the very market economy itself.

This is no small challenge. So why would you want to engage in a dance with a force that would as soon eat you as dance with you? For those individuals whose stories we tell in this book, the underlying reason is simply that our common future depends upon it — the future success and prosperity of our organizations and communities, the future well-being of our children and grandchildren, and the future possibilities of humankind and countless other species.

In *The Natural Step for Business,* we suggested that humanity is now engaged in a challenge of evolutionary proportions. We further suggested that ecological factors must become integral to our understanding of what it means to be successful in the organizations of the 21st century. Men and women in their roles in corporations, governments and non-governmental organizations, and as citizens, householders, and parents, are challenged to become conscious of the evolutionary role that our organizations and communities play in the future of the human race and life as we know it. We are all called upon to move beyond blame and to take responsibility for the conscious evolution of our human systems. We need to begin holding ourselves, and others, accountable for contributing to a more sustainable direction for humanity.

The individuals, organizations and communities featured in this book choose to dance with the tiger because it is a monumentally important task and challenge. Ultimately, it is the most vital, and many would say, the most exciting dance of all. This is the definitive dance of change: the transformation of the global system from one that is on an unsustainable trajectory to global misery and a fortress world, to one that leads the way to a vibrant, healthy, secure and prosperous future for all humanity. The purpose of this dance is not to change the tiger's stripes. The purpose is to inoculate the tiger with a new idea known as "sustainability" in order to ensure its future health, so that it can express its power, leadership, influence and creative energy in new, enlivening, and more sustainable ways.

It is our privilege to tell the stories of skillful performers — choreographers and dancers in the guise of employees innovating more sustainable practices on the production line, baristas in cappuccino bars selling fair trade coffee and saving coffee grounds for compost, municipal planners creating comprehensive sustainability plans, engineers designing closed-loop manufacturing systems — who are dancing with a force that holds promise and sometimes risk for them personally and for their organizations. These choreographers and dancers perform this dance in a variety of ways and for a range of reasons, but they share the following traits:

- They are aware that the health of global economic, ecological, and social systems is integrally interconnected and interdependent.

- They realize that sound business, strategy, and management decisions — whether implemented for financial profit, social profit or in a government agency —— ignore the realities of these interconnections and interdependencies at their peril.

- They operate with an expanded sense of social responsibility that is based on the belief that "doing the right thing" needs to be a deep-seated core value of any citizen, community or organization in the 21st century if we are to create a vibrant and prosperous future, and that integrating more sustainable practices *is* the right thing to do.

- They take personal responsibility for the conscious evolution of their organizations and communities in a more enduring and sustainable direction.

The following chapters invite you to join us as witnesses to the dance, and hopefully will inspire you to take up the dance yourself or add new steps to your existing repertoire.

In chapter 2 we explore the choreography of sustainability: how the dance of sustainability is put together. This chapter is divided into two parts. In the first part, we examine some of the insights that arise when we use systems thinking to understand the nature of sustainability; we outline a step-by-step strategic planning model for moving an organization toward more sustainable practices; and we look at how various approaches and strategies to sustainability and the growing array of tools, actions, metrics, and monitoring and reporting systems for sustainability, fit together in a complementary set to help organizations improve their sustainability performance. We also provide examples of how these approaches, strategies, actions, tools, and measuring and reporting systems are being used in diverse organizations. In the second part, we explore some of the symptoms: the warning signs that provide us with vital information about the state of health of our current global systems. Some readers will already be familiar with the details of these symptoms and may want to skip this section. If you do not have this familiarity, we urge you to look at the material and explore the sources we cite for more information.

In chapter 3 we introduce the main stories that we tell in this book, stories from Nike, Starbucks, Whistler and CH2M HILL, stories of the many individuals, teams, and departments engaged in this path-breaking work of sustainable development. We also explore the dynamics of the transformative change in which they are engaged: how new ideas and concepts spread and take hold in organizations (innovation diffusion), how change agents identify which steps to take in their dance (finding leverage in the system), and where to intervene in the system for the most profound results (prioritizing action).

In chapters 4 through 7 we take an in-depth look at the sustainability experiences of three global corporations, Nike, Starbucks, and CH2M HILL, and one community, Whistler. Each is a tiger in its own domain. None of the corporations in this book is now functioning in an ecologically or socially sustainable manner. None could pretend to do so. However, we focus on the many people, policies, and practices within these companies that support and encourage an authentic quest to integrate sustainability into their operations.

The chapter on Whistler, British Columbia, North America's premier four-season mountain resort community, provides insights into the experience of how a community can consciously choose to make ecological, social, and economic sustainability the foundation stones for its future well-being and prosperity despite the seeming paradox inherent within the concept of being a "sustainable destination resort." We recount the experience of several key organizations: the Resort Municipality of Whistler (the municipal government), Whistler/Blackcomb Ski Resorts, (a division of Intrawest, North America's leading developer of four-season, village-centered mountain resorts), the Fairmont Chateau Whistler (Whistler's icon flagship hotel), Tourism Whistler (the global marketing board for the resort), and AWARE (the Association of Whistler Area Residents for the

Environment, a community environmental activist organization), and we tell the stories of some of the individuals who are leading the dance, and inviting others in the community to join.

In chapter 8 we summarize some key sustainability themes, lessons, and insights that emerged for us as a result of working with these and other organizations. We focus on six themes that have emerged from our work with the organizations featured in this book as well as those in *The Natural Step for Business;* explore four dynamics that we have observed that influence the velocity and direction of change in organizations; and provide examples of steps that some additional organizations have taken toward instituting more sustainable practices.

In chapter 9 we look to the future and discuss critical issues of sustainable development and social and environmental responsibility for today's organizations. We consider some of the clear benefits experienced by organizations today as they authentically engage and experiment with sustainability in their operations, and consider these as guideposts on our way to creating the kind of world that we would want to bequeath to our children and the generations to follow.

In the appendix we include some basic background on The Natural Step framework for sustainability and the basic science upon which that framework is built.[5]

As you read the stories in the following chapters, remember that sustainability is a journey. We recognize that the organizations featured in this book are still at the beginning steps of this journey. They are not perfect. They have a long way to go, as we all do. However, we can say for certain that there *are* people operating within each of these organizations who understand how important this work is and who are genuinely making a difference in many ways in which the organizations conduct their affairs. We also ask you to remember that ultimately we are all walking in the tiger's realm. Even if we choose not to dance directly with the tiger, if we choose to confront the tiger in other ways, at the end of the day we are all engaged in the same dance as the tiger — the dance of sustainability and survival.

Finally, we offer this excerpt from a popular song written by Mark D. Sanders and Tia Sillers and performed by LeeAnn Womack that captures some of our own sentiment and the spirit we hope you find in the stories you are about to read:

I hope you never fear those mountains in the distance

Never settle for the path of least resistance

Livin' might mean takin' chances but they're worth takin'

Lovin' might be a mistake but it's worth makin'

Don't let some hell-bent heart leave you bitter

When you come close to sellin' out reconsider

Give the heavens above more than just a passing glance

And when you get the choice to sit it out or dance

I hope you dance. . .[6]

Even if it means dancing with the tiger.

CHAPTER 2

A COMPLEX CHOREOGRAPHY

While we still have a chance, let's face the music
and dance. — Irving Berlin[1]

L IKE A COMPLEX AND INTRICATE form of dance, the art and science
of sustainability is learned with effort, applied with concentration, and appreciated in its artful execution. In our consulting work
with the case subjects of this book — Nike, Starbucks, CH2M HILL,
and the leading players in the resort municipality of Whistler, as well
as in many other venues — we have frequently reflected on why it is
often so difficult to define and work with the concept of sustainability, and to learn the necessary steps to perform this new dance
gracefully, skillfully, and effectively.

We are now clear that the practice of sustainability is as much an
art as it is a science. It is the human factor that stands between the
unsustainable present and a future sustainable world, not the science,
engineering or technology. It is only through people — through the
heart, mind, and will of each individual — that the innovation of sustainability will be diffused and adopted within our corporations, our
governments and ultimately throughout our world. We have
observed that three challenges in particular need to be overcome as
we engage in this unfamiliar, and sometimes unwelcome, dance of
sustainability.

LEARNING NEW STEPS FOR A NEW DANCE

First of all, the prospect of humanity living in an unsustainable relationship with nature on a global scale is unique to our time. We are
faced with an unprecedented danger, and a challenge of planetary
proportions. Our perceptions of the world have not yet caught up
with the reality of the world in which we live. Throughout most of
human history, we have survived by reacting to threats that can be

experienced directly through our five senses. When we saw, felt, smelled, tasted or touched danger, our response was to fight or flee — the experience was immediate. The challenge facing us today is distinctly different. By the time we are certain of the threat we face because we can confirm it with our five senses, we may have crossed ecological thresholds that are irreversible. We will already be in the jaws of the tiger before we even know it is there.

Secondly, we need to employ a different mode of thinking than the way we were taught to think about, and thus perceive, the world. We need to become systems thinkers. We are currently taught in school, and elsewhere, to perceive the world primarily in terms of objects that can be individually studied and understood. This approach suggests that in every complex system the behavior of the whole can be understood from the properties of its parts. In contrast, our growing understanding of how systems work reveals that a complex system is a collection of parts *and* their interrelationships that interact over some period of time and produce a behavior. This behavior is an *emergent property* of the system. "Wellness," for example, can be seen as an emergent property of the healthy relationships among the parts that make up the human body. If a part is not healthy, the system is not healthy. If an important relationship among the parts is not functioning, the system is not healthy. Although the system cannot exist without its most vital parts — a healthy human body cannot exist without its heart, for example — an emergent property of the system, in this case, wellness, cannot be found solely in its parts. This means we cannot understand or guess the behavior of the system based exclusively on our understanding of the properties of the individual parts. A system's emergent properties arise from the pattern of interactions and relationships among the parts. When you dissect the system, you destroy this pattern of relationships.

Systems develop as nested hierarchies (systems within systems, networks within networks) of increasing complexity. For example, the nested hierarchy of living systems can be described as including cells, organs, organisms, groups, organizations, society, and supranational systems. In such a nested hierarchy, each higher level of complexity exhibits properties that do not exist at lower levels. Cells and their relationships contribute to the formation of organs, organs and their relationships contribute to the formation of organisms, organisms and their relationships contribute to the formation of groups, and so on.

Sustainability — and unsustainability for that matter — is an emergent property of a nested hierarchy of socioeconomic and ecological systems, just as wellness is an emergent property of a nested hierarchy of cells, organs and systems (e.g. circulatory, respiratory, cardiovascular) within the physical body. In other words, sustainability emerges from the interactions and interrelationships of multiple subsystems in the global socioeconomic-ecological system. This means we need to look at the parts *and* the relationships among the parts that make up the global socioeconomic-ecological system to begin to understand sustainability. Because sustainability is an emergent property of the highly complex and interwoven global system, it is inaccurate to suggest that we can create sustainable companies or sustainable communities if society is unsustainable at the global level.

Although sustainability emerges at the global system level, our sphere of influence, control and action resides in the subsystems that make up the larger system: our households, organizations, and communities. If we want sustainability to be the emergent property of the larger socioeconomic-ecological system, we need to figure out what relationships among the parts are most likely to produce that outcome. We cannot create sustainable organizations and communities. We can, however, create organizations, communities and interrelationships that contribute more to the possibility of a sustainable global socioeconomic-ecological system outcome than an unsustainable one. In other words, we can make decisions and take actions that increase the probability of a sustainable global society.

These concepts have important implications for how we think about the world. For example, rather than seeing the world as independent parts that can be best understood through specialized analysis, systems thinking involves:

- Seeing the living world as a network of relationships and thinking in terms of networks and interconnections;
- Seeing that living systems are more than parts, they are patterns in an intricate web of relationships;
- Seeing beyond what appear to be isolated and independent incidents to those deeper patterns;
- Seeing every structure as the manifestation of underlying processes (systems thinking is always process thinking);

- Seeing knowledge as a network of interrelated concepts and models;
- Developing the ability to shift attention between systems levels; and
- Developing the ability to shift attention from objects to relationships.

A particular challenge posed by systems thinking is the need to develop an integrative as well as an analytical approach to understanding the systems in which we live. Unfortunately, an integrative approach can make us feel uncomfortable because:

> [K]nowledge of the system is always incomplete. Surprise is inevitable. There will rarely be unanimity of agreement among peers — only an increasingly credible line of tested argument. Not only is the science incomplete, the system itself is a moving target, evolving because of the impacts of management and the progressive expansion of the scale of human influences on the planet.[2]

We would naturally prefer to have certainty, not surprises; stationary, not moving targets. So it is easier to fall back on more familiar modes of thinking and behavior because they make us feel more secure and sure, and they have helped us succeed so far. The challenge is that these modes of thinking are inadequate to help us understand the problems of the 21st century and to think our way through to sustainable solutions.

A third reason why sustainability and systems thinking are challenging to define and work with is that we do not have a common language to describe and understand these terms or the phenomena they represent. We have a rich vocabulary to describe the objectives, policies and success indicators that are related to economic growth because we have more than two centuries of history that equates progress with seeking and achieving growth. We do not have a similarly shared vocabulary for sustainability or sustainable development. We are just beginning to develop, learn, use and share that language.

As things stand today, in the world's dominant system, growth is still considered to be the hallmark of progress and a paramount goal of human endeavor. The new dance in which we are engaged asks us to reconcile that goal of growth with the limitations of a finite natural environment given that

> [T]he sheer scale of human enterprise — the number of people, the growing levels of material consumption and production — may exceed the carrying capacity of the planet. Human lifestyles and the industrial systems that support them threaten to change the climate, degrade ecosystems and deplete the earth's biological wealth, altering the natural environment on a global scale. And the 21st century may consign billions of the yet unborn to an existence of poverty, hunger and hardship. The destitution of multitudes amidst unprecedented levels of wealth and comfort for the privileged could portend social unrest and violence on unprecedented scales, challenging the very notion of global civilization.[3]

So if the concepts of sustainability and systems thinking are so new and unfamiliar, if we do not have a shared language to describe and understand these concepts, and if sustainability is an emergent property of a system that we can only influence on the level of its subsystems, how can we even pretend to make sense out of what actions and decisions we should take as responsible citizens, organizations and communities?

Given the discussion above, it is not surprising that a consensus definition of sustainability does not exist. One of the most commonly cited definitions of sustainability originated with the World Commission on Environment and Development (the Brundtland Commission) in 1987 and states that development is sustainable if it "meets the needs of the present without compromising the ability of future generations to meet their own needs."[4] More recent attempts to define sustainability focus on harmonizing ecological, social and economic dimensions of human activity in such a way that we pursue economic growth in a way that is consistent with long-term ecological and social health and integrity. This perspective has been popularized as the "triple bottom line" of sustainable development — economy, ecology, and social equity — first articulated by John Elkington.[5] For a definition that is succinct, easy to remember, and captures the essence of sustainable development, we like the one adopted recently by the City of Seattle stating that sustainability means "improving the quality of life within the means of nature."[6] The Seattle definition is very compatible with The Natural Step's four System Conditions for a sustainable society as described below.

What distinguishes a systems approach is the focus on connections within the system. The parts of any system are connected according to core principles that define the system. Seeing those connections opens the door for exploring opportunities for change and improvement that can move the larger system in the direction of sustainability rather than unsustainability.

MAKING THE CONNECTIONS: A SUSTAINABILITY SCHEMATIC *(or, Learning How the Dance is Put Together)*

To draw the connections in our socioeconomic-ecological system, it is helpful to start with what Dr. Karl-Henrik Robèrt, founder of The Natural Step, calls the core or "first-order" principles that define the system and through which all other principles or details of the system can be described or ordered.[7] We can turn to any game to demonstrate what we mean by first-order principles. When you want to play a game you haven't played before, you begin by asking what the rules are and what constitutes a successful outcome, i.e. what will it take to win it? For example, in a game of football the principle for a successful outcome is very simple: score more goals than the other team. This outcome is achieved within specified parameters that include an explicit environment (a football field), a restricted number of players and teams, and a set of rules that govern movement and direction within a defined time period. Understanding the rules and definition of success for the game gives us the first-order principles of the game. To become a good player, the starting point is to learn these rules and objectives well. All the strategies and skills you need to play the game skillfully are then elaborated, or ordered, as consequences of these first-order principles.

A sustainability schematic, depicted in Figure 2.1, provides some perspective on how to make sense out of working on the level of the subsystems while seeing the connections that influence the emergent properties of the larger system. The model begins by looking at first-order principles using a systems-based, scientific understanding of the planet and the biosphere to find the rules of the game; and deriving four core System Conditions for a sustainable society that describe what constitutes a successful outcome for the game — in this case the conditions for achieving global socioeconomic-ecological sustainability (Figure 2.2). Chapters 2 and 3 of *The Natural Step for Business* elaborated on the basic science behind The Natural Step framework and explained how the System Conditions are derived from that scientific understanding. We include a brief discussion of The Natural Step framework and its scientific background in the appendix of this book. If you are not already familiar with this background information, it would be useful for you to read it before proceeding.

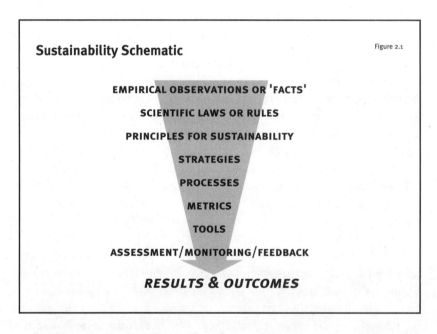

Sustainability Schematic

Figure 2.1

EMPIRICAL OBSERVATIONS OR 'FACTS'

SCIENTIFIC LAWS OR RULES

PRINCIPLES FOR SUSTAINABILITY

STRATEGIES

PROCESSES

METRICS

TOOLS

ASSESSMENT/MONITORING/FEEDBACK

RESULTS & OUTCOMES

Once we have a solid understanding of the rules of the game and what constitutes a successful outcome for that game, we can develop strategies, evolve processes, take specific actions, employ useful tools, set targets and assign metrics that contribute to achieving our ultimate goal: winning the game — creating a sustainable global society. A key point to remember is that as your knowledge and experience in playing the game develops, and as conditions surrounding the game change, your strategies, actions, tools and metrics are also likely to develop, change, and become more sophisticated. The rules of the game and the successful outcome for the game remain unchanged. They are non-negotiable.

Figure 2.2

The Four System Conditions for a Sustainable Society

In the sustainable society, nature is not subject to systematically increasing...

1.   ...concentrations of substances extracted from the Earth's crust,

2.   ...concentrations of substances produced by society, or

3.   ...degradation by physical means;

and in that society . . .

4.   ...human needs are met worldwide.

The four system conditions are based on a systems approach that recognizes the interdependence and interrelationships between society and the rest of nature. They articulate the basic conditions that the global socio-ecological system must meet to continue in a state of both social and ecological sustainability.

For a more detailed discussion of the science behind The Natural Step frame-work for sustainability, and an explanation of how the system conditions are derived from that scientific understanding, please see Chapters 2 and 3 of The Natural Step for Business or the Appendix to the present volume.

Source: The Natural Step

In the long run, how do we know whether we are moving closer to winning or losing, to sustainability or unsustainability? We keep score and compare our results to the criteria set for winning. If the four System Conditions represent the parameters of the successful outcome, then we assess the results of our strategies, processes, actions, tools, and metrics against the four System Conditions in order to determine whether we are contributing to a more or less sustainable outcome for the global system. On a subsystem level, we check our results against our objectives and strategies to determine whether we need to adjust our approach.

Today, a host of strategies, processes, actions, tools, and metrics are evolving to help organizations and communities connect their individual systems to the global socioeconomic-ecological system in a way that contributes to the potential sustainability of that larger system. We expect that many more will develop as humanity increases its understanding and competence with respect to sustainability. Because we are dancing in such new territory, it is easy to become confused between the various levels in this sustainability schematic. For example, we often see confusion arise between principles and strategies and between strategies and tools. It is also easy to get caught in the trap of "competing ideas" by seeing these various levels as competing with one another for primacy or importance. This issue is addressed in a recent paper representing a collective effort of several of the individuals who have pioneered some of these many tools and approaches including Dr. Karl-Henrik Robèrt of The Natural Step, Paul Hawken of the Natural Capital Institute, Bio Schmidt-Bleek of the Factor 10 Institute, and Mathis Wackernagel of Redefining Progress and co-creator of the ecological footprint concept. The objective of the paper is to show how these tools and approaches relate and build upon each other in planning for sustainability. The authors point out:

> The number of tools and approaches to develop sustainability is growing rapidly. Sometimes they are presented as if they were in mutual contradiction or in competition. A systems approach that is consistent with basic principles and requirements of sustainability, however, shows that these tools are complementary pieces of the puzzle that can be used in parallel for strategic sustainable development. In fact, it is only when using these approaches outside of the systemic context of sustainability, that they become contradictory.[8]

Within this model for thinking, no one level is more important or more relevant to sustainability than another. We need to look at this system of thought with the understanding that it is the relationships among these approaches that move us toward sustainability. For example, it is all well and good to know what it is going to take to win a game, but if you do not play the game, you have nothing but a fine theory. Conversely, we can certainly focus on a specific strategy or tool and think that we are working on sustainability, but unless the strategy or tool is implemented with reference to the principles for a successful outcome (in this case, the four System Conditions for a sustainable society), there is no way of telling whether or not we are moving closer to our sustainability objectives. It would be like executing some of the moves involved in playing football without reference to what we need to do to win the game. We would certainly get a lot of exercise and feel that we had spent our time in stimulating activity, but in the end we may be no closer at all to winning.

Consider environmental management systems. Many organizations point to the fact that they have an environmental management system (EMS) as evidence of their progress toward sustainability. However the relationship between an EMS and sustainability is frequently not clear. Although an EMS is a tool designed to help a company achieve and demonstrate improved environmental performance, if the goals and objectives of those improvements are set without reference to a framework for societal sustainability, it can be difficult to determine whether those improvements are indeed contributing to winning the sustainability game on a global societal scale. To continue with our game analogy, it would be like getting better and better at passing the ball without reference to the relationship between passing the ball, for example, to a specific player who can make the score, and winning the game. You could certainly measure and document improvements, but those improvements may not be related to the ultimate goal.

In *Natural Capitalism*,[9] Paul Hawken and Amory and Hunter Lovins suggest four central strategies to help companies and communities contribute toward sustainability:

- *Radical resource productivity*, which means obtaining the same amount of work from a product or process while using less material and energy. This is an idea that has been evolving, particularly over the past decade. It was most clearly articulated in the fall of 1994 in the *Carnoules Declaration* (Figure 2.3) issued by a group of environmental and development leaders, known as the Factor 10 Club, which met for the first time in Carnoules, France, at the initiative of the German think-tank, the Wuppertal Institute.

Figure 2.3

Carnoules Declaration

In Brief:
Economic progress and national wealth continue to be measured in terms of Gross Domestic Product (GDP); economic policies still aim at increasing labor productivity and production volume. But many factors that constitute real wealth have not increased — or are even declining — in industrialised countries since the mid 70s.

Ecological disruption is increasing, as are global natural resource consumption and population. Current environmental and social policies have not been able to stop this trend. As a consequence, we are losing natural capital at increasing speed, and we are losing the freedom to shape the future of humanity. Before long, many more resources will have to be invested in survival strategies.

Obviously, these problems must be addressed urgently.

While this paper does not suggest that all the answers are known, some practical solutions are identified that should be implemented without further delay.

Among these are:

1. In industrialised countries, the current resource productivity must be increased by an average of a FACTOR of 10 during the next 30 to 50 years. This is technically feasible if we mobilise our know-how to generate new products, services, as well as new methods of manufacturing.

2. The relative cost of labor will have to decrease in industrialised countries. This is possible by revamping subsidy systems and through taxing resource consumption instead of work. The aim is to preserve resources for future generations by making planned transitions now rather than facing abrupt and unplanned changes later.

Source: the Factor 10 website: http://www.factorten.co.uk/carnoules_extract.htm

- *Biomimicry*, which Hawken and the Lovinses describe as "reducing the wasteful throughput of materials — indeed eliminating the very idea of waste . . . by redesigning industrial systems on biological lines."[10] A term coined by Janine Benyus (Figure 2.4) in her 1997 book *Biomimicry, Innovation Inspired by Nature*,[11] biomimicry is a design strategy that seeks sustainable solutions to human problems by studying and emulating nature's time-tested patterns and strategies.

Figure 2.4

Bi-o-mim-ic-ry

[From the Greek bios, life, and mimesis, imitation]

1. Nature as model. Biomimicry is a new science that studies nature's models and then imitates or takes inspiration from these designs and processes to solve human problems, e.g., a solar cell inspired by a leaf.

2. Nature as measure. Biomimicry uses an ecological standard to judge the "rightness" of our innovations. After 3.8 billion years of evolution, nature has learned: What works. What is appropriate. What lasts.

3. Nature as mentor. Biomimicry is a new way of viewing and valuing nature. It introduces an era based not on what we can extract from the natural world, but on what we can learn from it.

- *Service and flow economy*, encompassing strategies to create a service economy in which goods are rented or leased rather than sold outright to consumers. In this approach, products are designed either to degrade back into nature or to be reincorporated into technical cycles as nutrients for other products or processes.

- *Investing in natural capital*, which is essentially a strategy of maintaining and restoring the Earth's living systems.

Natural Capitalism is rich with examples of how companies are already employing these strategies with great success. As our understanding of sustainability advances and as we master these strategies, we will no doubt develop even more sophisticated strategies to reach our goals. For now, this set of four broad strategies provides a valuable starting point for companies that want to institute more sustainable practices.

A number of processes and tools have also been developed such as life-cycle assessment (LCA), design for environment (DfE), ecological footprinting (EF), green procurement guidelines, environmental management systems (EMS), including the ISO 14001 standard, ecological and social accounting systems, LEED (Leadership in Energy and Environmental Design) standards, and sustainability management systems (SMS). For greatest effectiveness, we use these processes and tools to carry out the strategies we have developed to meet our ultimate objective: contributing to sustainability. All of these eventually lead to actions that put these strategies, processes and tools into practice, and metrics, which measure our degree of success in meeting our objectives.

Using such a sustainability schematic, we can begin to see the connections between principles, strategies, processes, actions, tools, measurements and outcomes. By taking this approach, we can align our decisions at each level with the ultimate goal of meeting the conditions for a sustainable society. The more organizations and communities that engage in this approach, and that we can individually and collectively influence to engage in this approach (for example, through demands we make in our supply chain), the more likely it is that sustainability will become an emergent property of our global socioeconomic-ecological system.

Having a sustainability schematic is extremely useful, but it does not automatically translate into knowing how to apply that model. For that reason, The Natural Step has developed a model for planning termed simply the A-B-C-D model for sustainable development.

The A-B-C-D Model — Learning to Dance Step by Step

The Natural Step framework uses a step-by-step approach to strategic planning that is called the A-B-C-D model for planning in complex systems (Figure 2.5). It consists of (A) developing an awareness of why our current socioeconomic system is unsustainable (aspects of A are covered in more detail in the next section of this chapter); (B) understanding what the minimum success factors are for a sustainable relationship between the global socioeconomic system and the global ecological systems (the four System Conditions), and assessing the current reality of each organization or community with respect to those success factors; (C) imagining future scenarios in which both the success factors for sustainability (the four System Conditions) and the success factors for the organization or community are being met; and (D) using a planning method called "back-casting" which enables the organization or community to identify the most effective investments, strategies, and actions to meet its sustainability and business or community objectives.

In back-casting, we begin with the end in mind. In back-casting for sustainability, we start with the understanding that if the future is to be sustainable, we need to be part of a society that operates with different assumptions about the interrelationships between society and nature. If we use the current situation to predict the future (forecasting), we simply extrapolate our current assumptions into the future; we try to solve our problems with the same thinking that created them.

To engage in back-casting for sustainability, we first align our assumptions with the first-order principles for a sustainable society. Then we envision our desired future state based on those new assumptions. For example, we imagine what our organization or community would look like in a sustainable society — a global socioeconomic-ecological system that is operating in a sustainable relationship. To create this vision, we can make the assumption that this future society operates in alignment with the four System Conditions: that nature is not subject to increasing concentrations of substances from the Earth's crust, or substances produced by society, or degradation by physical means; and that in that society human needs are met worldwide. We can make a further assumption that the successful organizations and communities in that sustainable society also operate in alignment with the four System Conditions so that they, individually, do not contribute to the accumulation in nature of substances from the Earth's crust, and so on. Aside from complying with these four System Conditions, the possible scenarios for an organization's or community's future are limited only by our imaginations.

Once we have a picture of where we want to be in the future, we return to the present and assess our current reality with respect to that future scenario. We can then begin to explore the strategies, processes, actions, and tools that we need to use in order to contribute to that desired future state of socioeconomic-ecological sustainability.

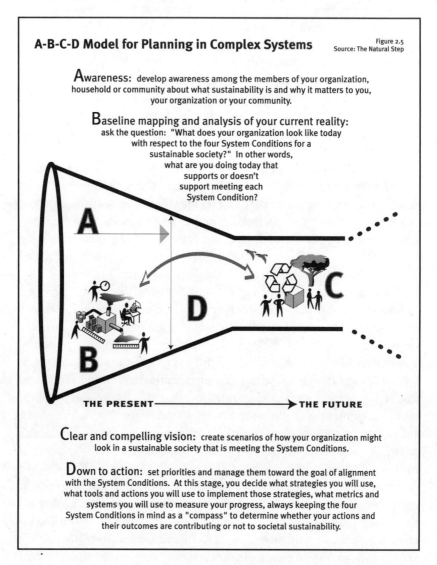

A-B-C-D Model for Planning in Complex Systems

Figure 2.5
Source: The Natural Step

Awareness: develop awareness among the members of your organization, household or community about what sustainability is and why it matters to you, your organization or your community.

Baseline mapping and analysis of your current reality: ask the question: "What does your organization look like today with respect to the four System Conditions for a sustainable society?" In other words, what are you doing today that supports or doesn't support meeting each System Condition?

A

D

C

B

THE PRESENT ——————————> THE FUTURE

Clear and compelling vision: create scenarios of how your organization might look in a sustainable society that is meeting the System Conditions.

Down to action: set priorities and manage them toward the goal of alignment with the System Conditions. At this stage, you decide what strategies you will use, what tools and actions you will use to implement those strategies, what metrics and systems you will use to measure your progress, always keeping the four System Conditions in mind as a "compass" to determine whether your actions and their outcomes are contributing or not to societal sustainability.

In step D of the A-B-C-D model, we implement processes and systems in ways that are consistent with best management practices. For example, Figure 2.6 illustrates how we can combine the conventional plan-do-check-revise pattern of successful management practice with this sustainability schematic. Ultimately, we assess our progress against our core strategies (did we achieve what we set out to achieve with that strategy) and against the successful outcome for a sustainable society by using the four System Conditions. In this way we create alignment throughout the entire system.

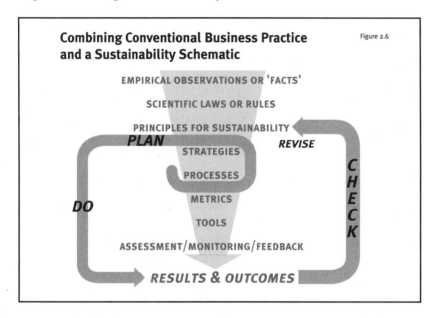

Combining Conventional Business Practice and a Sustainability Schematic

Figure 2.6

One of the advantages of any professional education, whether it is engineering, law, medicine or another, is that we are taught an approach to problems, a disciplined way of thinking, that has proven effective in problem solving over generations of reflective practitioners. Very often this way of thinking is highly analytical as we learn how to define a challenge and break it down into its many components and sub-components in order to deal with the problems piece by piece. The challenge of sustainability is that the problems are so complex and so interwoven that a different way of thinking, a new approach to problems, is called for, one that is integrative rather than analytical, one that leads to synthesis rather than dissection. All of our current thinking tools will, of course, be needed, but we also must learn to see our socioeconomic-ecological systems from this much broader, integrative perspective.

We hope that the intellectual frameworks discussed above will be helpful to you as a way of thinking about the complex issues facing humanity at the beginning of the 21st century. For those readers who would like more information on the current state of the natural world and the implications for the future of humanity, information that will help to create a better awareness of our planetary situation, corresponding to part A of the A-B-C-D model of sustainable development, the next section will provide you with some of that information. Readers already familiar with many of the alarming facts of our current global ecological situation may want to proceed directly to chapter 3.

Setting the Stage for the New Dance

The modern era of environmental awareness is often said to have begun in 1970, the year of the first Earth Day celebration and the establishment of the Environmental Protection Agency in the United States under the Nixon administration. In a little more than one generation, the world we live in has undergone profound and fundamental shifts. Compared to earlier times, ours is one of extreme disruptions in the traditional ways of doing things worldwide, a time of rapid change, complexity and uncertainty; a world in which human impacts on ecosystems have reached unprecedented global proportions and implications. The Natural Step framework depicts this global situation metaphorically as a funnel of *decreasing opportunities for humankind on a global basis.* This funnel (A in the A-B-C-D model) is defined by the fact that the Earth's major life-supporting resources are declining, while at the same time human consumption of, and pressure on, those resources continues to rise. *All major life-supporting systems on the planet are in decline.* From our oceans, topsoil, forests, prairies and savannahs, all major life-supporting systems are in decline. We are the first generation in human history to be confronted with this reality on a global scale. Humanity, whether it is ready or not, is now engaged in a totally new dance, one that calls for new choreography and new steps on a global scale.

A number of recent reports and studies help us understand what the funnel metaphor means in more concrete terms. For example, according to the *Living Planet Report 2000,* a joint publication of the United Nations Environment Programme's World Conservation Monitoring Centre, the World Wildlife Fund International, Redefining Progress, and the Centre for Sustainability Studies of the University of Xalapa in Mexico, over the last 30 years the state of the

Earth's natural ecosystems has declined by about 33 percent (Figure 2.7) while the ecological pressure of humanity on the Earth has increased by about 50 percent over the same period (Figure 2.8). This report quantifies changes in the state of the Earth's natural ecosystems over time, measures the human pressures on the natural environment arising from the consumption of renewable resources and pollution, and analyzes the geographic patterns of those pressures. The report indicates that the natural wealth of the Earth's forests, freshwater, ocean and coastal ecosystems has rapidly declined over the past 30 years. As Figure 2.8 illustrates, and the report further concludes:

> In 1997, the ecological footprint[12] of the global population was at least 30 percent larger than the Earth's biological productive capacity. *At some time in the 1970s, humanity as a whole passed the point at which it lived within the global regenerative capacity of the Earth*, causing depletion of the Earth's natural capital as a consequence (although locally this has occurred many times and in many places throughout human history). This is the ultimate cause of the decline in the natural wealth of the world's forest, freshwater, and marine ecosystems . . .[13] (emphasis added)

This means that we are consuming the natural capital that supports not only our species but also countless other species. We are eating not only the apples; we are eating the apple trees. How long can we continue to tear and trample the whole fabric of living systems upon which humanity is so fundamentally dependent before it unravels all around us to mark the end of life as we know it?

The *Living Planet Report 2000* is only one of several current initiatives that map and document the ecological impact of the dominant species on the planet. A distinctive collaboration of the World Resources Institute, the World Bank, the United Nations Environment Programme and the United Nations Development Programme recently produced *World Resources 2000-2001*, a report that explores the health and the viability of the Earth's ecosystems to continue to support growing human demands. Based on the results of a unique study, the report examines five major ecosystem types that are home to the majority of the world's population and cover the greater part of the Earth's land area and a significant portion of the ocean area:[14]

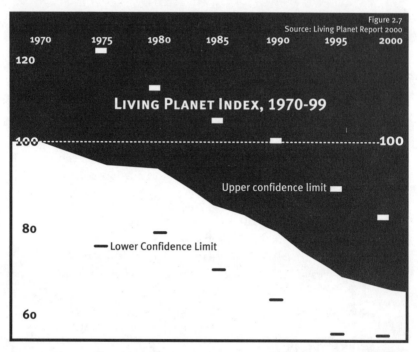

Figure 2.7
Source: Living Planet Report 2000

LIVING PLANET INDEX, 1970-99

Upper confidence limit

Lower Confidence Limit

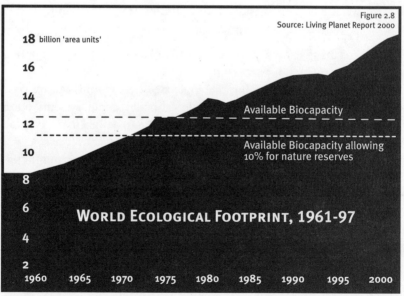

Figure 2.8
Source: Living Planet Report 2000

18 billion 'area units'

Available Biocapacity

Available Biocapacity allowing
10% for nature reserves

WORLD ECOLOGICAL FOOTPRINT, 1961-97

1. Agricultural ecosystems that cover 20 percent of the land surface (excluding Antarctica and Greenland) and account for $1.3 trillion in output of food, feed, and fiber, and for 99 percent of the calories humans consume.

2. Coastal ecosystems (including marine fisheries) that cover approximately 22 percent of the total land area in a 60-mile (100-kilometer) band along continental and island coastlines, as well as the ocean area above the continental shelf. The coastal zone is home to roughly 2.2 billion people or 39 percent of the world's population and yields as much as 95 percent of the marine fish catch.

3. Forest ecosystems that cover 22 percent of the land surface (excluding Antarctica and Greenland) and contribute more than two percent of global gross domestic product (GDP) through the production and manufacture of industrial wood products alone.

4. Freshwater systems that cover less than one percent of the Earth's surface but are the source of water for drinking, domestic use, agriculture, and industry; freshwater fish and mollusks are also a major source of protein for humans and animals.

5. Grassland ecosystems (including shrublands) that cover 41 percent of the land surface (excluding Antarctica and Greenland) and are critical producers of protein and fiber from livestock, particularly in developing countries.

The Pilot Analysis of Global Ecosystems (PAGE)[15] on which the report was based assembled the best information available on the extent of each ecosystem and the modifications that have been made. The research began with an analysis of the location of the ecosystem, its dominant physical characteristics, how it has changed over time, and what pressures and changes it is currently experiencing. Each ecosystem was then evaluated by examining the condition of a range of goods and services it produces. For each good or service, the researchers studied the quantity of the service being produced (and its value, where possible), and whether the capacity of the ecosystem to produce that service was being strengthened or diminished over time.

The study concludes that the capacity of ecosystems to continue to produce many of the goods and services needed by humankind is decreasing. In all five ecosystem types, capacity is decreasing over a range of goods and services, and significant modifications are increasing through forestry, pollution, biological invasions, and other human-produced causes including human-associated alterations in the basic chemical cycles upon which all these ecosystems depend. In the meantime, commodity production from these ecosystems to meet human needs continues to grow at the increased expense of the ecosystems that support that production. How long could we afford to run our businesses or communities based on such a dramatic depletion rate of capital? The difference is that we are depleting the natural capital required for the continued flourishing, and even survival, of the human race.

Among other indications of human-created ecosystem challenges, the report points out that the scale of human impact on freshwater systems is massive. Humans currently use more than one-half of accessible fresh water runoff and, by 2025, demand is projected to increase to more than 70 percent of runoff. About 70 percent of the water currently drawn from available runoff is used for agriculture. The result is that less and less of the world's freshwater is available to the other species with whom we have co-evolved and with whom we share this planet.

The erosion of global biodiversity is also alarming. To appreciate the vital importance of biodiversity to the future of humanity, we can think of it as providing the back-up systems needed to ensure our survival on Spaceship Earth, in the same way that space vehicles have redundant, back-up systems to ensure that if one system fails another can still perform the needed function for the human crew. With the loss of biodiversity, our planetary back-up systems on Spaceship Earth are being continually weakened. In the last few decades, significant losses have occurred in virtually all types of ecosystems. Forest cover has been reduced by at least 20 percent and perhaps as much as 50 percent worldwide. Some forest ecosystems are virtually gone. More than 50 percent of the original mangrove area in many countries is gone. Globally, wetland areas have been reduced by one-half. Grasslands have been reduced by 90 percent in some areas. Approximately 20 percent of freshwater fish species have become extinct, endangered or threatened.[16]

In 2001, the Worldwatch Institute joined with the United Nations Environment Programme, for the first time, to produce its report, *Vital Signs 2001,* the latest edition of the annual publication examining trends that are shaping the future of the Earth and its inhabitants. In 2001,

Vital Signs reached a milestone because, as of the year 2000, the trends the publication follows could be viewed from the perspective of half a century, as most of the data sets on which the report is based began in 1950. Here are some of the trends recorded in this milestone volume:

- In 2000, the global population topped 6 billion people, up 3.5 billion people since 1950. Most of this growth took place in the developing world. While the global population has more than doubled in the past 50 years, the growth of urban population has increased fourfold.

- The world economy has grown nearly sevenfold in the past 50 years and has led to important improvements in living standards for certain areas of the world's population. Nevertheless, 1.2 billion people still live in severe poverty and an estimated 1.1 billion do not have clean, safe water to drink.

- The world grain harvest has nearly tripled since 1950, providing increased nutrition for billions of people. However, this increase has come at the high cost of the erosion of our natural capital, resulting in falling freshwater aquifers and severe water pollution from extensive use of fertilizers and pesticides. Despite the increase in production, more than one billion people are under-nourished while paradoxically another billion are overnourished. While one-sixth of the world's population suffer from malnutrition and starvation, another one-sixth experience conditions of overweight and obesity.

- Emissions of carbon dioxide, the leading greenhouse gas, have risen nearly 300 percent since 1950. The concentration of CO_2 in the atmosphere, now at its highest level in at least 420,000 years, is approximately 30 percent higher than at the beginning of the Industrial Revolution. New scientific studies project dramatic climatic changes in this century that will produce increased storm intensity with consequent damage, agricultural losses, and economic and social disruptions.

- The world has lost more than one-half its wetlands and more than one-quarter of its coral reefs. Approximately 60 percent of the world's coral reefs are now endangered. These losses are accelerating. Species dependent on these habitats are also in decline. Of the approximately 9,900 bird species that have been identified, 12 percent are threatened with extinction.[17]

In January 2002, the North American Commission for Environmental Cooperation (CEC) issued its realistic, that is to say gloomy, report, *The North American Mosaic: A State of the Environment Report*. The CEC was established under the provisions of the North American Agreement on Environmental Cooperation (NAAEC) between the Government of Canada, the Government of the United Mexican States, and the Government of the United States of America, which itself was created as a complement to the environmental provisions of the North American Free Trade Agreement (NAFTA). In our opinion, this 100-page comprehensive report on the state of the North American environment, with commentary on the economic and social implications, should be mandatory reading for every citizen of North America. A sampling of some of the disturbing findings of this official report of the CEC includes the following:

- North America's diminishing biological diversity has profound consequences. Because the loss is irreversible — species lost are lost forever — the potential impact on the human condition, on the fabric of the continent's living systems and on the process of evolution is immense.

- Many of North America's estuaries, rivers, streams, lakes and groundwater reserves are polluted by industrial discharges, agricultural runoff and insufficiently treated municipal wastewater.

- Marine ecosystems suffer from a growing tide of municipal, industrial and agricultural wastes and runoff, as well as deposition from air pollution. Eighty percent of marine pollution in Canada, for example, is from land-based activities. About sixty percent of world fish stocks are currently either over-fished or fully harvested. We are now "fishing down the food chain," in many cases catching the food needed to rebuild depleted species.

- Income and social inequality, combined with environmental and other pressures, undermine the sustainability of social structures, disproportionately affecting people on the lowest social and economic rungs.

In looking to the future, the CEC calls for a major shift in North American society to one that embodies the principles of sustainability. The CEC comments: "The transition will not be easy. It will require adapting policies, institutions, technologies and lifestyles. It will mean

altering deep and enduring attitudes, values and behaviors that underlie our economic and social systems."[18]

Are these alarmist projections or are they evidence of trends that
are happening so quickly that we are only now beginning to grasp
their meaning? These conclusions are drawn from rigorous research
conducted by some of the world's most respected scientific and governmental research institutes. What is more, these reports are only a
sampling of the many serious attempts to understand the current
state of the ecosystems on which we depend and the trends that lead
us to question their viability in the future to continue to support not
only the lifestyles to which we aspire, but to support life as we know
it at all.

Although this information is widely available, at least in the industrialized world, our perception of our relationship with nature seems
to lag behind this reality by at least 20 to 30 years. We might even say
that as a global society we are stuck on the stage of 20th century
thinking when the dance of global sustainability requires us to move
to the 21st century. We still think of natural resources primarily as an
inventory of commodities to be exploited for human use. Our
actions, particularly in the so-called advanced industrialized world,
suggest that we still look at pollution as an unpleasant side effect of
our lifestyles — something we do not want in our own backyards —
so we export it to other people's backyards; and we convince ourselves, or pretend, that the problem has gone away and cannot affect
us. We still act as if the ecosystems on which we depend can provide
unlimited resources and absorb unlimited waste. We behave individually and institutionally as if the world were not an integrally
interconnected system ecologically, socially and economically.

Some progress is occurring, however slow it may seem. Over the
past 30 years we have not been totally blind to the challenge of the
rapid ecosystem deterioration. In 1972 the United Nations held its
first conference on the environment in Stockholm and called global
attention to the need "for a common outlook and for common principles to inspire and guide the peoples of the world in the
preservation and enhancement of the human environment."[19] The
focus of the conference was on human protection, improvement, and
management of the natural environment to ensure the meeting of
present and future human needs. The declaration that came out of
the conference emphasized the human role as manager, improver and

preserver of the environment. The environment was still perceived as an external "thing" to be acted upon by humans. Little emphasis was given to the real challenge: managing and improving ourselves.

In the early 1980s, The World Commission on Environment and Development, headed by the former President of Norway, Gro Harlem Brundtland, was set up by the United Nations as an independent body of politicians, civil servants and experts on the environment and development. The purpose of the Commission, later known as the Brundtland Commission, was to examine the critical environment and development problems in the world and to formulate proposals to solve them. The fundamental premise was to ensure that human progress could be sustained through development without bankrupting the resources of future generations. The Brundtland Commission report[20] was primarily concerned with securing global equity and redistributing resources towards poorer nations while encouraging their economic growth. The report posited that there are three fundamental components to sustainable development: environmental protection, economic growth and social equity. The Commission's report, issued in 1987, formulated the definition of sustainable development that is still widely cited today: development that meets the needs of the present without compromising the ability of future generations to meet their own needs. The terms "sustainability" and "sustainable development" began to receive greater attention in public, intellectual, and policy discourse.

The view of sustainability presented by the Brundtland Commission provided the intellectual backdrop to the second United Nations Conference on Environment and Development, the Rio "Earth Summit" in 1992, at which more than 178 governments adopted the Rio Declaration on Environment and Development, the Statement of Principles for the Sustainable Management of Forests, and Agenda 21, described as "a comprehensive plan of action to be taken globally, nationally and locally by organizations of the United Nations system, governments and major groups in every area in which humans impact on the environment."[21] Agenda 21 begins with the statement:

> Humanity stands at a defining moment in history. We are
> confronted with a perpetuation of disparities between
> and within nations, a worsening of poverty, hunger, ill
> health and illiteracy, and the continuing deterioration of

the ecosystems on which we depend for our well-being. However, integration of environment and development concerns and greater attention to them will lead to the fulfillment of basic needs, improved living standards for all, better protected and managed ecosystems and a safer, more prosperous future. No nation can achieve this on its own; but together we can — in a global partnership for sustainable development.

Since the early 1970s, we have focused increasing attention on the environmental impact of human activities and since the late 1980s we have progressively used the term "sustainability" and ascribed three dimensions to sustainable development: social, economic, and environmental. A decade has now passed since the 1992 Earth Summit in Rio. Have we seen any progress?

Canadian Maurice Strong, Secretary General of both the Earth Summit in 1992 and the Stockholm Conference in 1972, wrote recently in his autobiography, *Where On Earth Are We Going*, about the Earth Summit:

> When the conference was over, [the world leaders] all flew home to confront their own peoples and their own problems, and I went back to my own business. The Halifax G-7 conference came and went, the fiftieth anniversary of the United Nations, Rio+5, more G-7 meetings, as the years passed. The Kyoto meeting on global warming and climate change ended with an agreement, but a feeble one. I watched and waited. On the substantive issues, the determination that Rio had helped express seemed to slip away, the momentum dissipating. *On the really tough issues there was very little progress at all.*[22] (italics added)

Why, if the evidence is mounting, do we find it so difficult to make the fundamental shift in priorities and behaviors around issues that are arguably some of the most significant that humanity has ever faced? Why, if the term sustainability and its tri-dimensional aspects have been part of our discourse since the late 80s, do we find the concept so difficult to understand and use?

Perhaps it is because the dance of today's generations is what eco-philosopher Joanna Macy calls the Great Turning. "It is the epochal shift from an industrial growth society, dependent on accelerating consumption of resources, to a life-sustaining society."[23] Macy suggests that it is a great privilege to be alive right now "when all the wisdom and courage we ever harvested can be put to use and matter supremely."[24]

While it may be a privilege, it is not a comfortable one. Most of us still operate in a state of unconscious incompetence when it comes to sustainability. As Stephen Haines points out, a state of unconscious incompetence is "a very dangerous place to be. You are not conscious of the things you cannot do and you probably are not even concerned about this lack of competence."[25] In other words, *we don't even know what we don't know*. However, as awareness increases with respect to sustainability matters, as it has over the past 30 years in some quarters, we enter a stage of conscious incompetence. We are more aware of what we didn't know before. We also become aware of the limitations in our knowledge and experience, yet we are not sufficiently skilled, nor do we yet have the necessary new knowledge and experience, to change our behavior easily or even to know what behaviors to change, to what degree, and toward what results. We feel inept and unskilled; an extremely uncomfortable feeling at best, particularly for individuals hired to provide clear leadership, direction and solutions in their organizations and communities.

As we continue to develop the knowledge and skills to understand and work with sustainability, we eventually move to a stage of conscious competence. This stage only comes through much practice, through experimentation and innovation, through making and learning from mistakes; but the knowledge and associated actions are not yet second nature to us. That happens when we have integrated sustainability thinking so well into the way we live and run our organizations and communities that we take sustainable practices for granted as simply the way that things are done.

Another reason why we find it so difficult to shift our priorities and behaviors to more sustainable practices is that, barring a disaster or threat that mobilizes our attention and resolve, awareness is a necessary, but not a sufficient, cause to motivate change. We live in a world of competing demands for our time and attention. Like the leaders Strong refers to, our lives are filled with the tyranny of urgencies: keeping our jobs, feeding our families, meeting sales targets, delivering quarterly returns, meeting deadlines and production schedules.

For many people in the world, particularly in developing countries, the most urgent concern is simply staying alive.

Nevertheless, we can see evidence over the past 30 years that the institutions in society, including corporations, non-governmental organizations (NGOs), and governments *are* climbing a steep sustainability learning curve. We are becoming more aware of the data and trends that now appear in reports such as the *Living Planet Report 2000* and *World Resources 2000-2001*. Today tens of thousands of organizations, institutes, multinational companies, small and medium-sized enterprises, foundations, educational institutions, NGOs, churches, civic organizations, outdoor clubs, land trusts, and government agencies engage in research and action to understand the dynamics of the global system we are creating so that we can consciously design a sustainable and positive future. An increasing number of corporations are incorporating "sustainability" into both their policies and operations, setting up departments with names such as "corporate responsibility," "corporate social responsibility," "environmental," "sustainability" and "sustainable development." They are issuing sustainability reports and corporate responsibility reports based on a "triple bottom line" of social, economic and environmental dimensions. A coalition of approximately 150 international companies from more than 30 countries and 20 major industrial sectors join in The World Business Council for Sustainable Development[26] to express a shared commitment to sustainable development.

At the same time, many people are becoming more personally aware of the vast global inequities that have evolved within our social and economic systems, and are becoming more concerned about the implications of another phenomenon that has recently entered public discourse, becoming one of the most charged issues of our time: "globalization." The International Forum on Globalization observes that as we become more aware of the consequences of the intricate interdependencies of our global systems, we also become more concerned that the world's corporate and political leaders are "undertaking a restructuring of global politics and economics that may prove as historically significant as any event since the Industrial Revolution. This restructuring is happening at tremendous speed, with little public disclosure of the profound consequences affecting democracy, human welfare, local economies, and the natural world."[27] We are beginning to ask questions about how the products and services we have taken for granted in the developed world affect the quality of life of the people who make the running shoes and clothes or who grow the coffee — people who live predominantly in the developing world. We are beginning to make more demands on the companies that provide these goods and services.

Globalization, like sustainability, is a term that many thoughtful observers are struggling to define. Both terms refer to our growing awareness of the interdependencies of the global socioeconomic-ecological systems of the 21st century. In 1999, the United Nations Development Report, *Globalization with a Human Face*, argues that although globalization is not new, "the present era of globalization, driven by competitive global markets, is outpacing the governance of markets and the repercussions on people."[28] The report further suggests that although global markets, global technology, global ideas and global solidarity can enrich the lives of people everywhere, the challenge is to ensure that the benefits are shared equitably and that this increasing interdependence works for people — not just for profits.

The growing turmoil over globalization has resulted in demonstrations against the World Trade Organization, the World Bank, the International Monetary Fund, and many other meetings of global leaders worldwide, and has led to growing scrutiny of the operations and practices of multinational corporations, particularly those with widely recognized brands.

Figure 2.9 attempts to capture some of the pressures, changes and responses that are driving the velocity, trajectory and slope of the sustainability learning curve. Although this graph does not by any means include all of the pressures, changes and responses that have occurred over the last 30 years, we highlight some that we feel characterize the general nature of these drivers.

We included an earlier version of this learning curve in *The Natural Step for Business*. That learning curve applied specifically to businesses because the focus of the book was primarily on corporations. However, the sustainability learning curve also applies to other societal institutions and organizations. It illustrates, in brief, the immense learning challenge in which we are collectively engaged. It also suggests that, on this learning curve, society and its institutions are moving through progressive stages of learning — from unconscious

Sustainability Learning Curve

Figure 2.9

Stages of Learning →

	Unconscious Incompetence	Conscious Incompetence		Conscious Competence	Unconscious Competence
		1ST ERA COMPLIANCE	**2ND ERA BEYOND COMPLIANCE**	**3RD ERA ECO-EFFICIENCY**	**4TH ERA SUSTAINABLE DEVELOPMENT**
	Widespread use of DDT	*First Earth Day*	*Brundtland Commission*	*Rio Earth Summit (UNCED)*	*Growing concern over globalization*
	Burning rivers in Europe	*Environmental legislation*	*Bhopal catastrophe (India)*		*Rio+10*
	Rachel Carlson publishes: "Silent Spring" ushering in the modern environmental movement	*Toxic contamination of Love Canal residents (USA)*	*Exxon Valdez oil spill (Alaska)*		TNS/Biomimicry/Design for Sustainability Sustainability Management Systems
		UN Conference on the Environment (Stockholm)	*Chernobyl nuclear disaster (USSR)*		Expanded CSR/Natural Capitalism/Factor 10 Triple Bottom Line Accounting/Environmental Footprint
				Environmental Cost Accounting	
				Product Stewardship/DFE/LCA	
				TQEM/Environmental Management Systems	
			Stakeholder Participation		
			Pollution Prevention/Waste Minimization/Education/Incentives		
		Regulation/Pollution Control/Compliance			

Response	BEFORE 1970s Unprepared	*1970s* Reactive	*1980s* Anticipatory	*1990s* Proactive	*2000s* High Integration
Goals	NONE	MEETING REGULATORY STANDARDS	COST AVOIDANCE • Impact reduction • Pre-emption of regulation • Leadership • Legitimacy protection • Partnerships • Competitive edge	PROFIT CENTER APPROACH • Eco-efficiency • Dematerialization • Strategic environmental management	EXPLICIT MAINSTREAMING OF SUSTAINABILITY • DFE/LCA • Environmental cost management • Resource productivity • Products of service • Culture change • Learning from nature • Systems thinking

incompetence toward an ideal state of unconscious competence. We expect that this latter stage will not take hold until some time in the future. We are moving from an era where "legislating sustainability" is necessary because, as a society we still don't know what we don't know, to one where integrating sustainability into the way we think about and operate in the world becomes second nature to us. Between these two extremes we find the difficult and sometimes frustrating process of learning: thinking in different ways, learning new skills, trying new approaches. We feel like we are dancing with two left feet: an uncomfortable and perilous situation when dancing with a tiger.

CHAPTER 3

THE STORIES WE TELL,
THE WORLD WE CREATE

A culture cannot evolve without
honest, powerful storytelling.
— Robert McKee[1]

It's all a question of story. We are in trouble
just now because we are in-between stories.
The Old Story — the account of how the world
came to be and how we fit into it — sustained us for
a long time. It shaped our emotional attitudes, provided
us with life purpose, energized action, consecrated
suffering, integrated knowledge, and guided education.
We awoke in the morning and knew where we were.
We could answer the questions of our children.

But now it is no longer functioning properly,
and we have not yet learned the New Story.
— Wendell Berry[2]

STORIES HELP US MAKE SENSE out of our experience. In fact, how we experience life often depends upon the stories we tell ourselves about it. Is ours a heroic tale? Is it a tale of being a victim, helpless against the circumstances around us? Is it a story of beauty and hope? This chapter introduces the stories that we tell in this book. It explains why and how we are telling them, and what it means to us to share these stories with you. This chapter also has a story of its own: the story of how human systems learn and change and the role of the individuals within those systems that enables the process to happen.

It seems only fitting to begin this introduction to the stories in this book with a story of its own — one by Julie Reder Fairley:

Ianu's Dance[3]

In the heart of Africa there lived a precious little girl named Ianu. Ianu loved life and life appeared to love her as well. She displayed the countenance of one who wonders, but is not skeptical; dreams but does not fabricate; and laughs but never sneers.

On this new day Ianu watched her father as he hunted for their dinner. She noticed his stealth and grace as he approached a herd of antelope. Having speared his prey, her father knelt and prayed for its spirit before skinning it. He told Ianu, "God provides the antelope for our dinner, and tonight the antelope will dine with God."

Back at home she helped her mother who was making a basket. Carefully she wove each reed so that the basket was not just a container, but also a seamless circle of recurring patterns, which told a story. Her mother explained, "Weaving a basket is hard work, but the story gives the basket life, and makes it more than just a container. So, the work does not seem burdensome."

Later that day Ianu visited the village high priest who was grinding berries in a small bowl. "Are you preparing dinner?" questioned the naive child. "No, I am grinding these dried berries to mix with roots and water in order to have paint to color our faces for a ceremony we will be having soon. Berries, like many other gifts from nature, serve us in several ways."

That night, as the village settled in for gentle conversation around a communal fire, the elders heard a strange noise. They followed the sound through the thicket to the edge of a clearing. Uncertain of the source of the strange sound, they approached the clearing in silence. What they beheld made them stop in awe.

Close to a small fire, Ianu was dancing around the skull of the antelope. The skull lay in one of her mother's baskets and the pattern of the basket was replicated on Ianu's legs and arms and face and also on the head of the animal. After watching the small child dance for a while, the chief of the tribe asked, "Who taught this child to dance?" At first no one responded. Then her father said, "I taught her about the spirit of the antelope." And her mother said, "It was I who spoke to her of the story baskets." And lastly, the high priest acknowledged his instruction about the berries. "But," the father asserted: "we still have not found the person who taught my daughter to dance." The wise chief smiled before congratulating his people. "As legend foretold, it has taken our whole village to educate this child. Each of you has been a muse, teaching her an important lesson about life. One of you taught her to respect all beings; another to find meaning in work; and yet another to seek and celebrate hidden beauty. To these teachings the child has brought the inner rhythms of her own soul and she has found that dancing will always be her way of exalting the gift of life."

❖ ❖ ❖

It follows: Now and then, it takes a child to teach a whole village.

We are a storytelling and a story loving species. Every culture and sub-culture has its fundamental stories: stories that unify and define the culture and provide a sense of understanding, meaning and purpose. Stories describe and explain our distinctiveness. They also reveal what is universal. We tell stories to teach, learn, share and understand our differences as well as our connections. Whether the story is of our individual lives or the global challenges and possible solutions of the 21st century, it helps us make meaning of our experience and to create shared meaning with others. Mary Catherine Bateson, renowned writer and anthropologist, writes: "When you pass strangers on the street, the unfamiliar faces blur. When you let your lives touch and make the effort of asking questions and listening to the stories they tell, you discover the intricate patterns of their differences and, at the same time, the underlying themes that all members of our species have in common."[4]

For example, generations of us have grown up in the United States and Canada entranced and influenced by the story of the magnificent woodsman, Paul Bunyan, with his mighty ax and trusty ox, Babe. As children, we marveled at the story of how he strode across the frontier, conquering the savage wilderness, turning empty forests into valuable lumber with which to create civilization from the wilds. We learned from this story that the conquest of nature was a noble undertaking, something of which to be proud. Other such stories of noble heroes, from Davy Crockett to John Wayne, taught us that the march of the iron horse, the taming of the wild, the subduing of the "savage Indians," were all right and good, part of our manifest destiny. We learned that turning forests into farms, and prairies into parking lots, was progress and part of the march of civilization.

Kenneth Burke, the noted philosopher, who is often cited as the father of cultural studies, viewed stories as "equipment for living."[5] Stories about others help us to try out their experiences so we can expand our understanding of the possibilities that are open to us. This process helps us to empathize with the lives of others, or alternatively, to revile them, depending upon the stories that we are told or we tell ourselves. Therefore, we need to become mindful of the stories we tell and the attitudes and behavior that they engender. Stories can also help us develop ways of celebrating, coping with, or changing the circumstances in which we find ourselves. Bateson asserts that we practice the *art of living* when we tell stories, and that one of the ways we find wisdom is "through our overlapping lives and the resonance we find between our stories."[6]

We offer the stories in the next four chapters in the same spirit that Ianu learned to dance. There is no story we can tell you about "the sustainable company" or "the sustainable community." The truth is, we cannot imagine how a company or community can be sustainable in an unsustainable global society. Those inside these organizations would be the first to tell you that sustainability is not a destination, it is a journey, and they have only taken, often hesitantly, their very first steps in that journey. They, as we all do, have a long way to go. Rather, we urge you to follow Ianu's example and learn something from each chapter. From the stories of Nike, Starbucks, Whistler, and CH2M HILL, take what is of value to you, just as clever Ianu learned something from her mother, her father, and the village high priest.

One of the reasons we tell these particular stories is that we have had the privilege of both witnessing them, and participating in them, first-hand. Thus, we can speak with some confidence about the processes, lessons, struggles and rewards that they represent. We have also had the opportunity on many occasions to reflect with the leaders, change agents and practitioners inside these organizations about their experience, and even ask them, as we did for this book, to provide their best advice for others who want to join them in the dance of discovering how to live, work, and play in a sustainable way.

No story exists in isolation; it derives its meaning from context. Gregory Bateson, noted biologist, philosopher and anthropologist, might ask us to consider what pattern connects us to these stories? Bateson points out that "the right way to look at the pattern which connects is to think of it *primarily as a dance* of interacting parts,"[7] (emphasis added). Context is a pattern that exists and moves through time. "Without context," Bateson asserts, "words and actions have no meaning at all. . ."[8] Nor do our stories. The interesting thing about context though, is that context and story exist in a co-creative relationship with one another. The context provides meaning for, and helps create, the story while the story helps create, and provides meaning for, the context.

Each of our four case chapters is organized to offer a system of stories and contexts that are nested within each other as illustrated and explained below (Figure 3.1).

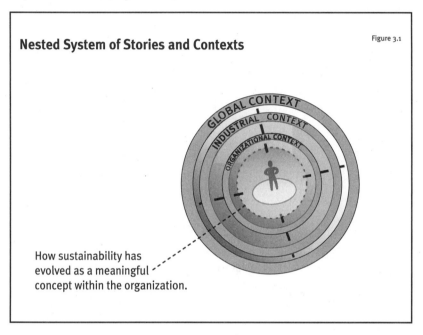

Nested System of Stories and Contexts

Figure 3.1

How sustainability has evolved as a meaningful concept within the organization.

The first level of context we provide is laid out in chapter 2: the context is global society and the story is about the current course of global society that is inherently unsustainable due, in part, to the stories that give meaning to the culture currently dominant in the global system — that culture is ours. At the second level, the context is the modern, Western-based economic/industrial system. The story is about the history and structure of each industry within which players operate and find their identity and success. At the third level, the organization provides the context, and the story focuses on the history of the organization, how and when it was founded, how it has developed, what constitutes its distinctiveness, and what can be said about the internal stories that perpetuate its unique culture. At the fourth level, the context is the concept of sustainability and the story is about how sustainability has evolved as a meaningful concept inside each organization. At the fifth and final level, the context is the individual change agent, and the story is about the experiences of numerous change agents and early adopters as they find personal relevance in the challenges of integrating sustainability into their lives and their organizations, and in their attempts to influence the contexts in which they, their organizations, and their industries live and operate. By putting all of these stories and contexts together, we can begin to see the critical challenge that we face in the early 21st century is to find a New Story and/or to change the context that gives meaning to our present stories. Journalist Patrick Mazza asserts:

> If life is a story, and story is a context flowing through time, then dealing with the trouble in our world story involves making new contexts. This has a strong correlation to the concept of ecology. Ecology is itself the study of contexts. It seeks to examine the dynamic of relationships, in as full a way as possible, within a system. Ecology is known as the science of community. *It might as well be known as the stories of how different beings live with one another* (emphasis added).
>
> Changing the context ecologically involves many different levels, redefining the pattern so our story will unfold in a healthy manner. It means changing our networks of community context so we meet our needs and desires in a sustainable way.
>
> Ultimately, changing the context ecologically involves a different vision of what the world is. Are humans the only (reputedly) intelligent life form on the planet, or is all life imbued with an intelligence of which we are a part? What's the story here? And if we choose to live the context of Gaia, our common planetary life, how are we to know it except as our own personal story, the universal life breathing, speaking words and living stories through us, in our own individual and sometimes quirky ways?[9]

At each of the levels described above we can find tigers, forces that can threaten, constrain or obstruct our ability to change or influence the context or to create the new story of a world that is heading not only in a sustainable direction, but in a vibrant, inviting, and desirable direction. It is our challenge to learn how to dance with these tigers so that the forces they represent can contribute to the transformation of both context and story. As the character Ishmael points out, in Daniel Quinn's book of the same name, if six billion people are intent on "conquering nature," the story of modern times, before long nature will be lying dead and beaten at our feet.[10] In contrast, the stories in the next four chapters are about people and organizations learning how to perform the dance of sustainability in harmony with nature and all humankind.

There are three observations that we would like to make with respect to the intersecting contexts and stories that may be useful for you to keep in mind as you read the four cases to follow.

The first observation is that by virtue of the very complex phenomena involved, the stories in this book can only present a limited perspective on the wider reality of the forces that operate in the global social, economic and natural systems that make up the stage on which we are doing our dance. Think of these case stories as a verbal map presented with the explicit understanding that "the map is not the territory" as Alfred Korzybski, originator of the field of general semantics, was fond of pointing out.[11] A map does not contain everything that is in the territory it represents, and these stories do not contain all the forces, influences and issues experienced by the people, organizations and industries we describe. A question that arises for us in presenting these cases is "what details do we put on the map and what do we leave out?" Gregory Bateson reminds us that "we face a world which is threatened not only with disorganization of many kinds, but also with the destruction of its environment, and we, today, are still unable to think clearly about the relations between an organism and its environment."[12] Our stories focus on the paths that the organizations and individuals within them are taking to think more clearly about these relations. These are the details we include. But they are still maps and as such will feature some aspects of the territory while not showing others.

The second observation is that no matter what our intentions with respect to making a difference in the world, we are constrained by what is within our actual power to control and within our power to influence, no matter how extensive our areas of concern may be as individuals and organizations. Often the stories we tell about ourselves and each other focus on our differences of opinion and belief about what we can, should or expect one another to do in these varying circles of control, influence, and concern. For example, we may all share a concern about the destruction of the natural environment upon which all life depends, or a concern about the personal, social, and economic costs of the increasing disparities in the world, but to be effective we also need to understand what is within our real power to control and influence in these areas.

As you read these case stories, it is useful to ask what are the spheres of actual control for each organization, and how each is operating within or seeking to expand those spheres of control with respect to sustainability. Next ask what are the spheres of real influence for each organization to enable it to affect the thinking or actions of others in their industry or on the global stage with respect to sustainability, and how the organizations are exercising or expanding that sphere of influence. Finally, ask what are the spheres of concern for each organization with respect to sustainability, and how each of the organizations is expanding its area of sustainability concern.

It is extremely interesting to observe the frequent disconnection, or non-alignment, between a company's own perception of its sphere of control or influence in the world, and that of the public. For example, while Starbucks has a very visible and well-known brand, particularly in the U.S. and Canada, it buys only around one percent of all coffee grown in the world. So Starbucks' perception of its own sphere of control and influence may differ markedly from that of the public. However, as the public voices its sense of concern and calls for greater and greater engagement by corporations in issues of ecological and social sustainability, in addition to the financial sustainability with which corporations have traditionally been concerned, then a company may have to undertake a change in behavior and expand its sphere of influence, and certainly its sphere of concern, with respect to these ever more pressing issues. Therefore, the perceptions of what is, or should be, included in the spheres of control, influence, and concern of a given individual or organization may vary considerably among its stakeholders. Furthermore, these perceptions have significant bearing on the stories we tell about the ethics, authenticity and effectiveness of the dance both individuals and organizations are performing on the path to sustainability.

The third observation is that there is a pattern to the kind of change required of organizations to create and live a new story, or create and perform a new dance — particularly when the issue is as complex and multidimensional as sustainability. If we understand the pattern of organizational change and work with it, we increase our likelihood of success as change agents. There is, in fact, a whole field of inquiry that is devoted to understanding how new ideas spread and take hold. Innovation diffusion theory, introduced into the communication field by professor Everett M. Rogers in the early 1960s, suggests that the adoption of a given innovation in a social system follows a predictable pattern. According to Rogers, innovation is a special type of information, an idea, practice or object that is perceived as new by the individual or group.[13] In our cases, the innovation is the knowledge and practice related to sustainability. A social system, whether in an organization or a community, consists of people in formal and informal groups or organizations working toward a common goal. Diffusion is the way the innovation makes its way through the social system.

Research done by Rogers and others[14] indicates that generally an innovation starts with a small group, sometimes even a single individual who has a "new" idea, that is, an idea that is new to the culture of the population. The innovation spreads slowly at first through the work of change agents who actively promote it. As more change agents in the social system adopt the innovation and communicate it to others, more early adopters join the process until a critical mass is reached and the idea takes off. A similar phenomenon is observed in epidemiology where the critical moment in an epidemic when critical mass is reached is referred to as the "tipping point." Author Malcolm Gladwell applies this concept to social issues in his book, *The Tipping Point*.[15]

The process of innovation diffusion picks up speed as more people adopt it. Eventually it reaches a saturation point where everyone who is going to adopt it has done so. Moving the innovative idea to the point of take-off is of vital importance in any social system change initiative. If it is a good idea, it will then develop a life of its own.

As you read the cases and stories to follow, look for this predictable pattern of innovation diffusion. Consider where and how the concept of sustainable practice was introduced, how it spread, what factors the stories have in common. How are they different? Look for the factors that seem to make the spread of this idea easier. Observe how much time it seems to take. It often happens that one department may be the change agent within a large organization, then that department consciously seeks early adopters within other branches of the same organization to join it in diffusing the desired innovation.

The diffusion of an innovation usually follows a normal, bell-shaped curve that illustrates the rate of adoption over time by certain categories of adopters based on their degree of innovativeness (Figure 3.2).

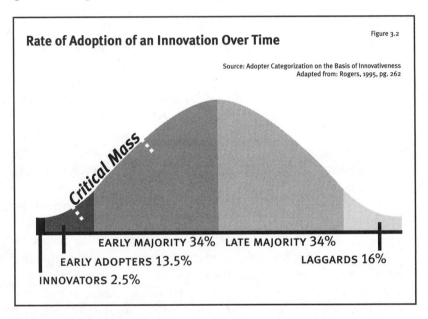

Rate of Adoption of an Innovation Over Time

Figure 3.2

Source: Adopter Categorization on the Basis of Innovativeness
Adapted from: Rogers, 1995, pg. 262

Critical Mass

EARLY MAJORITY 34% LATE MAJORITY 34%
EARLY ADOPTERS 13.5%   LAGGARDS 16%
INNOVATORS 2.5%

The adoption of a new idea results from information exchange through interpersonal networks. The first adopter of an innovation discusses it with other members of the system, and each of these adopters passes the new idea along to others. The diffusion curve begins to level off after one-half of the individuals in a social system have adopted the innovation, because each new adopter finds it increasingly difficult to tell the new idea to a peer who has not yet adopted it. Adopters can be characterized by their degree of "innovativeness": innovators, early adopters, mainstream (early majority and late majority), and laggards. The segment of the diffusion curve between 10 to 20 percent adoption is "critical mass" or the "heart of the diffusion process" and represents the transition from the "early adopter" level of innovativeness to the "early majority." Reaching this "critical mass" is the focus of an effective innovation diffusion strategy.

The strategy succeeds by focusing on identifying, working with, and supporting the early adopters. These individuals tend to be respected by their peers, are role models, and are well integrated into the organization's social system. In other words, it is essential that, in order for them to be effective, they must have and maintain "institutional credibility." This is yet another example of dancing with the tiger in pursuit of sustainability, as effective change agents and early adopters who earnestly desire to move their organizations in a more sustainable direction must nevertheless temper their enthusiasm with the hardheaded recognition that maintaining credibility in the eyes of their professional peers and clients is an essential aspect of their being successful in innovation diffusion

Another important aspect of this process is to recognize that an individual's decision to adopt an innovation is usually not an instantaneous act. Rather, it is usually a process that occurs over time, consisting of a series of actions and decisions. Rogers' model of the innovation-decision process, views this process as consisting of five stages (Figure 3.3).

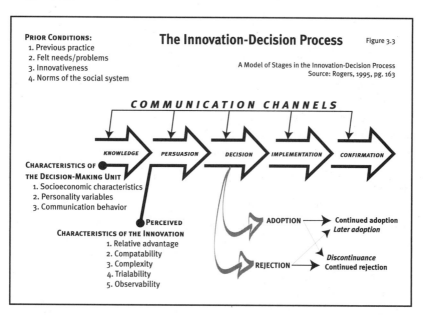

The innovation-decision process is "the process through which an individual (or other decision-making unit) passes from first knowledge of an innovation, to forming an attitude toward the innovation, to a decision to adopt or reject, to implementation of the new idea, and to confirmation of this decision."[16]

It is valuable as you read the following stories to remember that context plays a powerful role in the effectiveness and velocity of the idea's adoption. The structure of the social system within the organization, or within the wider social/political/economic system, can impede or enhance the diffusion and adoption of an innovation. Norms (the stories we tell ourselves about the patterns of behavior that are considered normal) establish which behaviors in any social system are tolerated and which are not. Opinion leaders also affect the social climate and the rate of adoption. These elements are part of the context; and, as Gladwell points out, the power of context suggests that behavior is often less a function of individual dispositions than of the particular setting in which the individual resides.[17] Anyone who has experienced the political and social overtones and undercurrents of any working environment with two or more people knows exactly what he means. *Small changes in the setting can produce large changes in behavior.*

As you read the next four chapters, look for evidence of the context within which these particular change agents and early adopter organizations are spreading knowledge about the innovation of sustainability. Of course, the purpose of spreading this knowledge is to integrate this understanding into new practices, in other words, to shift from less to more sustainable behaviors. Changes in behavior are influenced by what a person knows and how he or she thinks. One of the fundamental steps in the adoption of more sustainable practices is sharing an understanding of what sustainability is and what constitutes sustainable practices. The first adopter of an innovation shares it with other members of the system, and each of these adopters passes the new idea along to other peers.

Also bear in mind that although knowledge is certainly necessary, it is not sufficient to produce behavior change. Perceptions, motivation, skills, and factors in the social environment also play important roles. Look for evidence of how change agents spread the knowledge of sustainability in their organizations and how they convert that knowledge into behaviors that are meaningful within the organization's context and that are compatible with their spheres of control and influence. Also look for evidence of how the ideas and practices spread and are integrated into operations, communications, purchasing and supply chain management, and internal incentive systems.

We realize that these stories can only make sense within the context of your own story. We urge you to look for patterns and relationships, not only within each story, but also between these stories and your own life experience. As author and scientist, Fritjof Capra, points out: "Since relationships are the essence of the living world, one would do best if one spoke a language of relationships to describe it. This is what stories do. What matters in stories is not the plot, the characters or the scenery. What matters are the relationships between them."[18]

What's in a story? Everything. As poet Muriel Rukeyser reminds us, for human beings our "universe is made of stories, not atoms."[19] Story is a powerful way that we organize and share our own experience and explore and co-create shared realities. Our psyches and cultures are built upon and filled with "story fields" (mutually reinforcing stories such as myths, memories, news, movies, fiction) and story-like phenomena (such as roles, metaphors, images, and archetypes). "A story field paints a particular picture of how life is or should be, and shapes the life within its range into its image."[20] We are the stories we were told, we continue to tell ourselves, and we tell each other. What does this have to do with sustainability? Everything. For, as Mary Catherine Bateson points out, "Hope for a sustainable future depends on reshaping the life cycle — not the individual life cycle alone but the overlapping and intersecting cycles of individuals and generations, reaffirming both the past and the future, not only in families but in the institutions we build and share."[21]

We now invite you to explore the stories that we have to tell, to take from them the lessons that provide value to your own story, and like Ianu, to create a dance that exalts the gift of life.

CHAPTER 4

NIKE
INFUSING "JUST DO IT" WITH "DO THE RIGHT THING"

Dancers are the athletes of God.
— Albert Einstein[1]

If you have a body, you're an athlete.
— Bill Bowerman

TO MOST OF ITS EMPLOYEES, Nike is more a state of mind than it is a place of work. Born out of innovation and irreverence for the status quo, Nike remains a mindscape as much as it has become a part of the landscape of global commerce. To its legions of fans and customers, Nike is more than just a company; it is a cultural icon and creative engine dedicated to the triumph of the athlete and a celebration of the human spirit. To its activist critics, Nike has come to symbolize the many failings and deficiencies of an inequitable global market system. In attempting to understand Nike and its step-by-step movement through increasing corporate responsibility toward sustainability, we are thrown directly into the startling disparities and paradoxical nature of global society and market capitalism in the early 21st century.

So it should not come as a great surprise that difficult and soul-searching questions are being posed internally by more and more Nike employees about all aspects of the company's business — from product concept, to research, design, development, manufacturing, shipping and retailing. "How do you create a superior athletic product, then profitably manufacture it, distribute it, and eventually reclaim it, so that no damage occurs whatsoever to our world playground? And how do you do the right thing for everyone involved with our products at every stage of the process?" asks Darcy Winslow, the dynamic global head of Women's Footwear, a billion-dollar component in Nike's dominant Footwear division, and who, in her prior role, was the first general manager of Footwear Sustainability. "We all love this beautiful blue-green planet so much, so profitably aligning all of the products and processes of a global industrial system to the inherent design of our natural world is an idea whose time has come." With nearly $10 billion[2] in annual revenues, over 22,000 of its own employees, and more than 550,000 persons making Nike products in more than 50 countries, and approximately 750 sub-contracted manufacturing facilities around the world, this is no small thought.

Yet asking paradigm-breaking questions is an inherent part of Nike's culture and one of the very reasons for its enormous success. Nike has consistently made room for rebels and independent thinkers, perhaps because the co-founders of the company were two such characters. From University of Oregon Coach Bill Bowerman's cooking rubber waffles on his wife's waffle iron in search of the perfect running sole, to Phil Knight's 1960s Stanford MBA thesis on establishing a marketing-based global corporation with all manufacturing overseas, the independent thinker has been essential to Nike's ongoing growth and development. Today, there is another wave of status quo-busting creativity and innovation swelling within the design studios, research labs and corporate offices of Nike as the company grapples with an undeniable paradox. Nike's essence is the ascendance and even transcendence of the human spirit through athletics, yet its actual down-to-earth impact calls attention to some of the most challenging social and environmental issues that humanity faces.

This paradox gives rise to internal questioning, which is made more urgent and relevant to the business as watchful critics in activist organizations around the world criticize the labor practices of the contract manufacturers who produce Nike products. These criticisms focus on a range of issues including child labor, wages, health and safety of workers, and workers' rights — concerns that working people share worldwide. Many of the criticisms are well founded, acknowledged by the company itself, and have become part of the contemporary Nike story. The social impacts of Nike's global operations have drawn the most attention and negative commentary in recent times. Dusty Kidd, Vice-President of Compliance for Nike, and a thoughtful individual who struggles day in and day out with these issues, comments:

The social dimension is part of sustainability, and any look at Nike and sustainability that doesn't look at the struggles that we've had with these issues internally will be bankrupt. And anything we do that doesn't acknowledge that this has been a real hard issue for us is just not honest. Year after year and month after month the larger and larger challenges we face trying to come to grips with our responsibility in this area, and prioritizing the work we do, grow harder every time we look at the problems. I don't think any one company is up to the challenge here. What we're trying to do is to understand the issues, figure out what we can do, prioritize our actions, acknowledge that we're not going to be perfect, and get at the things that matter the most.

The paradox that Nike faces, we face as a society because many of the goods and services we acquire to enhance the quality of our lives come to us with social and environmental costs that generally remain invisible to us — and those costs are accumulating. Consumers and producers alike are beginning to wake up to the reality that these goods and services have environmental and social effects in our own backyard as well as the backyards of others. We are becoming more aware of the systemic, as well as the personal, implications of our decisions and actions, and we are beginning to take responsibility for them and demanding that the organizations in which we place our trust and do our business take responsibility as well.

The heart and soul of Nike always has been, and most employees believe always will be, the soaring spirit and transcendent greatness of the athlete pressing against and exceeding the known limits of human performance. The genuine human magnificence of a Michael Jordan, a Tiger Woods, a Mia Hamm or a Lance Armstrong touches our hearts and inspires our spirits. Yet it is not just their victories that inspire us. Every athlete knows that for every triumph, there are countless times when performance falls short. What also inspires us is the sheer determination that drives countless hours of unglamorous, sometimes tedious, often grueling practice that yields aching muscles and occasional injuries as well as greater skill and higher performance.

We have come to expect something special from Nike because Nike has convinced us that it *is* special. Believing in that specialness, and true to their inspired heritage, an authentic, grassroots movement for environmental and social responsibility, with support and endorsement from the senior leaders of the company, is gaining momentum within the organization; a movement with science, compassion and long-term, good business strategy on its side. A growing number of initiatives of both a social and environmental nature are emerging inside Nike, led by some independent and innovative thinkers scattered throughout the company and around the world, to help reconcile its transcendent vision with its sometimes less than inspiring impacts on the ground. The balance of this chapter is an attempt to capture the stories of some of these sustainability champions, and to place them within the context of the unique corporate culture and complex global industry in which each of them works and devotes so much of his or her intellectual and emotional life.

We hope to give you a flavor of the authentic re-examination of Nike's way of doing business that is occurring within every part of this constantly evolving organization. Nike's new maxim of "Do the Right Thing" daily becomes more and more taken to heart throughout the company and is increasingly being reconciled with two better known Nike-isms: "Just Do It" and "There Is No Finish Line." Today, if Nike is going to just do it, it wants to ensure that whatever it does, it does the right thing. What is more, Nike is learning that the concept "there is no finish line" applies both to the nature of the commitment needed to contribute to social and ecological sustainability and to the ideal outcome of sustainability: a civilization that does not crash and burn, but one that thrives and plays indefinitely.

GLOBAL SYSTEMS CONTEXT

Nike operates, and we all live, in a world characterized by gross disparities between extreme wealth and extreme poverty. These global inequalities have been rising steadily for at least two centuries, and they remain one of the greatest challenges facing the global economy and global society. Measured by the Human Poverty Index,[3] more than one-quarter of the 4.5 billion people in developing countries still do not have life's most basic securities: a reasonable expectation of living past 40, or access to clean water, food, personal security, minimum private and public services or education. Roughly 15 million children die each year as a result of poverty. Approximately 41,000 children die every day, or almost 2,000 an hour — about the time it will take you to read this chapter. About 840 million people are malnourished. An estimated 1.3 billion people earn less than one dollar per day.

In contrast, the 20 percent of the world's people who live in the richest nations of the world have 74 times the income of the world's poorest 20 percent. The assets of just the three richest people in the world are greater than the combined Gross National Product (GNP) of the 49 least-developed countries — countries with more than one billion inhabitants. The assets of the 200 richest people exceed the combined income of 41 percent of the world's people, that is, more than two billion human beings. A contribution of a mere one percent of the wealth of these 200 richest people could provide access to primary education for all (estimated to cost $7 to $8 billion per year).[4]

These are the realities of the world that humanity is creating. They are also the realities of the international global market system. Another reality of the international global market is that these growing wealth and population disparities also create disparities in wage and labor conditions. In part, wages are low and working conditions are poor in developing countries because the supply of unskilled labor is abundant and the demand for labor is weak. There are limited alternatives for employment. In the countries of South Asia, for example, where the majority of the world's poor live (outside of China), more than one-half of the labor force is self-employed and only a small proportion is regularly employed.[5] Labor-intensive production, such as garment and footwear manufacturing, has developed as an economic lifeline for many of these countries and millions of people. Developing countries specialize in the export of products like garments and footwear because these products are labor-intensive; and because these countries have abundant low-wage labor, they can produce high-labor content articles for the global market at competitive rates.

The high consumption rates of the developed countries are made possible, in part, by this global production and trade structure. Well over one-half of U.S. imports come from developing countries in Asia, Latin America and the former Soviet Union. Apparel, footwear, toys, and sporting equipment account for a large portion of these imports. Worldwide, some 80,000 factories employing millions of workers provide the goods purchased by consumers in the developed world. In other words, we are all implicated in this inequitable global system. We each support it with almost every purchase that we make.

IF YOU HAVE A BODY, YOU'RE AN ATHLETE[6]

While Nike's story is now inextricably interwoven with the global pattern of relationships between the so-called developing and developed worlds, the story begins much closer to home. Early in its 30 years of existence, Nike became the world's leading sports and fitness company, an entrepreneurial legend, and one of the most recognized brands in the world. The roots of the company began when Phil Knight, a business student and runner at the University of Oregon, and his coach, Bill Bowerman, started a company named Blue Ribbon Sports, in 1962, based on Bowerman's innovative ideas on how to improve his runners' performance and Knight's innovative business idea to import high-tech, low-priced athletic shoes from Japan and sell them in the U.S. market to compete with the German-made shoes that then dominated the market. The focus then, as it is now, was on creating high-performance gear for athletes to help them maximize their potential.

After he completed his MBA at Stanford University, Knight decided to take time out to travel around the world. While he was in Japan, he contacted Onitsuka Tiger Company and convinced them that there were great marketing opportunities in the United States. When asked what company he represented, Knight simply made up a name, Blue Ribbon Sports. Knight then ordered shoes that were delivered to his parents' garage. He and Coach Bowerman each contributed $500 to pay for the product; they shook hands, and the company was born. This was the beginning of their extraordinarily successful business relationship, one that would thrive for decades.

Bowerman worked constantly on ways to improve the shoes and Knight pushed the boundaries of creativity to build the business. By 1968, a Bowerman-modified design, the Cortez, became Tiger's best-selling shoe. Between 1962 and 1971, revenues in the business grew from $8,000 to $1.96 million, and the number of employees grew from zero to 45.

In 1972, Blue Ribbon Sports ended its partnership with Onitsuka Tiger and would no longer sell Tiger brand shoes. Knight and Bowerman renamed the company Nike after the winged Greek Goddess of Victory and went into business to design, have manufactured, and market their own brand of shoes under the new Nike label. Nike was the brash and exciting challenger company on the scene with an "in-your-face" attitude. The timing and image were perfect, riding the growing interest among baby-boomers in physical fitness and jogging. Through

continued innovative design and business strategies, as well as high energy and self-confidence, by 1980 Nike had captured 50 percent of the
growing U.S. running shoe market. That year, with 2,700 employees
and a successful track record, Knight took the company public. The
company continued building its brand through a steady focus on high-
performance athletes. Athletes were responding: by the end of 1982,
every world record in men's track, from the 800 meters to the
marathon, had been set by athletes wearing Nike's high-performance
sports shoes. It was an astounding achievement for the young company.

By 1984, revenues had grown to $919.8 million. Nike continued to
produce innovative advances in design as it expanded its range of product offerings. In addition, through strategic sponsorships, Nike became
associated with high-performance athletes in a range of sports. Today
these Nike heroes include Michael Jordan, Pete Sampras, John
McEnroe, Carl Lewis, Mia Hamm, Joan Benoit-Samuelson, Monica
Seles, Michael Johnson, Andre Agassi, Tiger Woods and Lance
Armstrong. In 1990, Nike had grown to 5,300 employees and $2 bil-
lion in revenue. Between 1993 and 1997, the company scored record
growth, tripling in size. By 2001, the company had grown to more than
22,000 employees operating on six continents and almost $10 billion
in revenue. Through its network of suppliers, shippers, retailers, and
service providers, Nike provides employment for close to one million
people worldwide. (See Figure 4.1 for Nike's recent revenue history.)

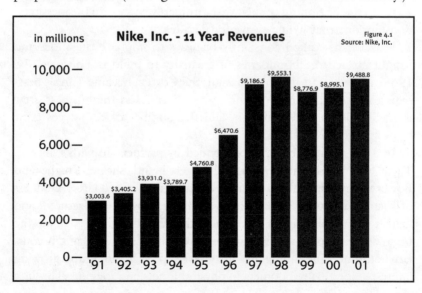

Nike, Inc. - 11 Year Revenues
Figure 4.1
Source: Nike, Inc.

Nike's organizational culture is about sports, fitness, performance, risk, excellence and winning. It is a competitive culture that attracts sports-oriented, competitive people who pride themselves in being performers. At Nike the athlete is king, and making cool products for athletes is the ultimate achievement. Boldness is a core competency. The company is fast paced and creative. As a result, there is little patience for a long-term perspective. Nike is not, and has never been, a "top-down" organization. Its successes are based on people having good ideas and making them happen: an attitude of "just do it" permeates the company's culture. Rarely at Nike do you get a management mandate to do something; you get financial support and then it is up to you to make it happen. It is firmly understood that real innovation doesn't come from upper management. It is truly a culture that admires high performance heroes who defy the odds.

In its meteoric growth and rise to prominence as a globally recognized brand, Nike has become a "big company," despite the fact that at heart many employees, particularly those who have been with Nike for some time, still view it as an agile, even rebellious company. However, in many ways, Nike has gone from being the brash challenger to being the corporate establishment. In the process, the company's spectacular growth outpaced its organizational capacity and the company needed to turn its attention to building greater internal capacity. At the same time, Nike found unwanted prominence in a new arena: it became a symbol of globalization and the controversies that surround it. Nike's brand recognition and offshore manufacturing network make it a favorite target of activist groups who want to bring attention to the challenges and inequities inherent in the global market system including the current system of global manufacturing out-sourcing.

Nike's business model still depends upon producing high-performance product — footwear, apparel, and equipment — through contract manufacturers, that is, through manufacturing facilities not owned by Nike. These contract manufacturers are located primarily in developing countries. This means that Nike's business is deeply entrenched in some of the most pressing and difficult business, social and environmental issues of the 21st century. Many of the countries Nike operates in compete aggressively for this business as it provides much needed wage-based employment in situations where unskilled labor is abundant and alternatives are limited. These countries represent a diversity of cultures, traditions, and social, economic, political, regulatory and enforcement structures. These new challenges also mean that Nike needs to develop capacity and expertise in areas that go quite beyond those conventionally attached to business.

This is thorny and uncharted territory where many critics demand overnight solutions to extraordinarily complex problems that defy the quick fix. Added to that is the complication that although Nike has some degree of control over what happens in the factories, since it doesn't own them, it is often limited to exerting influence on what happens in them. The degree of influence Nike can exert also varies. It is highly challenging in this situation to figure out how to actually "do the right thing" as required by one of Nike's recently adopted maxims. Simply withdrawing their business will not change the practices and conditions that exist in the factories. In fact, the loss of Nike's business would likely only exacerbate the difficult conditions faced by the workers. Added to the challenge of finding the right leverage in each of these domains of control and influence is the sheer magnitude of the task. Vice-President of Compliance, Dusty Kidd explains:

> Three or four years ago, our biggest challenge was try-
> ing to figure out the basic compliance issues: compliance
> around age, wages, overtime and benefits. Those were
> our biggest issues. So we put most of our resources into
> trying to get factories into compliance with their local
> labor law and with our code, whichever was tougher. As
> we learned more and peeled off more layers, we won-
> dered if maybe the bigger issues aren't compliance issues
> as much as they are people management training issues,
> and so we put a huge amount of work into just basic
> management training, not even training on specific labor
> standards, but on how to help factory managers manage
> people.
>
> Now if you have one factory, that is a fairly discrete
> piece of work, and you can probably do it pretty well
> over the course of a year or two. We're trying to do that
> sort of basic training of management skills to help fac-
> tories across 58 countries and in 700 or 800 factories.
> So you're not only peeling the layer off the onion,

you're peeling the layers off 700 or 800 onions. At the same time that you're trying to bring some standardization to the process, the reality is that each of those factories is a unique living environment. They are all different, so you try to bring standardization, you try to bring bang for the buck, you try to bring consistency, while the reality is that the field in which you are operating has all sorts of different issues that are different factory by factory.

So it is a real challenge to master the management of that sort of responsibility. Now we're in a third phase — and all these are actually happening simultaneously — we are really going into the health and safety aspects of a manufacturing facility and trying to understand the risks and the rewards of making clinics the highest level priority or looking at the workplace production lines and attacking the occupational health issues that come with all of that. Another aspect is there are some huge people impacts that aren't so much about the workplace as they are about having a collection of people working together: cultural issues, women's empowerment, looking at education outside of the workplace, and really making the job a foundation for helping young women to improve their situations. Take all that together and multiply that again by 700 or 800 places.

Almost overnight in organizational terms, Nike has become a complex social system organized on the basis of regions, global functions, categories of business, functional business units, and dealing with some of the most problematical issues of our time. Now, as at its inception, Nike's goal is to produce the best and most innovative line of products. At the same time, Nike is involved in a different quest for excellence: exploring what it means to play and excel on the field of corporate responsibility.

SUSTAINABILITY EVOLUTION

In the late 1980s, Phil Knight asked a group of people in Nike to suggest some scenarios for Nike's future. Some of the participants at that meeting mentioned that Nike needed an environmental program. They were concerned particularly with the environmental impact of manufacturing. Although Knight agreed that Nike should look at environmental issues, he also expressed some doubt as to whether Nike could get the factories to change.

> *Nike's place as a global company is evolving. We are looking at a much larger picture, one of becoming a sustainable business, of sound labor practices, of being a responsible global and corporate citizen.*
>
> — Phil Knight, CEO and Co-founder

A steering committee was formed and eventually concluded that Nike needed an environmental department. In 1993, the Nike Environmental Action Team (NEAT) was formed. The focus for NEAT in the first few years was mainly on compliance, manufacturing, monitoring, and creating an innovative recycling-based program called Reuse-A-Shoe.[7] In 1995, Sarah Severn, then the Director of NEAT, took her staff to hear Paul Hawken speak about his new book *The Ecology of Commerce*.[8] Severn recalls that after hearing Hawken she felt her staff had received their marching orders. "The message seemed simple. The planet's living systems are in decline and without them there is no such thing as society, let alone business. Our choice as a business seemed clear — continue to contribute to the decline, or enter a new era of commerce where human and business needs stop depleting living systems."

By 1996, NEAT began to focus on supplier education, pollution prevention, and the greening of materials used in the manufacture of their products. In that same year, Nike established its labor practices group. Nike first became involved with The Natural Step and its approach to sustainable development in June 1997, when the company hosted a one-day introductory workshop on sustainability at their corporate conference center. By 1998, the company had adopted The Natural Step framework as a foundation for sustainability learning. The main focus was to use it as an educational tool in learning programs and forums. Severn remarks:

> The key benefits to Nike of The Natural Step framework for sustainability are:
>
> • It provides a shared language and set of guiding

principles both within the company and between ourselves and other organizations with whom we do work on sustainability;

- It is scientifically robust;

- It uses a "systems perspective" — thinking about cause and effect and linkages through a whole system rather than just analyzing discrete units of the system;

- It is non-judgmental; and

- The principles work across different cultures.

That same year, Severn brought Bill McDonough and Michael Braungart of McDonough Braungart Design Chemistry (MBDC)[9] to Nike to speak to some of the Research, Design and Development (RD&D) staff. Darcy Winslow, then Global Director of RD&D for Footwear, recalls: "After hearing and meeting Bill McDonough and Michael Braungart for the first time, it dawned on me that we are investing five years upstream, which eventually affects one to ten to 10,000 different products. And what we do upstream has a down-stream effect — good, bad, or indifferent. If we don't consider all aspects of a product's life cycle, and work on the solutions upstream, we are going to be cleaning up after ourselves." McDonough and Braungart generated a lot of excitement and interest in more sustainable ways of creating product, especially among designers in Footwear. Sustainability initiatives began to emerge that focused on product design within both the Footwear and Apparel business units.

In 1998, Nike made a strategic hire by bringing in Maria Eitel as Vice-President for Corporate Responsibility, which signaled that the issues around corporate responsibility and sustainability were considered important at the senior executive level. This raised the profile of corporate responsibility in the company. Severn and her team at NEAT began to explore ways to bring sustainability awareness to the wider Nike community. This presented a set of big challenges: how to provide meaningful sustainability education in a large and global organization that is characterized by a very fast-paced, creative, and competitive environment; how to design this process so that it makes sustainability practice immediately relevant to the business; and how to ensure that this business relevance is demonstrated in measurable improvements in both sustainability practice and business performance. NEAT set out to create a process that would address these challenges.

Nike developed and then launched its environmental policy in September 1998. This event produced a groundswell of energy, interest, enthusiasm and passion among Nike employees. At the launch, Paul Hawken reminded Nike employees that at its core, "Nike is about life," a message that resonated with the positive image Nike employees hold about their work. Bill McDonough told employees that Nike could send a signal to the world that the power of developing a new design is not about "being less bad tomorrow," it is about designing products that are part of the solution in a sustainable society. Tom Clarke, then President of Nike, made a commitment to the next steps and encouraged the individual ingenuity of Nike employees: "This sustainability challenge is dependent on education. We're going to be providing education through our NEAT team. But it is through our collective curiosity and our individual curiosity that we're going to get discoveries that will allow us to be what we want to be in the future."

Although NEAT was designing the educational program to be rolled out in the summer of 1999, it was clear that the business units, particularly Footwear and Apparel, were eager to move ahead more quickly. By February 1999, the Footwear and Apparel groups each conducted sustainability workshops in their business units. From August 1999 through April 2000, NEAT launched a remarkable and ground-breaking global sustainability education and integration process based on The Natural Step framework for sustainability. The sustainability integration initiative not only provided education for sustainability champions across the company, it also generated more than 65 sustainability-oriented pilot projects across all areas of Nike's business and provided inspiration to hundreds of Nike employees.

During 2000, two other significant processes took place at Nike with respect to sustainability. First, the company leadership engaged in serious soul-searching about what it means to be a "truly great company" in the 21st century. Nike had already become the pre-eminent sports and fitness company in the world. What was next? Particularly in light of its struggles around labor practices, Nike turned inward to explore the values that would carry it successfully into the new millennium as a leading global corporate citizen. In the midst of this exploration, Nelson Farris, who in many respects functions as Nike's institutional memory, remarked: "We're really trying to build what we think should be the world's best corporation in this new millennium. Following the same thinking of the early Nike, we are at the point of doing the remarkable, hoping to achieve the exceptional, and eventually to achieve the inconceivable. The inconceivable is what this is: we don't know what it means to be a great corporation of this millennium, and so we're trying to figure this out. The remarkable is what we are going through right now: we're trying to refocus the company." This exploration resulted in the creation of eleven Nike "maxims" released in the spring of 2001. The purpose of the maxims is to help shape the culture of the company for a new way of doing business in the 21st century. One of these maxims is "Do the right thing," which includes a focus on corporate responsibility and sustainability.

Secondly, Nike began drafting its first corporate responsibility report. CEO Phil Knight remarks in his introductory letter to the report that "Nike for the first time has assembled a comprehensive public review of our corporate responsibility practices." Reflecting on the changes that have been taking place in Nike, he says:

> Things change. We are still passionate and focused. We are still about sports. But our world has become much bigger, our impact felt beyond sports. In January 2001 we redrafted our mission and values to reflect this evolution of Nike, to recommit to our fundamental truths while identifying opportunities for growth as a business and as a citizen. We call these truths our maxims. Among these maxims, we state that as a sports brand, 'Nike exists to bring inspiration and innovation to every athlete in the world.' As a global corporation, we have somewhat broader goals; 'Nike exists to pursue opportunity and to enhance human potential.' As a citizen of the world, Nike must Do The Right Thing — try to be transparent about what we are doing right, and about what we are doing wrong; embrace diversity; drive sustainability.[10]

The report, now available on the Nike website,[11] is the company's first attempt to provide a transparent accounting of its approach and activities with respect to the environmental and social aspects of sustainability. This is a very comprehensive document, perhaps a landmark in the field, and is a good reference for anyone interested in the field of corporate responsibility.

It is important to realize, when reading about the substantial progress that Nike has made over the past ten years in corporate responsibility and sustainability, that Nike really had no idea at each stage of the journey what the territory two or three stages down the road would be. It has truly been a step-by-step progression. Yet at each stage, decisions had to be made to determine what the next steps would be and there were often many alternative courses possible. Nike has been a pioneer, and like all pioneers, it has faced undiscovered territory, with potential pitfalls and rewards at every turn. At each major branch point in the journey, decisions were juggling acts balancing many factors, including desired programs, available funding, general corporate priorities, departmental priorities, internal staffing, and stakeholder concerns.

Sustainability Integration: Step by Step[12]

The evolution of corporate responsibility and sustainability in Nike has been driven by internal employee concern and by external stakeholder pressure. Both dynamics were vital factors in moving Nike in a more socially responsible and sustainable direction. In the 1980s, a few Nike employees expressed their concerns about Nike's environmental impacts. This led to the creation of NEAT and ultimately to the early stages of integrating sustainability thinking into product and process design and to incorporating sustainability into the company's core values. External pressures have pushed Nike to re-examine its values and will continue to help Nike "keep its eyes on the prize."

At the heart of it, however, the dance toward sustainability in Nike has been a grassroots process. It has received the endorsement of senior leadership and their support in the form of financial resources, permission to explore, and the dedication of personnel time to learn the dance, but it is the passion, drive and genius of individuals across the company that brought the process to life and carries it today. Leadership commitment made it possible for more than 100 employees from around the world to participate in an intensive sustainability education process and to bring back what they learned to their functions and business units so they could convert it into meaningful business practice. Leadership in sustainability emerged on all levels of the organization in this process as individual employees and teams of employees began to translate sustainability concepts into design principles and to apply them to internal logistics and operations. In this section, we explore some of the steps that Nike has taken with respect to leadership commitment, integrating sustainability and social responsibility into policy statements, board commitment to these principles, the commitment of time and resources, education, and actually walking the talk by integrating principles into practice.

> *Our commitment to corporate responsibility has to come from every level of Nike and be a part of every aspect of our business.*
>
> — Dr. Jill Ker Conway, Chair, Corporate Responsibility Committee, Nike Board of Directors, September 2001.

Leadership Commitment

Leadership commitment in any organization is expressed through the internal and external statements of the top executives of the company, through the policies that guide company behavior, and through the provision of financial and human resources to get the job done. The top leaders of Nike have expressed their commitment to sustainability and corporate responsibility on many occasions: in public speeches, in internal speeches, in internal videos and in public as well as internal confidential reports. Some examples of what leaders in Nike are saying include:

Phil Knight, CEO, President and Chairman

> We have a strong interest in the environment and sustainability at Nike. Especially among middle management, and our younger employees, who can teach the rest of us, including me, how to use sustainable business practices to make us a better business. All of us know intuitively that making decisions based on what is good for future generations will help us create a company that is built to last.

Mark Parker, President, Nike Brand

> We are committed to sustainable design. It is not something that's simply in next year's business plan; it is

something that's a long-term, ongoing, never-ending commitment. Employees should feel that if they want to make a deeper commitment that the company will be there, that we are looking for input, we are looking for ideas. It is exciting to me, as a part of senior management at Nike, to see my peers and others corporately really being a lot more conscious about what we're doing, the impact of better understanding the decisions we are taking on the environment and really putting a lot more thought into that aspect of our business than ever before. It's a commitment throughout every phase of the product process.

Jerry Karver, Divisional Vice-President, Footwear Operations

Historically, people say, 'Well you have the environmental issues here, and you have the business issues there, and they're diametrically opposed and never will the two meet.' But the reality is that the idea of sustainability is one of the best business strategies we could adopt. There are so many companies out there that couldn't do this; even if they wanted to with the best intentions, they couldn't do it. But when I think about Nike, and when I think about our ability to change, our ability to think, our ability to innovate in so many ways, I look at sustainability and say, we can do this. The real progress that is being made is that the idea is taking hold. And in a company like this when an idea like this becomes part of our basic values, of who we are, the power of it is unleashed.

Maria Eitel, Vice-President, Corporate Responsibility

The word 'sustainability' has been thrown around a lot. What it means to us is not seeing things piecemeal, not stressing business issues in one piece and sustainability issues in another. To us sustainability means running our business while being conscious of, and addressing, its impacts, and addressing them everywhere.

Curt Roberts, Vice-President, Global Strategic Planning

I am continually, though pleasantly, surprised by how

intrinsically motivated Nike people can be to do good work and the right thing. They don't necessarily need somebody at the corporate level to hammer it home. It is a fairly motivated bunch that way and you will see product designers and other people putting effort into what they otherwise could blow off because it might not be in their performance review. But they'll do it anyway because they just know that it's important and that's one thing about this place that I think is a good characteristic. If you ask people to express a degree of confidence that the work that we are doing in this regard would pay off in a financial sense, you'd get a very mixed response. Some might even argue that it doesn't have to, that doing the right thing is the right thing to do whether it pays off or not.

Dusty Kidd, Vice-President, Compliance

The thing that started Nike on the path to great success was the quality of the people. The people came for a reason and it was a mission. It wasn't about a job and earning money and being popular as a brand. It was because they really thought that we had a mission to provide great sports products and really connect with the athlete. That same thing is true in a growing way in the areas of corporate responsibility and sustainability. Our younger generation here is very keen on that and they care about it and if we weren't concerned about it as a company they wouldn't be here either.

Another important indicator of leadership commitment is the way that sustainability shows up in official corporate policies that signal to internal and external stakeholders what the company stands for:

Nike Corporate Environmental Mission and Policy

Through the adoption of sustainable business practices Nike is committed to securing intergenerational quality of life, restoring the environment and increasing value for our customers, shareholders and business partners.

NIKE WILL ENDEAVOR TO:

- Integrate principles of sustainability into all major business decisions.

- Scrutinize our environmental impacts in our day-to-day operations and throughout every stage of the product life cycle.

- Design and develop product, materials and technologies according to the fundamental principles of sustainability.

- Promote our practices through the supply chain and seek business partnerships with suppliers who operate in a manner consistent with our values.

- Educate our employees, customers, and business partners to support our goal of achieving sustainability.

- Turn awareness into action by integrating environmental responsibility into job responsibility.

- Partner with experts and organizations that contribute to our knowledge about sustainability and stewardship of our outdoor playground.

- Contribute to quality of life in the communities in which we operate.

- Monitor, measure and report progress.

- Strive for continuous improvement in everything we do.

- Comply with all applicable and relevant regulations wherever in the world we do business.

Nike Forest Products Policy

Nike will give purchasing preference, where price and availability allow, to wood and paper products that originate in forests that have been independently certified as being well-managed. Nike will recognize only those certifications issued by organizations accredited by the Forest Stewardship Council (FSC).

- Nike will eliminate from its purchasing practice those materials derived from wood or pulp originating in native old growth or frontier forests. Examples of products that may derive from such wood or pulp include (but are not limited to) paper, paperboard, lumber, furniture, cellophane tape, and acetate.

- Nike has become a member of the Certified Forest Products Council (CFPC) and will work with CFPC to develop an action plan that will help us define, develop and implement responsible forest products purchasing practices and work with our suppliers to meet our needs.

- Nike will benchmark its paper consumption to determine paper usage, types, and origins. Targets will be set for reducing per capita paper usage and for increasing, where feasible, the use of tree-free papers. Nike will conduct a similar benchmarking process for non-paper forest products.

Procurement Policies

Nike is developing a comprehensive Strategic Sourcing Initiative: a system that will not only track indirect spending, but also integrate environmental language into proposals and contracts with its suppliers. Nike has been purchasing only energy-saving computers, copiers, printers and other office equipment for years. They are now helping to close the loop by choosing products that have recycled content and can be recycled again, avoiding items with excessive packaging, and using their influence to "green" other products.

Board Commitment

In September 2001, Nike brought its commitment to corporate responsibility and sustainability to the board level through the unanimous approval of the creation of a board-level Corporate Responsibility Committee. The new committee is responsible for reviewing, reporting and making recommendations to the full board of directors regarding the company's business strategy and practices and their alignment with corporate responsibility commitments. The committee will review Nike's efforts in the area of labor compliance initiatives, environmental practices, community affairs programs, human resources, diversity issues and philanthropic efforts.

Dr. Jill Ker Conway, a Nike director and visiting scholar with the Massachusetts Institute of Technology's program in Science, Technology and Society, chairs the committee. Dr. Conway is also an author and former president of Smith College. Former Nike president, attorney and Nike director Richard K. Donahue and Dr. A. Michael Spence, Nobel Prize winner and former Dean of the Graduate School of Business at Stanford University, also serve on the committee.

> *The board's creation of this committee reaffirms Nike's commitment to corporate responsibility at every level of our business. The key to a sustainable business, from our perspective, is keeping in mind that we are accountable for not only our financial results, but also for the overall footprint we leave behind, both environmental and social.*
>
> — Phil Knight, CEO & Co-founder

The establishment of this committee means that corporate responsibility is a regular item on the board agenda as a vital factor of doing business and corporate responsibility practice is formally reported by Nike staff to the board on a regular basis.

Commitment of Time and Resources

One of the indications of Nike's leadership commitment is the support that it provides in the form of resources, particularly time and money, the positions dedicated to moving sustainability forward in the organization, and the placement and levels of those positions within the organization. The growth of both NEAT and Labor Practices provide excellent examples. In 1993, NEAT had three full-time positions. By 2000, NEAT had 20 positions in the United States, two in Europe and seven in Asia. In addition, sustainability-oriented positions had been created in the business units: Footwear had five positions in the United States and two in Asia; and Apparel, a smaller business unit, had one position in the United States and by 2001 had four positions. The Labor Practices department started in 1996 with three people and now has more than 40 people in 15 countries. Corporate responsibility and compliance — focused primarily on labor practices — are represented at the divisional vice-presidential level with Maria Eitel and Dusty Kidd.

Nike has experimented with several organizational approaches to draw the right balance between signaling the separate and clear importance of these issues to the company and integrating these concerns effectively into business practice. The three areas of NEAT, Labor Practices, and Community Affairs were first consolidated under Corporate Responsibility in 1998. In 2001 there was an internal re-organization between NEAT and Labor Practices in response to the needs of the organization — in part due to the success of the Footwear and Apparel divisions taking on some of this work, and also because Nike needed to become more sophisticated in the way that it integrated social and environmental matters. The Labor Practices group became Compliance and took on all of the Asia environmental positions, and NEAT transitioned into the Sustainable Development unit, focused on the development of stakeholder engagement, continued integration of sustainability into the business, and corporate reporting. This mandate spans both environmental and social issues. With the promising integration of environmental sustainability concerns occurring in the business units, the corporate level function has shifted more to a support function for those business activities, particularly through continuing education, and to more concerted work with stakeholder engagement and corporate reporting. These functions of corporate level Sustainable Development, together with Community Affairs, now fall under the umbrella of the Corporate Communications department.

With respect to the Compliance group, Kidd points out, "The work of compliance is so complex and so difficult that we need to really focus it in a way that makes it most likely that we will succeed. So one aspect is to take the best people vertically and horizontally and put them in one group, and then to put them where they can have more impact than they've had out on an island of responsibility. Put the responsibility where it will have more leverage on the factories. Where is the most leverage? In the business unit that has the most factories." Therefore, the Compliance group has been relocated in the Apparel business unit in order to have more direct influence on business decision-making and to exercise greater authority. Although Apparel is a smaller unit in terms of gross revenues generated, it has a comparable worker count to Footwear, approximately 250,000 workers, and has by far the largest factory base: a ratio of more than ten to one compared to Footwear, approximately 700 Apparel factories to 60 Footwear factories. Although located in Apparel, Compliance personnel in other business units such as Footwear and Equipment report to Kidd as well.

These are only a sampling of the level and types of resources that Nike is dedicating to corporate responsibility and sustainability. Overall, the company is committing hundreds of employees around the world and tens of millions of dollars each year to enable it to become increasingly effective in dealing responsibly with the many extremely complex issues in this arena. As the following sections demonstrate, Nike has also committed significant resources to education, to building partnerships with external stakeholders, and to experimenting with what all these concepts mean in real business applications.

Education

Leadership arises from many places in an organization. This is particularly true in Nike's culture where boldness, creativity and innovation are the lifeblood of the organization. Until fairly recently, environmental sustainability principles and applications were foreign to the vast majority of Nike employees. There was a need, first of all, to communicate that sustainability is part of everyone's job. In order for people to know what that means, it was clear that Nike needed to educate its people on the issues. As often happens with people and business teams within Nike, NEAT developed an ambitious goal: to start with a relatively small group of sustainability champions, provide intensive education in sustainability concepts to this group, and send them back to their business units and functional departments where, as sustainability leaders and coaches, they could help change the business culture and practices of the corporation. These champions would each work on projects, primarily with teams that would integrate what they learned into practice. This would require that the champions develop and exercise leadership and communication skills needed to share the knowledge they had gained and to demonstrate its business value. The goal was to develop a critical mass of change agents to individually and collectively lead the transition to sustainability for Nike.

The sustainability educational process took place over a period of nine months. At four four-day off-site sessions, participants learned from some of the world's leading thinkers in sustainability such as Dr. Karl-Henrik Robèrt, Paul Hawken, Bill McDonough, Amory Lovins, Janine Benyus, and Ray Anderson. They then spent two to three days each session exploring a variety of frameworks, strategies and tools such as The Natural Step framework for sustainability, natural capitalism strategies, systems mapping, management systems, and metrics. They developed leadership, communication, and coaching skills to help them work with their teams. They heard from a variety of practitioners from other corporations and examined a number of case studies to learn how aspects of sustainability could be applied. During the time between these sessions, participants received coaching, they shaped and defined a salient business issue, then convened an action team around the business issue, applied their newly acquired knowledge of sustainable principles to it, and ultimately presented the outcomes of their work or "work in progress" to the wider Nike community. This active learning approach was designed to facilitate the integration of the learning outcomes from the off-site sessions into each participant's normal business responsibilities. Upon completion of the nine-month sustainability training, each participant received a CD, containing training and presentation material on The Natural Step framework, to be shared with their Nike colleagues around the world.

As the sustainability education and integration course proceeded, NEAT rediscovered an age-old truth: Rome wasn't built in a day and you can't change a corporate culture overnight. NEAT found that their original goal to transform this complex global corporation through 100 change agents in a short period of time was overly optimistic. However, the process did create a strong network of people who learned how to think of Nike as a complex system, rather than just a group of distinct, "siloed" departments. In addition, each participant convened a team of peers who were not a core part of the program and identified business issues to set goals against. More than 65 projects were initiated or affected by this process, with environmental sustainability as a key consideration.

Nike hit one of the challenges of grassroots movements: the middle of the organization was moving faster in the understanding and direction of sustainability than the organization's leadership. Energy, excitement and ingenuity were being stimulated to design and implement more sustainable practices, but they were finding an uneven reception across the company. Although many of Nike's leaders were engaged and committed to the process, others did not give it the support, priority and attention that team captains needed and expected in order to move forward effectively. The process helped Nike find and nurture early adopters on all levels and sections of its system, but it was not, in the limited time of nine months, able to reach critical mass.

> *When I think about sustainability, I look at the ideas, the concepts, I look at the organization, I look at the training, I look at the commitment we've made to people, money, resources, training, and time. I say this is cool. This is how we get at this issue.*
>
> — Jerry Karver, Divisional Vice-President, Footwear Operations

We believe that it is still too early, almost two years after the completion of the sustainability education initiative, to accurately assess the success of the process with respect to its ultimate influence on changing Nike's corporate culture and business practices. As pointed out in chapter 3, the diffusion of any innovation does not happen overnight. It takes time to build critical mass, and the point at which one more shift or change, design or statement becomes the tipping point of that critical mass is not possible to predict. The evidence is clear, however, that between the end of that program in April 2000 and the present, January 2002, corporate responsibility and sustainability have become more and more integrated into the operations of Nike's business units, into conversations about the business and in company decisions. Has the whole system changed yet? No. Is it near the tipping point? Maybe. Phil Berry, Technical Director, Footwear Sustainability, comments: "We were ahead of a long curve and the Sustainability Initiative actually raised that curve. The whole education component clearly raised people's awareness, raised the bar, and got a whole lot more people involved with more meaningful tools."

More sustainable practice occurs on the level of personal day-to-day decisions and actions. Therefore, one of the best ways to assess the effect of participation in the sustainability education and integration initiative is directly from some of the participants:

Miro Peters, Sustainability Project Coordinator, Europe

> I think it has shown to people who were directly involved, and those people who got word of it, that Nike

is seriously trying in its own way to be proactive about sustainability. I think it has helped to put sustainability on the map. Even if people don't know what it is about in detail, they still have been exposed to it somehow and the threshold to participate has been lowered. I think it was a very brave start.

Liz Rogers, Director of Nike's Global Intranet

Although I considered myself a 'sustainability person' before participating in this initiative, I have learned more factual information about what it takes to be sustainable, how to measure return on investment (ROI), apply metrics, etc. to all aspects of projects. I have integrated sustainable thinking; this means I no longer put on my 'sustainable lens' now it's becoming part of my everyday work. We still have a long way to go, however it's a tremendous start, there are more people in the business practicing sustainability, even in Internal Communications (previously the word wasn't in their vocabulary), we are seeing the majority of IC's work being done on the web and much, much less material is being print produced and delivered to employees. This alone is a huge accomplishment.

Jim Stalknecht, Senior Designer, Special Projects, Nike Europe

It became a new way of thinking. With everything I do, I ask myself, what the impact for the planet will be and also try to bring that over to others by talking about it. When I do presentations, I always encourage people to behave more sustainably.

With respect to the Sustainability Initiative's impact on Nike, Stalknecht believes that it created more awareness both inside and outside of the company:

More people know that Nike works on the environment. People get enthusiastic about it and want to participate. People are proud that Nike does this. Also, outsiders are happily surprised that Nike works on sustainability.

Mary Margaret Briggs, Creative Director, Hong Kong

The Sustainability Initiative increased my awareness of sustainability when making decisions about product or processes. It has made Nike a better company with a bigger heart and soul. It has added value to our brand, and made us a company that we can feel more proud of.

Rick MacDonald, Apparel Innovation Director

It's not like everyone in every department is sitting around integrating sustainability into their every task or project. The fact that sustainability is called out in the 'maxims' is a step in the right direction and indicates that the Initiative has had a positive impact on the company, but until the environment is written into every product brief and project description, we have a way to go.

Jane Pallera, Design Director for Kids Footwear

It has made a huge difference. It's empowered conscientious individuals to feel that they can make a difference regarding their impact on the environment: every little bit counts.

Kjell A. Krane, Packaging Manager

During the months that the Sustainability Initiative was actively underway, I was startled at the powerful, deep convictions that so many of my fellow participants shared regarding the loss of natural resources and the steady, unrelenting damage to clean water and air, even here in Oregon. I still can't decide if these values were so evident because many of us had volunteered for this project and already had these shared concerns or does it possibly exist in the majority of Nike's employees? I'm convinced that a very significant percentage of Nike employees are seriously alarmed about the man-made threats to water, air and land quality that are all too recognizable on all continents. However, the Sustainability Initiative gave us the courage and optimism to openly discuss it with our coworkers and even our supervisors.

The Initiative truly legitimized our personal concerns for the environment and gave us the forum to openly bring these concerns to the workplace.

Dave Newman, Claims Manager, Nike Logistics

The Sustainability Initiative has affected me personally through using systems thinking versus the old model of linear thinking. Sustainability has allowed me to bring a passion into my work, permission to think differently, or ask better questions on current processes. For me, the impact has been life-changing, both in my work and home. As for Nike, I see and hear people talking about sustainability as I never had before. The biggest hurdle will be continuing to present the business case for sustainability, which allows funding current and new projects

Partnerships

Another area where Nike is demonstrating its commitment to more sustainable and responsible practices is through the many partnerships it is creating. Nike's core competence is business and so it turns to partners with competencies in environmental and social issues to learn how to more effectively address those issues. These are just a sample of the many partnerships Nike is forming:

McDonough Braungart Design Chemistry (MBDC)

In 1998, Nike and MBDC formed a partnership to explore the chemical composition and environmental effects of the materials and manufacturing processes that Nike uses and then to develop recommendations on how to move to more benign materials and processes. Through scientific research, if chemicals are determined or suspected to have adverse effects on human health or biological systems, they are targeted for replacement. Ultimately the goal is to develop a "positive list" of substances that can either be reintroduced into a technical cycle or naturally metabolized into nature's biological cycles. The partnership involves a two-phased effort between Nike, MBDC and Nike's vendors to establish replacement guidelines and acceptable thresholds for use during manufacturing. The first phase began in the fall of 2000 and included auditing all Nike's major material suppliers, focusing on the chemicals in Nike's products that are targeted by legislation in at least one country in the world. The second phase conducted in 2001 focused on chemicals used in Nike's manufacturing processes.

The Global Alliance[13]

The Global Alliance is a consortium of organizations designed to help corporations develop ways to respond to worker needs and aspirations on a factory-by-factory basis. Workers, most of whom are young females, are directly involved in the project. The Global Alliance is starting out in Southeast and East Asia. Over time, it will expand to other regions. The primary goal of the Global Alliance is to build a sustainable assessment and development process, and the infrastructure to ensure it lasts, focusing on identifying worker aspirations and workplace issues, assessing worker/community needs; developing and implementing programs that respond to identified needs; implementing management training programs and providing regular public reports.

The Coalition for Environmentally Responsibility Economies (CERES)[14]

Nike was accepted as an endorsee of the CERES principles in late 2000. CERES is a coalition of more than 70 environmental, investor, and advocacy groups working together for a sustainable future. The CERES principles that Nike commits to are: protection of the biosphere, sustainable use of natural resources, reduction and disposal of wastes, energy conservation, risk reduction, safe products and services, environmental restoration, informing the public, management commitment, and audits and reports.

The Global Compact[15]

Nike is an endorser of The Global Compact, which was initiated by Secretary General of the United Nations, Kofi Annan, at the World Economic Forum held in Davos on January 31, 1999. Annan challenged world business leaders to embrace and enact nine principles in a Global Compact. These principles cover topics in human rights, labor and the environment.

Fair Labor Association (FLA)[16]

In early 2001, the FLA board accepted Nike as a participating company. The FLA is a non-profit organization established to protect the rights of workers in the United States and around the world. It is a coalition of apparel and footwear companies, NGOs, and human and labor rights organizations. The FLA has created a Charter Agreement, the first industry-wide code of conduct and monitoring system. The agreement lays the foundation for the creation of an independent monitoring system that holds companies publicly accountable for their labor practices, as well as those of their principal contractors and suppliers around the world. The FLA accredits the independent monitors, certifies that companies are in compliance with the Code of Conduct, and serves as a source of information for the public.

World Wildlife Fund (WWF) and the Center for Energy and Climate Solutions[17]

In the fall of 2001, Nike entered into a new partnership with the World Wildlife Fund and the Center for Energy and Climate Solutions to reduce Nike's greenhouse gas emissions (GHG) worldwide in a program called Energy Savers. Through this program, Nike is pursuing practical activities that both reduce emissions of greenhouse gases and achieve energy efficiency goals. The global emission of greenhouse gases is considered to be the principal cause of the climate change that threatens the survival of many plants and animals as well as the well-being of people around the world. Under the new agreement, the WWF and the Center for Energy and Climate Solutions are working with Nike to achieve the following climate-saving targets:

- Reduce carbon dioxide (CO_2) emissions from business travel and Nike-owned facilities and services 13 percent below 1998 levels by the end of 2005. Nike intends to achieve this goal by pursuing energy conservation projects, purchasing green power and investing in community energy efficiency projects. As the earliest year for which reliable data and information exists regarding Nike's greenhouse gas (GHG) emissions, 1998 will serve as the baseline for reductions.

- Create baselines for Nike's major subcontracted footwear and apparel manufacturing facilities by year-end 2003. Extending reduction efforts to its global network of business partners, Nike will investigate, evaluate and distribute best practices to its major subcontracted manufacturing facilities. A GHG emissions reduction strategy for these facilities will be determined in 2005.

- Examine Nike's supply chain, from packaging to mode of transportation, for opportunities to improve logistics efficiency and reduce GHG from supply chain activities. By 2005, Nike will determine how to proceed with a GHG reduction strategy for logistics.

In addition, Nike will continue its already existing program to eliminate the greenhouse gas sulphur hexafluoride (SF6) and has committed to complete elimination of SF6 by June of 2003. Sarah Severn, Director of Sustainable Development, Corporate, comments on these GHG initiatives: "We take very seriously the effects of climate change on our planet. Nike's reduction of greenhouse gas emissions will illustrate how environmental strategies can align with business goals and will hopefully inspire more businesses to address climate change."

WALKING THE TALK

As is evident by now, Nike is undertaking sustainability improvements across all areas of its global system, both from a social and an environmental perspective. The company is, in fact, involved in literally thousands of individual initiatives, most of them completely invisible to the consumer, which are designed to improve the quality of life of the people manufacturing Nike's products and to reduce and eventually eliminate any harm to the natural environment from the production or disposal of Nike products. For example:

- Bio-Baby, a shoe design for Nike Kids, was created as a direct result of the Sustainability Initiative. The project goal was to design and develop a completely sustainable shoe. It inspired the project team to think differently about how Nike designs and develops footwear for children. The Bio-Baby incorporates life-cycle thinking and seeks to achieve zero waste, zero toxic materials, and a closed-loop production design. This project has evolved into more Nike products following the same innovative thinking process.

- The marathon singlet, first designed for the 2000 Sydney Olympics, marries high performance with elements of sustainability. The project goal was to develop an environmentally friendly state-of-the-art performance running garment for use in the Sydney Olympics and beyond. It has an innovative energy-efficient textile production process, uses post-consumer content from recycled soft drink bottles (one singlet used the material from approximately one and one-half recycled 1.5 liter PET, polyethylene terephthalate, soft drink bottles), eliminates an energy-intensive yarn-spinning stage of production, and uses sonic welding minimizing the need for sewing thread. The garment is made from a single polymer with recyclable potential, and sells at the same or lower price as a comparable product. The fabric has generated a new family of performance fabrics for Nike.

- Nike is now blending organic cotton into much of its cotton apparel, such as lightweight jersey t-shirts, to reduce the use of pesticides, herbicides and fertilizers in a way that supports the nascent organic cotton industry, and sources the cotton closer to production in order to reduce transportation costs and CO_2 emissions. Approximately 90 percent of Nike's shirts produced domestically now contain an amount of certified organic content and Nike's organic cotton use in Europe is growing exponentially.

- The Air Essential III, a sustainability advance in Nike's line of walking shoes, demonstrates that traditional products can be improved without significant redesign. The goal was to increase Nike's understanding and integration of sustainability thinking by minimizing toxic chemicals and waste, while at the same time being on a par or superior to its predecessor in performance, value, and profitability. Business partnerships in this effort were crucial — the factory and key suppliers pushed the envelope to reduce waste and find a benign replacement for non-sustainable materials such as chromium-tanned leather.

In designing the Air Essential III, my objective with looking at an entire product was to create a vehicle that could be used for demonstration purposes internally. To show people that you could get somewhere if you just put your mind to it using existing technologies. There wasn't anything new that we did here. It's just being conscious of what was possible with current technologies. Let's do something, anything. The whole point was to be able to demonstrate to people that we could actually create a more sustainable product if we put our minds to it.

— Larry Eisenbach, Product Creation Director for the
Walking Category

- The company is working to eliminate solvents with volatile organic compounds (VOCs).[18] Nike has for several years been collaborating with manufacturing partners and chemical suppliers to develop water-based alternatives to adhesives, primers, degreasers, and mold release agents containing petroleum-based solvents. In 1998, Nike held an open forum, called "Leaving Organic Solvents Behind," for footwear manufacturers in Bangkok, Thailand. Nothing was held back — all information around Nike's innovations was shared with competitors, including a tour of a Nike factory that had implemented the advances. Along with being the right thing to do, Nike found that the hazardous chemicals replaced by May 31, 2000 had resulted in $4.5 million savings in raw materials alone, not counting those related to labor, storage, and shipping. Nike has eliminated more than 1.6 million gallons of solvent each year, equivalent to more than 32,000 barrels of oil, and has made environmental improvements that benefit 180,000 workers in 37 Asian factories.

- Nike is phasing out polyvinyl chloride (PVC). PVC, or vinyl, over the past 50 years has become ubiquitous in our society, being used in packaging, sports equipment, pipes, toys, flooring, and thousands of other products. However, PVC has recently come into increasing disrepute as studies have shown the following: the vinyl chloride monomer (used to make the PVC polymer) is a carcinogen; PVC incineration can result in dioxin emissions and dioxins are persistent, highly toxic, bio-accumulative substances; pthalates, a group of compounds used to soften PVC have been identified as endocrine disrupters; additives used in PVC contain toxic heavy metals such as lead and cadmium that do not remain bound in the final product; and PVC is not easily recyclable once it has become waste. Based on the scientific literature and an extensive investigative process, Nike decided to phase out PVC from its products. Finding replacement material has proven a challenge and has required partnering with suppliers in joint research and development efforts.

- Other projects focus on many aspects of supply chain sustainability, such as reducing packaging, and reducing greenhouse gases associated with all Nike operations, travel and product transportation. The company has also established an extensive internal recycling program and is employing state-of-the-art green building practices for new construction and renovation.

- All of Nike's contract factories must abide by Nike's Code of Conduct. It defines contractors' obligations to workers and to the company. The Code is translated into the language of the worker and manager, and prominently displayed in all Nike contract factories. A laminated pocket-sized summary version of the Code has been provided to workers in their languages. In addition to its internal monitoring process called SHAPE (Safety, Health, Attitude of Management, People Investment, and Environment), Nike has instituted compliance with its Code of Conduct through independent external parties including the Fair Labor Association (FLA). The FLA is working to ensure that all factories adhere to strict standards in terms of human rights, including the freedoms of association and collective bargaining for wages, working hours, and benefits. One successful monitoring program for Nike has been conducted in Vietnam by the Center for Economic Studies and International Applications (CESAIS) which conducts private focus groups with workers on a regular basis and provides feedback to the factories and Nike.

- Nike created and launched an education initiative in 1997 to provide opportunities for contract workers to receive a higher education. In 1998, CEO Phil Knight pledged to organize formal education programs in all contract footwear factories by the end of 2001. To date, Nike has contributed $1.3 million to this effort. By year-end 2001, 85 percent of all footwear factories offered education programs to the workers. These include both formal, government-accredited middle or high school programs, and informal vocational and business training. Nike understands that a higher education for workers in developing countries can have a marked positive impact on their future. In China, Nike and World Vision[19] have partnered to create after-hours, free education programs for workers in footwear factories.

- In Pakistan, Nike is a member of a coalition dedicated to eliminating child labor in the soccer ball industry and to placing Pakistani children into schools. This initiative is being coordinated under the International Labor Organization's International Program on the Elimination of Child Labor (IPEC)[20] with the participation of the Save the Children Fund, [21] United Nations Children's Fund (UNICEF),[22] and more than 50 soccer products companies.

- In Thailand, Nike and Union Footwear, a major manufacturing partner, are working with the Population and Community Development Association (PDA),[23] a local non-governmental organization (NGO), to develop a "Nike Village" concept for rural areas. In these areas, stitching centers are established in the villages as a hub for employment while other opportunities, including vegetable and tree banks, women's counseling, education programs, and other micro-enterprise projects, are available.

Many of the Sustainability Initiative projects saved money, some innovated new processes and product ideas, and a few might even revolutionize the way we do business in the future. Perhaps the most important takeaway achieved by this program is the fact that momentum was achieved, and that momentum is heading in the right direction.

— Sarah Severn, Director, Sustainable Development, Corporate

The foregoing initiatives represent only a handful of thousands more, small and large, that Nike is undertaking in the area of corporate responsibility and sustainability. We urge you to explore Nike's highly informative website, and to examine in detail its remarkable self-disclosure document, the recently published Nike Corporate Responsibility Report.[24] This corporate responsibility document, a real milestone in Nike's journey to sustainability, sets new standards for the organization in terms of corporate transparency and public disclosure. The report also contains descriptions of numerous projects, many generated or strengthened by the Sustainability Initiative, including product creation, supply chain relations and management, internal operations and connecting with the consumer.

We have been actively engaged with Nike's sustainability efforts since 1999. We can say from first-hand knowledge that there are people in the company, many with significant authority and responsibility, who are deeply caring, knowledgeable and committed on the issues of corporate responsibility and sustainability. Nike is making authentic and impressive efforts to address the problems of worker rights, working conditions, worker benefits, toxic materials, carbon emissions, and a multitude of other serious concerns. Yet at the same time, many of these issues are so complex, that one company cannot do it all, even one industry cannot do it all. Many of these issues can only be solved by mobilizing whole industrial sectors and the international body politic. It is up to all of us as citizens to voice our concerns, not only to the companies involved, but also to our elected leaders to help mobilize the national and international will to make meaningful structural changes at the international level.

ADVICE ON THE SUSTAINABILITY JOURNEY

Having invested, and continuing to invest, significantly in the step-by-step processes of research, education and implementation of corporate responsibility and sustainability, Nike is now clearly a global corporate leader in the field. Several of the most knowledgeable and experienced people actively involved in these pioneering initiatives have agreed to share some advice to fellow travelers on the road to sustainability in business.

Phil Berry, Technical Director, Footwear Sustainability

- You must set up a system. Just like you set up any other business system. It isn't that tough.

- Sustainability has to be integrated into the business plan and not only integrated into the business planning process, it also has to be integrated into the overall process of risk and reward that goes on inside the business.

- Plan, set goals, do the things that are necessary to implement the goals and then audit to make sure you achieve the goals. You obviously cannot plan and develop without the people who are doing the implementing also being part of the planning process. You can't accomplish operations and implementation without having the people who helped you develop the plan involved in some way. Then there are several kinds of auditing. You do your internal auditing to make sure that as a corporation you are going down

the right road — your road — the one you determine to be right for your organization. You have
external auditors and NGO partners to make sure
your road fits within societal norms and goes in the
right direction.

- You've got to start with the vice-presidential level to
  ensure accountability, but you also need to push functional responsibility to the lowest possible level in the
  organization. There are two things that you want to
  do: ensure accountability through management
  involvement and have the people who are at the
  ground level actually tasked with accomplishing the
  work.

Heidi Holt, Global Sustainability Director, Apparel

- For Nike Apparel, the greatest challenge revolves
  around ensuring adequate supply of organic fiber and
  getting the right quality in the right region at the right
  time. We support "local for local" to the greatest
  extent possible, using cotton that is organically grown
  in an area for the supply of production in that same
  area. We want the infrastructure to be developed to
  support farmers in each particular region. We're
  becoming a very large player in the organic cotton
  arena, so we make pre-plant and longer-term commitments with the farmers. Establishing a high level of
  trust between Nike and the farmer is critical. This is
  their livelihood and it can't be approached in a cava-
  lier manner. If we make a commitment, we have to
  stick with it; there has to be a personal relationship
  and a high level of earned trust in order for a farmer
  to believe that a very large corporation has their long-
  term best interest in mind.

- At present, the business understands one bottom line,
  not a triple one. It is my responsibility to drive the
  awareness of a sustainable business model, both internally and externally, through very specific and
  concrete projects that have immediate impact and

return. In order to do that I had to understand what sustainability meant. Is it something we do just to feel good about ourselves as a company or do we do it because it also adds business value? Was there a business case for becoming sustainable or was it just something that we do, but at a cost to the business? I realized that unless sustainability in fact was sound business practice, it would only last while business was booming and would be one of the first things to be cut when business got tough.

- Any sustainability initiative — whether product or process based — has to work with our existing systems, infrastructure, supply base and business model, and it must have a return. What I'm seeing over time is that sustainability initiatives have a rate of return that we couldn't have calculated with a traditional finance perspective. Their positive impact on environmental health, long- and short-term human health, not to mention their contribution to smart business practices ultimately put us in a very competitive business position.

Dusty Kidd, Vice-President, Compliance

- First, start from the top. Get the CEO, Chief Operating Officer, and the key leadership in the company involved and signed off. It's not impossible, but it's certainly a much harder hill to climb if you start from the middle. Start from the top.

- Second, build sustainability into the structure of the business. It should be part of business planning and brand planning and all those key things that you do to drive your business forward.

- Third, do it in stages that are logical, digestible and provide you with some early successes.

- If I were in a small company or a company that had never tackled sustainability as a question before, I would try to take it in that order.

Bob Kreinberg, Divisional Vice-President, Global Logistics

- It takes a lot of work and a lot of background and a lot of buy-in for people to really understand what you have to do to drive sustainability through the company. If you want to get it started and want the company to pick it up, and go that way quickly, the place to start the education is just right up here at the top.

- When you do general education, you need to know what the next steps will be. If you don't have anything planned for people to follow up, then people just get frustrated.

- I think it's going to take a lot of initiatives that build in the same direction, but they have to be based on the proposition that you invest time and energy with the expectation of having a tangible, profitable impact on the company.

- The best way to get support for something is to show the results.

Sarah Severn, Director, Sustainable Development, Corporate

- Don't wait for senior leadership to get started, but seek their support once you have. I get very frustrated when I hear people saying this has to start with the CEO. It doesn't. When we were in the midst of the Sustainability Initiative, I remember Peter Senge saying (with apologies for inaccuracy), that we often confuse leadership with the senior executives in an organization, when in fact leadership is the capacity of a human community to create a new future. Leadership can come from anywhere within an organization. Nike's culture recognizes and enables this.

- Develop your skills of compassion and insight. You will need them when the going gets tough.

- Understand how sustainability/sustainable development connects to the values of your organization, because if that connection is missing, the business case alone won't get you there.

- Find well-respected allies in the organization who understand the benefits to business and who may be able to approach this from a different perspective that adds value to the message. If you work in a corporate function, make sure you collaborate with leaders in the business who can bring credibility to the work.

- Communicate using the language that your organization is familiar with since sustainability language can seem academic and elitist. Even more importantly, when bringing in experts who are external to your organization, find those who will not totally jar with the culture of your organization. You definitely need to challenge people's perceptions of current reality, and ensure you reach their blind spots since that's when real learning starts to happen. On the other hand, if the messenger not only turns their entire world view upside down but also is alien to the organizational culture, there is a very good chance that the message will be rejected.

- Challenge the organization to set outrageous goals, in the long run these will be more motivating. Hence the reason we have seen goals like zero waste and zero toxics emerge out of the product groups. They understand the value of setting the bar high.

Darcy Winslow, Director, Women's Footwear

- For the general population within a corporation, or whatever your sphere of impact is, you have to make it simple. And it takes a long time to make something this complex simple. I found that we started to make progress against that when we clarified the four long-range goals, and just made them sound bites — zero waste, zero toxics, closed-loop business processes — while addressing growth, and profitability in a more sustainable way. Then people can go away and say, okay, then what does that mean to the business from where I sit? Make it understandable in a way that somebody can sit down at their desk, whether they're a designer or an organizational expert or transportation, logistics, materials, whatever, they can take those and think about it and say, okay, I understand what this means and I can understand how I am connected to it. Then they become owners in the process more quickly. Put your stakes in the ground and state them simply and aggressively. Create tangible goals.

- Take a long-term approach and work with supply chain partners or business partners depending on what aspect you're attacking. Then you can start setting up partnerships and longer-range R&D where becoming more sustainable is built into the process rather than something additional to address. Build in the criteria, or the principles, into the natural course of creating whatever it is your company creates.

- Sometimes, you just have to work under the radar and work with the groups that really make things happen.

- One of the things I've learned over the last two years is some days you walk away from work thinking, 'Wow, have we made some great progress, we are really starting to get there'. And other days you walk away thinking, 'This has been a futile two years.' So you have to step back and look at the progress you've made from a very objective perspective. I think we've made huge progress toward getting something that's this large and this different embraced in a very complex corporate structure. This is not something that can be done even in a matter of five years or ten years. We'll never be done with this because we'll always learn more.

- You have to be very comfortable with taking risks and being looked at cross-eyed and really believing that what you're doing is right. Don't rely on yourself or a small team. Go out and find other leaders in the organization. Look for leaders in untraditional places. One of the keys to success is finding others who can help bring some of the messages or ideas to life. Look to many parts of the business. A drop here, a drop there, and a drop over here, once it comes together creates a waterfall. I think that is what is happening right now.

- It takes persistence and patience, and the patience piece is probably the most difficult because you can see the end so clearly, because that's all you do, you think about this day and night; others don't, and to help them through that, you have to become a teacher. You are a choreographer. Not everybody has to dance the same steps at the same time, but it has to look good when it's all together, and it takes a long time to get there.

Jill Zanger, Outreach Program Manager, Sustainable Development

- Coming from a communications perspective, the most important lesson I've learned in Nike's sustainability integration process, is to continually speak the language of the business culture regardless of the content and learning you're working to bring inside the organization. More than once our best-intentioned messages were misunderstood. It's human nature, really, to listen to and truly hear a message when it's delivered in a package you find appealing. However un-radical of an idea sustainability was to us in the beginning of the process, when we sounded as if we were coming from 'outside' ourselves, the results had the potential to be disastrous. We're still not perfect at this notion of talking about sustainability in Nike-speak, but the glassy-eyed stares in response to us are at an all-time low.

FINAL REFLECTIONS

How is Nike doing in this new quest for excellence: exploring what it means to play and excel on the field of corporate responsibility and sustainability? It is too soon to tell — sustainability is a very complex game that Nike has just begun to seriously play. What we can say is that Nike has never shied away from a challenge, and this is a new game on a new field, the biggest and most complex game that Nike or any other company has ever played. So Nike is on a steep learning curve to absorb all of these new inputs, these new variables, to figure out the new rules and develop the skills and competencies in order to win the game of business sustainability in the global arena of the 21st century. We know one thing for sure, Nike, by its own creation, is associated with the highest standards of performance and the struggle it takes to achieve them. In Nike's words: "We speak the language of aspiration, inspiration, and perspiration."[25]

In Nike's new Corporate Responsibility Report, CEO Phil Knight comments:

> In all of these areas of responsibility, how are we doing? I know what makes for good performance when I see it on the running track. I know it when I read quarterly results from the finance department. I have to admit, though, I'm not sure how we measure good performance in corporate responsibility. I'm not convinced anybody does. Why not? Because there are no standards, no agreed-on definitions.... Until then we have to figure it out ourselves, with the help of our business partners, local and national governments, international organizations, and other interest and consumer groups.[26]

What we do know is that Nike is dedicating hundreds of its players around the world and millions of dollars per year to figuring out the rules of the new game and learning how to play it well. This is a game that requires new knowledge and skills. It is a game that requires practice, perseverance, focus and determination. To play it well requires teaching others how to play inside and outside of your organization. Any athlete will tell you that for every win there are at least as many failures. Kidd reminds us that: "In his entire career, Michael Jordan failed half the time. He averaged about 50 percent success in shooting his field goals, and he is arguably the best player who's stepped onto the court." Nike aspires to be the best player, but it is still in the stages of early training and practice. As with any player, the only way to know whether Nike will achieve its aspiration is to observe how it plays in the game. Athletes are not great because they say they are, they become great by proving it on the field of play.

We have interacted first hand with scores of individuals and teams inside Nike who are genuinely trying to figure out what it means to excel in the area of corporate responsibility and sustainability and they are doing so with the blessing and encouragement of the company's senior management. They are "just doing it" because they personally and professionally believe it is the right thing to do, and they are able to do it because it has become a core value in the company. They, and many of their colleagues, are sincerely doing their best to "Do the Right Thing." It is not just a slogan, it is the real thing. However, like a single player in the NBA, Nike is but one player in a very complex global game. While it can influence the game, it cannot alone determine the outcome. It needs the help of all of us, our involvement, to change the rules of the global game — so that no one is excluded, everyone is a player, and everyone wins in the global game of sustainability.

CHAPTER 5

STARBUCKS
THE QUEST FOR AUTHENTIC
CORPORATE RESPONSIBILITY

*It is Starbucks mission to create hope, discovery and
opportunities in communities in all the regions and
countries we touch. To carry out this mission we strive
to integrate sustainable business practices and support
socially responsible causes. We don't do it for the
visibility, but because it is the right thing to do,
not only as a company, but as individuals.*

— Orin Smith, President & CEO

IN JUNE, 2000 we were invited by Sue Mecklenburg, now Vice-President of Business Practice, and Ben Packard, Director of Environmental Affairs, to help Starbucks conduct a sustainability assessment of its global operations. As long-standing Starbucks aficionados, we were intrigued by the opportunity. Living north of Seattle near Vancouver, B.C., we have been in the epicenter of the Pacific Northwest coffee culture ever since it began, and on many occasions as we left Starbucks in the morning with our latte, mocha, and carrot date loaf, we had wished that our favorite coffee company had a frequent flyer program for serious coffee drinkers. We would have flown around the world more than once on our Starbucks habit. When we began our consulting work with Starbucks, we immediately felt on intimate terms with the company as mainstream loyal customers.

The interesting thing was, although we knew we loved the place and sought out Starbucks wherever our travels took us in the U.S., Canada, and overseas, we actually didn't know much about the corporation itself. We just knew that for years it had been our coffee company of choice. As we conducted our research and interviews for the sustainability assessment project, and learned more about the company's values and the actions it takes in support of those values, the more our appreciation and respect grew. As we proceeded with our investigations and collaborative work with Starbucks 'partners,' as all employees are called (because even part-time workers receive stock options after working for the company for six continuous months), and as we learned in greater detail the stories of the people who started the company and those who work within and lead the company today, our appreciation and respect continued to grow.

> *The story of Starbucks is not just a record of growth and success. It's also about how a company can be built in a different way. It's about a company completely unlike the ones my father worked for. It's living proof that a company can lead with its heart and nurture its soul and still make money. It shows that a company can provide long-term value for shareholders without sacrificing its core belief in treating its employees with respect and dignity, both because we have a team of leaders who believe it's right and because it's the best way to do business.*

— Howard Schultz, Chairman, Author of *Pour Your Heart Into It*.

How a small coffee store in Pike Place Market in Seattle grew to become the largest specialty coffee retailer on Earth, with an increasingly recognized and global brand, and succeeded at the same time in creating a culture of caring for its people, its communities, and its world, is both a remarkable entrepreneurial story and a remarkable tale of corporate social and environmental responsibility. Over the past 30 years, the company has grown from a single shop to a network of more than 5000 locations, 16 million customers a week, and system-wide sales of $3.0 billion in 2000. At the same time, it has become the single most generous corporate donor to CARE in America with donations exceeding $1.7 million, and that is just one of many of Starbucks' community and environmental commitments.

Of all the corporations that we have worked with as advisors in the field of corporate responsibility and sustainable development in the United States and Canada, Starbucks is in that special circle of companies that has come the farthest in truly embodying an understanding of the *direct and immediate importance of sustainability* to the business strategy and profitability of the corporation — of seeing the direct connection between its business well-being and the well-being of the natural environment from which it sources its products, and of seeing the direct connection between its business well-being and the well-being of the communities in which it both sources its supply and to whom it purveys the delicious refreshments for which it is so famous. In speaking extensively with members of the Starbucks executive team, it is clear that as much as the average businessperson sees the immediate connection between his or her customer and profitability, Starbucks sees the clear and direct connection between its financial, community and environmental well-being.

In fact, Starbucks has every practical reason to be working toward the triple bottom line of sustainability — an integrated system of people, planet, and profit. Its primary product is agricultural and therefore depends directly on the health of the natural environment. Furthermore, its industry is inextricably intertwined with the dynamics of global economic and resource inequities and the consequent social disparities and dilemmas. Finally, Starbucks' financial health and future depends on continued access to high quality coffee, which in turn depends upon finding resolution to these ecological and social challenges. In our experience with Starbucks, it is clear that the company is well aware of the reasons why sustainability is a fundamental business strategy. It is also our experience that the Starbucks commitment to corporate responsibility has even more personal roots.

COFFEE IN THE GLOBAL SYSTEMS CONTEXT

Starbucks dances with tigers, lots of tigers. In fact, it is in a simultaneous dance with a multitude of tigers. It dances with the tiger of a global coffee industry dominated by four major players, the kings of this jungle, who purchase 40 percent of the world's coffee compared to Starbucks' one percent. It dances with the tiger of the specialty coffee market where competition is steadily growing. Starbucks faces yet another tiger because of the company's perceived influence and buying power: increasing pressures from many quarters to be responsible for changing the very structure of the coffee industry and the frequently brutal effects of the inequitably balanced global social and economic system. Although Starbucks may seem pervasive for someone walking in downtown Seattle or Vancouver, as noted above, it purchases only about one percent of the world's coffee. Yet the company's very success and high visibility have made it a favorite target for an array of social activist campaigns, ironically sometimes because of the very social conscience attributed to Starbucks customers and the high values that the company itself espouses. The biggest tiger of all is the structure of the global coffee system, which embodies some of the most troubling aspects of globalization, exemplifying the growing gap between the rich and the poor, and epitomizing the deep web of interconnectedness that is the basis of our global economic system.

Coffee is an ancient commodity and an integral part of our historical, cultural and social landscapes. This ubiquitous elixir is consumed on the order of 2.25 billion cups a day worldwide. The dark, rich brew has an equally dark and rich association with bustling cafés, creativity, progressive thinking, revolutions, the rise and fall of fortunes, and the wealth and poverty of nations. If you drink coffee, you are part of an extraordinarily complex system that stretches back in history well over a millennium, reaches around the globe, and affects the lives and livelihoods of millions, if not billions, of people.

One of the best-known legends about coffee relates that its properties were discovered by a young Ethiopian goatherd named Kaldi who noticed his goats' frenetic behavior after they ate the red berries of a bush. Kaldi was intrigued. He ate the berries and, upon experiencing a similar exuberance, began dancing with his goats. Henceforth the goatherd developed a habit of consuming the berries on a daily basis. The legend goes on to tell how Kaldi dutifully reported his discovery to the abbot of a local monastery who tried the berries and found that they kept him alert during the long hours of evening prayer. Pleased with this effect, he made a beverage with the berries and shared his discovery with the other monks at the monastery, and ever so slowly knowledge of the energizing effects of the berries began to spread to monasteries throughout the kingdom. Eventually use of the energizing drink reached the Arabian peninsula and continued its journey through time and to the rest of the world. What an extraordinary story of learning from nature and innovation diffusion!

By the mid-16th century, coffee had become so popular in areas around Constantinople and Mecca that people met in special areas to drink; creating the first coffee houses.[1] Although European travelers had experienced coffee in their travels to the Middle East and had commented on it in their journals, it was Venetian merchants who introduced coffee to Europe in the early 1600s. By the mid-1600s, coffeehouses had opened in Marseilles (1644), Venice (1645), Oxford (1650), London (1652), Paris (1657) and Vienna (1683). By the late 17th and early 18th centuries, coffee was by far the most popular of the three "temperance beverages" in England (the other two being tea and chocolate). Some 2000 coffeehouses, it is estimated, existed in London alone in the late 17th century. At times in European history, the dark brew outranked wine and beer in popularity.[2]

Coffee as a commodity played a role in the development of European expansion and long-distance trade. It also contributed to the inhumanity of colonial slavery in the 18th century. The spread of colonial empires led to the expansion of the coffee trade and new locations for the cultivation of coffee. It is believed that a coffee plant from the royal French botanical gardens was the source of most of the coffee found in the West Indies and the Americas.[3]

By the start of the 20th century, annual world production of coffee reached one million tons. Three-quarters of that was cultivated in Brazil. Today coffee is grown in Africa, Asia, South and Central America and the Middle East. It is the world's second largest legally traded commodity in export dollars, second only to oil, with worldwide sales of $55 billion.[4] The largest exporters are Brazil, Colombia, Vietnam, Indonesia and Mexico. The largest importer of coffee is the United States, accounting for about one-fifth of the total. Every day in the United States 450 million cups of coffee are consumed by more than 130 million people.[5] The average American consumes ten pounds of coffee per year.

The modern coffee industry is dominated by four multinational companies: Procter and Gamble Co., Philip Morris Companies Inc., the Sara Lee Corp., and Nestle, which account for 60 percent of U.S. retail sales and 40 percent of worldwide sales. Six multinational export firms control 40 percent of the world's coffee market.[6]

Coffee is the most important agricultural export for dozens of Third World countries. It is a highly labor-intensive crop that provides a livelihood for over 20 million people in more than 50 countries. Although some coffee is produced on large plantations, the majority of the world's coffee, approximately 70 percent, is still grown on family farms of less than five hectares (about 13 acres), all in the developing world. It takes five years for coffee bushes to produce their fruit. Generally the smallholders cannot export their coffee directly because they produce too small a volume of coffee to sell to the major exporters who buy bulk lots of hundreds of 150-pound bags, not just a few at a time.

In this complex system, coffee beans can pass through as many as 15 hands between shrub and cup, with price increases along each step of the way. Few companies actually know which farmers produce the coffee they buy. In between the farmer and the exporter are multiple middlemen each adding their costs to the price of the coffee. If farmers object, the middlemen simply turn elsewhere. If coffee is too expensive in one country, many buyers simply turn to another. Once protected by quotas, coffee is now traded openly, with prices that swing wildly, driven by speculators and weather reports alike. The vast majority of the world's coffee farmers live in desperate poverty, while the majority of those who benefit from the fruit of their labors live in industrialized countries. For many of the estimated 20 million households worldwide that produce coffee, the crop is the primary, if not the sole source of cash income. This juxtaposition makes coffee an obvious symbol of the asymmetries of global markets and the brutal impact of consistently declining commodity prices and persistent poverty in many regions of the world.

In 2001, coffee prices plummeted to a 30-year low, which had a devastating impact on many coffee-producing countries. These countries suffer from high levels of rural poverty, uncontrolled rural migration to already overcrowded cities, economic imbalances, social instability, and the inability to repay debts. Many countries such as Burundi, Ethiopia, and Uganda depend upon coffee for more than one-half of their export earnings. These low commodity prices will worsen the conditions of countless families who are facing more than a financial crisis: they face a crisis of desperation and survival. In the early 1990s, a price crash in coffee bankrupted many coffee farmers in Chiapas, Mexico. Many of them joined the Zapatista rebels. The same crash pushed Rwandan coffee farmers in Africa into desperate conditions.[7]

In 1989, trade liberalization efforts by the Reagan administration led to the collapse of the International Coffee Agreement, an arrangement between coffee producing and coffee consuming nations that for decades kept prices relatively high or at least stable. Since then, there has been no effective supply management. Each country increased production to increase coffee revenues. New arrivals, such as Vietnam, also added to increased supply. A decade ago, Vietnam was a marginal player in the coffee market; today it is the world's second largest exporter, surpassing Columbia and second only to Brazil. In Columbia and Bolivia, United Nations programs have encouraged farmers to switch from coca to coffee. Much of this new coffee is low-quality, or *robusta*, coffee. Since 1990, coffee production has increased by 15 percent, twice the rate of consumption. The market has been flooded with *robusta* beans, which are used in inexpensive blends and instant coffees. When the price of *robusta* fell, so did the price of *arabica* beans used in higher-quality blends.

Right now we have a worldwide coffee glut, which is perfectly understandable because each of the players, each of the countries, each of the individuals tries to maximize their own wealth, indifferent to the outcome for everyone. So there is too much coffee, and no one gets wealthy. There is no invisible hand, there's no one in charge of this to help smooth it out. There's no cartel. They fall apart because the individual players think they can do it better. So what we have is continual over-production. From a macroeconomic view you see that some of the producers will drop out, there will be a scarcity, prices will go up. But those producers are individual farmers who are land based. They don't have alternatives. They can't go into another industry. So while we talk about world markets and prices, the reality for the family farmers is a matter of losing their livelihoods and their land.

— Sue Mecklenburg, Vice-President, Business Practice

Total coffee revenues are lower today than they were in 1980. In Kenya, many farmers only derive pennies from producing a pound of coffee beans. Some Latin American farmers now receive just 15 to 25 cents per pound for berries, half of what they earned in 1999, and most of that is eaten up by costs. In Nicaragua, hundreds of coffee workers — almost the entire population of three villages — deserted their homes to go to the city of Matagalpa in the hope of some employment because they could no longer work in the coffee fields. Venezuela's coffee exports have nearly been cut in half, which led to street protests by angry farmers. Plantations in Brazil and Colombia are moving from lower-grade coffee to focusing on higher-quality beans, which hurts poor nations like Kenya that specialize in high-quality coffee. Many small-scale farmers cannot afford to continue to grow coffee because their production costs are sometimes double or more what they can expect to get for their crop. Many are deserting their land altogether. Others are clearing their land in order to produce alternative crops. They are cutting down coffee bushes, and the lush environment they thrive in, to open up fields for planting corn or raising cattle.

Switching to other crops or leaving the land altogether is creating environmental pressures. Small coffee farmers traditionally use sustainable growing methods that include composting coffee pulp, rotating crops, and growing coffee among other plants such as banana and nut trees to provide food security and additional income. This provides homes and food for wildlife. Generally the coffee grown by these farmers is organic. They do not use chemical pesticides and fertilizers, largely because they cannot afford them. Very little of this coffee is certified as organic, in part because of the expense involved in the certification process. In many areas the pressure to increase yields has led to the use of "modern" farming methods, specifically, sun cultivation. In the past, these methods have been promoted by agencies such as The World Bank and the U.S. Agency for International Development with the intention to increase crop yields and, consequently, to increase prosperity in producing countries. Unfortunately, this technification produced unintended negative environmental and social consequences. Sun cultivated coffee farming requires chemical inputs, destroys wildlife habitats, increases soil erosion, accelerates deforestation of rainforests, pollutes water supplies, and has driven many small farmers off the land.

Starbucks relies upon securing a growing supply of consistently high-quality coffee beans in a complex industry that has evolved over hundreds of years, an industry that affects the economies and politics of entire countries and the well-being of millions of people around the world, many of them small farmers who have very little land, very little collateral and very little access to credit.

Starbucks buys high-quality coffee, often dealing directly with cooperatives and farmers. It purchases coffee at a substantial premium above commodity prices, at least a dollar a pound or more, and tends to buy from the same people year after year. Sue Mecklenburg explains, "We buy coffee in large quantities and are looking for high-quality coffee from reliable sources."

The wider context is a big thing for us because unlike many industries, we don't have a choice about where we source our products. Many industries source products in less developed countries because the cost of living is cheaper, and therefore labor is cheaper. But we have a tropical product and we are inextricably tied to our suppliers, the coffee farmers, and to that income disparity, that wealth disparity. I mean, we have no choice, so it's just a pretty amazing place to be.

— Sue Mecklenburg, Vice-President, Business Practice

Working directly with farmers presents its own set of challenges. Despite their precarious position, farmers often tend to be overly optimistic about their next crop. This has made it very difficult in the past to get long-term contracts because the farmers always remember other days when prices were higher. They want to deal a year at a time. Mecklenburg remarks, "As prices have fallen to historic lows, however, farmers are more willing to enter into longer-term contracts." Mecklenburg estimates that Starbucks sources approximately one-half of its coffee directly from farms and co-ops and the rest through importers. The company has arranged some five-year contracts with farmers and created long-term relationships with importers who help Starbucks source coffee. So while Starbucks' business has become profitable, it has not been easy. This is particularly so as it is primarily based on an agricultural product purchased in fluctuating commodity markets in a system rife with great income and social disparities.

ONE CUP AT A TIME[8]

Starbucks, named after the coffee-loving first mate in Herman Melville's *Moby Dick*,[9] was created thirty years ago when Jerry Baldwin, Zev Siegel and Gordon Bowker opened a store called Starbucks Coffee, Tea and Spice in Pike Place Market in Seattle. The idea for Starbucks was born out of their experience with Peet's Coffee and Tea in Berkeley, California, an enterprise established in 1966 by Alfred Peet who had begun importing fine *arabica* coffees in the

1950s. Peet's store in Berkeley specialized in importing and selling exceptional coffees and teas, dark-roasting beans in a European tradition, teaching customers how to select and grind beans and to brew coffee at home for superior taste.

> *Holloa! Starbuck's astir," said the rigger. "He's a lively chief mate that; good man, and a pious; but all alive now, I must turn to." And so saying he went on deck, and we followed.*
>
> — GOING ABOARD, Chapter 21, *Moby Dick*

Starbucks was an immediate success. In the beginning, the three partners bought their beans from Peet, who mentored them in the art of coffee selection and roasting. Eventually, however, they set up their own roasting operations and developed their own roasting blends and flavors. In 1972 Starbucks opened a second location in Seattle and by the early 1980s there were four stores.

In 1981, Howard Schultz was the vice-president and general manager of U.S. operations for Hammarplast, a Swedish housewares company. Schultz, who was located in New York, became curious about Starbucks when he noticed its high-volume orders for a particular Hammarplast drip coffee maker. He visited the company and was immediately taken with the experience: the rich aromas of the coffee beans, the care with which the clerk ground and brewed a sample for him, the philosophy behind the company that placed its highest priority on coffee quality. This dedication to quality began with selecting superior beans, meticulous roasting, and educating customers so they could truly appreciate the qualities of the coffee. He was also impressed with the company's approach: to build customer loyalty pound by pound.

Schultz decided he wanted to be part of this company. He recalls, "There was something magic about it, a passion and authenticity I had never experienced in business."[10] After months of diligent pursuit, Schultz began work with Starbucks in September 1982, heading up marketing and overseeing the retail stores. He began by learning the business from the ground up: working behind the counters, tasting different coffees, learning about all aspects of the coffee business from beans to roasting to retail.

In the spring of 1983, while attending an international house-wares show in Milan, Schultz stopped into an espresso bar. The experience stirred his imagination. He spent time going from one espresso bar to another, each with its own distinctive characteristics, but all with the common thread of a *barista* who made the rich espresso drinks and engaged the clientele. Schultz noted that Milan was filled with espresso bars; in a city about the size of Philadelphia, there were 1500 espresso bars, and about 200,000 in all of Italy. He came back to Seattle with the idea that recreating this experience could be a significant differentiating factor for Starbucks. He saw that in addition to providing superior coffee, like the espresso bars in Italy, Starbucks could provide a rich sensory treat and a place for people to meet and visit.

Despite his enthusiasm, Schultz found resistance to the idea when he returned to Seattle. Starbucks was already successful. It was a retail-er of whole bean coffee, not a restaurant or espresso bar. In addition, Starbucks was about to purchase Peet's Coffee and Tea. The time was-n't right for trying out new ideas. It wasn't until April 1984 that Schultz was able to test out the espresso bar idea inside a new down-town Starbucks store. It was an instant success and within two months was serving 800 customers a day. Nevertheless, the Starbucks owners were still not comfortable with the idea. Baldwin told Schultz: "We're coffee roasters. I don't want to be in the restaurant business . . . Besides, we're too deeply in debt to consider pursuing this idea."[11]

Within a few months Schultz decided to leave Starbucks and to set up his own company based on the Italian espresso bar experience. He called it Il Giornale. Baldwin, one of the Starbucks owners, became Schultz's first investor in the enterprise and a director of the new com-pany, and Bowker, another Starbucks owner, served as a part-time consultant to help Schultz get started. By the end of January 1986, Schultz had raised $400,000 in seed capital and had raised $1.25 mil-lion in equity by the end of the year. The first Il Giornale store opened in April 1986 and served 300 customers on the first day. Six months later Schultz opened a second Il Giornale store in downtown Seattle and a third store in Vancouver, British Columbia in April 1987. By mid 1987, sales at the three stores had reached $1.5 million.

In March 1987, Baldwin and Bowker decided to sell the entire Starbucks operation (Siegel had left Starbucks in the early 80s) includ-ing the stores, the roasting plant and the name. Schultz raised the

$3.8 million needed to acquire the company and completed the transaction in August 1987. He merged Starbucks and Il Giornale under the Starbucks name for an enterprise totaling nine stores, and, at age 34, became president and CEO of the company. His vision was not only for Starbucks to become a national company, but a company based on clear values and guiding principles. He wanted to build a company that would make the people who worked there proud, a company that would be both profitable and a good place to work. Schultz's objective was to open 125 new stores within five years. He exceeded that expectation by opening 150 stores by 1992. Despite posting losses for three consecutive years (1987, 1988, 1989) during this early growth period, Schultz was able to raise new venture capital ($3.9 million in 1988, $13.5 million in 1990, $15 million in 1991). By 1990 Starbucks became profitable, and its profits have increased every year since then, excluding one-time write-offs in 2000 for Internet investments.

In June 1992, Schultz took the company public, and its initial public offering (IPO) turned out to be one of the most successful IPOs of the year. This capital infusion supported the expansion of the store network. The company's success helped stimulate both the demand and supply for specialty coffee products. Many competitors emerged: some imitated the Starbucks model; others found their market niche by differentiating themselves from the Starbucks model.

In 1992 and 1993, Starbucks developed a three-year expansion strategy and created zone vice-presidents to oversee the development of each region. Store launches became increasingly successful. In 1995, new stores generated an average of $700,000 in revenue in their first year compared to $427,000 in 1990. Existing stores continued to post year-to-year gains in sales. The company began to experiment with different store formats, with expanded product offerings, and with different partnerships such as the joint venture with Pepsico to create a bottled Frappuccino, or with Dreyer's Grand Ice Cream to create a new line of Starbucks ice cream. Nonetheless, the core focus was always on quality coffee. The company's retail sales mix remained predominantly coffee beverages (about 61 percent) and whole bean coffees (15 percent) while it diversified into food items (16 percent) and coffee related products and equipment (8 percent). In recent years, Starbucks has also begun selling jazz and blues CDs.

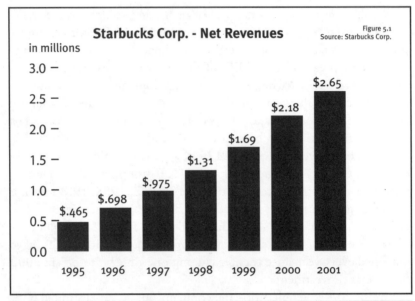

Starbucks Corp. - Net Revenues

Figure 5.1
Source: Starbucks Corp.

in millions

- 3.0
- 2.5
- 2.0
- 1.5
- 1.0
- 0.5
- 0.0

1995 — $.465
1996 — $.698
1997 — $.975
1998 — $1.31
1999 — $1.69
2000 — $2.18
2001 — $2.65

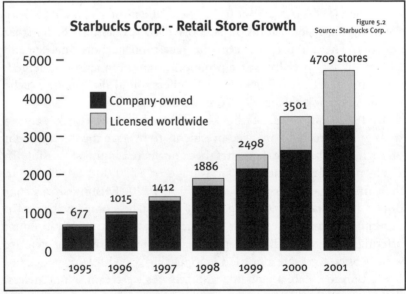

Starbucks Corp. - Retail Store Growth

Figure 5.2
Source: Starbucks Corp.

- 5000
- 4000
- 3000
- 2000
- 1000
- 0

Company-owned
Licensed worldwide

1995 — 677
1996 — 1015
1997 — 1412
1998 — 1886
1999 — 2498
2000 — 3501
2001 — 4709 stores

Starbucks predominantly owns its stores and rejects a franchise model. By owning stores, Starbucks maintains greater control over the quality of the product and is able to nurture the company's values and culture. In recent years, the company has entered into a limited number of licensing agreements for opportunities where it does not have the ability to locate its own stores. For example, Starbucks has an agreement with Host International, Inc. that licenses Host to operate Starbucks outlets in airport locations, and with Aramark Food and Services to operate stores on university campuses. Through other special arrangements Starbucks sells coffee beans to restaurants, airlines, universities, hotels, hospitals and business offices.

Starbucks' meteoric growth has presented the company with important management challenges: building an excellent top management team, putting systems into place to recruit, hire and train *baristas* and store managers who are the true heart and face of the company, and securing sufficient high-quality coffee beans to supply the company's growing needs; all the while ensuring the integrity of its hallmark, the quest for providing the perfect cup of coffee.

In 1994, Schultz decided it was time to change his role. "Managing day-to-day operations of a big company was not what I wished to do. It was beyond the scope of my skills and also fell outside my interests. I wanted, rather, to continue to create the vision, to anticipate the future, to experiment with creative ideas. That's the value I can add, and it's the work I love."[12] In 1994, Orin Smith, who had been chief financial officer since 1990, was promoted to become president and chief operating officer, while Schultz remained chairman and CEO. In June of 2000, Smith became president and CEO. Schultz became chief global strategist and remains chairman of the board.

CREATING A DIFFERENT KIND OF COMPANY

Howard Schultz's determination to build a company based on dignity and caring arises from very personal experience, in part, from witnessing the challenges of his father's life. Schultz describes his father as "a beaten man. In a series of blue-collar jobs — truck driver, factory worker, cab driver — he never made as much as $20,000 a year, never could afford to own his own home."[13] Schultz recalls the day his father died of lung cancer in 1988 as the saddest day of his life. His father died with no savings and no pension. "More important, he had never attained fulfillment and dignity from work he found meaningful."[14] When Schultz became president and CEO of Starbucks, he resolutely decided that he would create a different kind of company, a company that would not leave anyone behind.

On August 18, 1987, the day the new Starbucks was born, Schultz called employees together. He recalls telling them that all his life he had wanted to be part of a company and a group of people who share a common vision. He had seen that in Starbucks when he first came to visit them in Seattle, and he admired it. He said, "I'm here today because I love this company. I love what it represents." He told them about his vision of making Starbucks a national company and promised them that in doing so he would do nothing to dilute the integrity of the company. He promised, "I will not let you down. I promise you I will not leave anyone behind." He explained that he wanted to include people in the decision-making process, to be open and honest with them and that he wanted to build the company on guiding principles that would make them proud. He told them, "In five years I want you to look back at this day and say 'I was there when it started. I helped build this company into something great.'"[15]

In keeping with his promise, in 1988 Schultz convinced the board to approve the precedent-setting extension of health care benefits to part-time employees who worked 20 or more hours a week. Part-time workers constitute a significant part of the Starbucks workforce. Despite initial resistance, Schultz argued that it was the right thing to do. In addition, if treating employees well and with dignity helped cut down turnover, it would also cut costs of recruiting and training. Starbucks depends upon its employees to provide its public face and to make the connection that cements customer loyalty. Providing health care benefits was a way to demonstrate that Starbucks honored and valued their important role within the company.

Today these benefits include preventive care, crisis counseling, dental care, eye care, mental health care, and treatment for chemical dependency. Coverage is also offered to unmarried partners in a committed relationship. What Schultz recognized is that, although retail and restaurant businesses succeed or fail on the basis of customer service, employees in these sectors tend to have the lowest pay and worst benefits of any industry. He wanted Starbucks to be an employer of choice and he decided that the way to do that was to pay higher than the going wage and to offer benefits no one else offered.

In early 1990, Starbucks began a strategic planning process by creating a mission statement that would reflect the values of all employees. It was drafted by the senior executive team and reviewed by the employees. The remarkable thing about this mission statement is that its guiding principles place people ahead of profits. The fact that this is so unusual in our society is as much an indictment of our society's money-driven values system as it is another source of appreciation of the Starbucks approach.

STARBUCKS MISSION STATEMENT

Establish Starbucks as the premier purveyor of the finest coffee in the world while maintaining our uncompromising principles as we grow. The following six guiding principles will help us measure the appropriateness of our decisions:

- Provide a great work environment and treat each other with respect and dignity.
- Embrace diversity as an essential component in the way we do business.
- Apply the highest standards of excellence to the purchasing, roasting and fresh delivery of our coffee.
- Develop enthusiastically satisfied customers all of the time.
- Contribute positively to our communities and our environment.
- Recognize that profitability is essential to our future success.

Source: www.starbucks.com

Perhaps even more remarkable, to ensure that the company lives up to its promises, Starbucks set up a mission review team and an internal system that enables partners to be in dialogue across the company and to provide feedback on what is and is not working. Employees are encouraged to report concerns to the team if decisions and actions are not consistent with the company's mission statement. As the company has grown, Starbucks has assembled a team of people from different regions to review employee concerns, seek solutions, and report back at the company's Open Forums, which are held biannually in every geographic region. Senior managers meet regularly with interested employees to provide updates, answer questions, and hear their concerns and grievances.

By 1991, with the achievement of its first profitable year, Schultz introduced "Bean Stock," a stock option plan for all employees working at least 20 hours per week. Schultz says, "I wanted to find a way to share both ownership of the company and the rewards of financial success with the people of Starbucks." His plan was to link shareholder value with long-term rewards for employees and to make the connection clear between the contribution that employees made to the success of the company and the growing value of the company. Through this program, Starbucks granted stock options to over 700 employees while the company was still private. When the Bean Stock program was introduced, Starbucks dropped the term *employee* and began referring to all of those who worked for the company as *partners*. In 1995, Starbucks also implemented an employee stock purchase plan.

Starbucks takes social responsibility seriously. Still it faces the challenge that every company does in this arena: figuring out what really constitutes authentic social responsibility for a company. According to Schultz, his responsibility as CEO was "to the people of Starbucks: partners, customers and shareholders." He also feels a sense of responsibility to "those who came before me, those who created the legacy of Starbucks and built it into what it is today."[16] Schultz feels that it is Starbucks' responsibility, as an employer and as a public company, to sustain and grow its business and that it should also provide support in the communities where Starbucks stores are located and in the countries where their coffee is grown.

The challenge, of course, is to create a balance among these various sets of responsibility. Evidence of the company's responsibility to its shareholders (including many Starbucks employees) can be found in its fiscal responsibility and the strategic growth of the company. The company's health care coverage and its stock option and purchase programs indicate its respect and concern for its partners. The company's CUP Fund, Caring Unites Partners, provides another example of ways it seeks to be a different kind of company. CUP is a financial assistance program that helps Starbucks partners in times of special need, such as illness, not covered by insurance, death of a partner or family member, natural disaster, or other extreme circumstances (fire, theft, etc.). The CUP Fund is supported by partner contributions that are matched by the company.

The commitment of Starbucks to the communities in which it operates is listed as a guiding principle in the company's mission. The company has set up several programs to work toward that commitment. Starbucks encourages both its partners and its customers to be involved in their communities through a program called Make your Mark. The program matches partner and customer volunteer hours in non-profit organizations in their communities with cash and product donations to those organizations. Since the Make Your Mark program started in January 2000, Starbucks partners and customers have volunteered over 20,000 hours and generated nearly $40,000 for charities.

> *When I travel around the country and do these town hall meetings, and I do a lot of store visits, I work in stores because I think that's where the spirit is. It's not here at corporate headquarters. I think that's where it is, and it astounds me that almost without exception people just love this company. They love being part of it. Many employees who choose Starbucks don't necessarily choose it because it is a good corporate citizen, but in fact it's a big part of why they stay because once they get involved they understand what we're doing in our communities, how we support the world in these areas, how we support origin countries. They want to be part of that.*
>
> — Dennis Stefanacci, Senior Vice-President, Corporate Social Responsibility

Starbucks encourages partners to make financial contributions through a program called Choose to Give! This program supports Starbucks partners who provide financial contributions to community organizations. Partners may elect to make one-time donations or to give through payroll deduction, and Starbucks matches the contributions dollar for dollar up to $1,000 per partner. In the year 2000, with a match from Starbucks, partners contributed $500,000 to the communities in which it operates and its partners live.

Starbucks also encourages its executives to lend their management expertise to non-profit organizations by becoming board members for non-profit organizations. Examples of some of these organizations include The American Red Cross of King County, the Meany Theatre at the University of Washington, the YWCA of King County, the AIDS Housing of Washington, the Urban League of Seattle, the Alliance for Education, the Benaroya Research Institute of Virginia

Mason Medical Center, the Corporate Council for the Arts, the Seattle Chamber of Commerce, and the Trade Development Alliance.

In addition to these programs, in 1997 Starbucks established the Starbucks Foundation with the mission "to create hope, discovery and opportunity in communities where Starbucks lives and works." The Foundation focuses primarily on literacy programs based on the philosophy that reading is a fundamental building block for success. The company holds an annual All Books for Children book drive that collects new and used books to donate to local schools and literacy organizations in the United States and Canada. Since the program started in 1997, it has collected and distributed more than one million books. The goal Starbucks originally set for the year 2001 was 500,000 books. Starbucks has made arrangements with United Parcel Service to provide free pick-up of all the books collected at Starbucks locations and delivery to participating literacy organizations.

The company has also made a commitment to economically underserved communities through an innovative joint venture partnership with Earvin "Magic" Johnson's Johnson Development Corporation. Called Urban Coffee Opportunities (UCO), the joint venture is designed to bring retail vitality and economic opportunity to underserved neighborhoods. The program is based on the philosophy that "the presence of a Starbucks store can be a catalyst for other business development in a community as well as an inviting place to work and meet."[17] The UCO develops Starbucks stores through the United States, particularly in major metropolitan areas. The first UCO store opened in March of 1998 in south-central Los Angeles and is the top performing UCO store in the region. By year-end 2001, there were 29 UCO locations across the United States.

Schultz is well on the way to fulfilling his promise to himself and his partners: to create a truly different kind of company. One of its hallmarks is a conscious journey to discover what authentic corporate responsibility means. In November 1999, to lead and act in this quest, Starbucks formed a Corporate Social Responsibility department to organize all of the company's social and environmental efforts, contributions, and foundations under a single umbrella. To Starbucks, contributing what it can to a more sustainable global society is simply an inherent part of this corporate responsibility. Where will this journey lead? Just as the company is building its brand and customer loyalty cup by cup, it is taking this journey one step at a time.

SUSTAINABILITY INTEGRATION: STEP BY STEP

From that day in 1987 when Schultz promised not to leave anyone behind, to the present time, Starbucks has been progressively expanding its sphere of concern, and exploring what is within its power to control and influence, *in order to be not only a different kind of company, but a company that can make a difference.* We begin our examination of the steps Starbucks is taking with what its leaders are saying and how sustainability-oriented concerns show up in policy statements. One way that Starbucks expands its sphere of control and influence is through strategic partnerships that are focused on some of the difficult issues intrinsic to the coffee industry. Starbucks is very clear that it is a business organization, not an environmental, international development or humanitarian agency. So the company enlists the assistance of organizations with expertise in these areas to tackle some of the problems that enter its sphere of concern and to choose ways to best focus its influence and control. The corporate responsibility function covers local and global programs such as literacy programs, community volunteering, recycling efforts, shade grown coffee, Fair Trade coffee and international relief efforts. In this chapter we feature a cross-section so as to provide a sense of their scope in these areas.

Leadership Commitment

When you talk to people at the Starbucks Support Center in Seattle, the consensus is clear that the company's top leaders and the board are solidly committed to corporate responsibility. Dennis Stefanacci, Senior Vice-President of Corporate Social Responsibility comments, "The board through Howard Schultz and Orin Smith has said publicly, and has communicated to this company, that we want to be known as much for being a good corporate citizen as we are known for the quality of our coffee." At Starbucks, Stefanacci insists, these are " important and parallel and equal missions."

Sue Mecklenburg, Vice-President of Business Practice, points out that Smith is committed to corporate responsibility and sustainability because he "sees it not only as a part of what we ought to do, because of who we say we are and what we believe in, but really as essential for inspiring our partners to want to work for the company. If you look at it as a sustainability advantage, the sustainability of being in a business like this is dependent on a lot of part-time people. You need to inspire them to not only do the best for the company and stay with the company, but to carry that message out to our customers. They're our front-line people, so for Orin it is a comprehensive way of looking at and running a business."

Mecklenburg provides an example of the extent of Orin Smith's commitment to these issues. Smith was giving a speech at a Conservation International dinner in Washington, DC. Mecklenburg reports, "Orin pointed out that if Starbucks as a company could have most of its coffee shade grown — right now a little less than one-half of our coffee is shade grown — and we could set this up as a standard; and if we could do that with the one percent of that coffee that Starbucks represents out of all the coffee that is grown, we're not going to make a difference. But if that becomes a standard that other companies emulate, then this is an opportunity to change actual deforestation patterns and practices in the world. So Orin is looking at the big picture opportunity of being able to utilize our corporate values to influence industry practice. It's easy to get up every morning and come to work with a CEO who thinks like that. You come to work and get excited to do your day's work because you know that you are on track with what he wants the company to do."

Stefanacci believes the role of Corporate Social Responsibility is to be the "conscience of the company." He comments that Starbucks is "already a very moral and ethical company. Our role is to serve two functions: When decisions are made or public statements are going to be made or policies are going to be made that impact this company and the role it plays in being a good corporate citizen, our first function is to bring to the table all the players that are involved in making that decision so that when we make that decision or that public statement, it is made from an informed base. The second role we fill is to make sure we actually do those things and to keep all of the players across the whole institution committed."

Sue Mecklenburg's position in Starbucks as Vice-President of Business Practice is a far cry from her early training as a physical therapist. After raising her children, Mecklenburg dove into the non-profit sector by founding an advocacy organization for urban children and families and serving on the boards of several other non-profit organizations. She returned to school and got an MBA, with the ultimate goal of finding work with a socially responsible company. While enrolled in the MBA program at Washington State University, she was asked to help them set up a new program in environmental management and was at the university teaching and directing that program when Starbucks called asking for recommendations of people for a new position they were creating. So she said, "tell me about your job." Although the company was concerned that she had never worked in retail, she got the job anyway. They started her with a $50,000 budget. Now there are 12 people and a $6 million budget supporting a corporate contributions program, employee volunteer program, workplace giving program, partner relief fund and the Starbucks Foundation. Today Mecklenburg deals primarily with non-profit partnerships and activist groups. As for activists, she says, "I deal with all the people who have issues that we care about but maybe have a little different take on."

Think Systemically

Dennis Stefanacci believes an effective Corporate Social Responsibility (CSR) function brings a systems perspective to the organization's decision-making process and helps the company think out of the box. One way to achieve this is to build cross-functional teams to address issues. Stefanacci comments, "There is nothing we do that doesn't involve a cross-functional team. I don't care what piece it is of what we do, even to the point that there is a representative now from CSR that sits on every marketing group and committee so that they begin to think about how we're going to become the company that we want to be." He believes that the role of CSR is to work "across silos" so that the organization can understand that it is an interconnected system.

The following example demonstrates the importance of applying this approach to a seemingly simple organizational change toward more sustainable practices. In this case it was increasing partner use of reusable serve-ware during their breaks. Not only is this practice better for the environment, it was also an economically sound decision that saves money and reduces waste. Although it was simple, the change produced resistance. So Stefanacci went to the retail operations department and said, "Do you know that, in order to do this, we need to have an operational directive that requires our partners to use reusable serve-ware when they take the drinks in the store? It needs to become an operation directive." The first step was to present the recommendation to the operations council, which consists of the executive vice-presidents and the presidents of all the operations, and get them to say, "Yes, we want to do this." Stefanacci continues, "So we have to work with retail operations to first convince them this is not yet something else that the partners are being forced to do, but that this is the right thing to do because the savings from a paper perspective are very significant. Financially, we'll probably save one million dollars a year across the company-owned stores in the United States. More importantly, it saves 16 million paper cups. So that's what we start with."

The second step was to provide education and training. So Stefanacci worked with the Starbucks learning and development people to help reinforce why this one small change was important. They hoped that partners using reusable serve-ware would begin to ask the customers who take their drinks in the stores if they would prefer porcelain.

Finally, he went to the procurement group and said, "We are committed to this and we are going to do this. What do we have to do to make that happen?" Then he went to Store Development and said, "We're committed now as a company to doing this, so when you design new stores you need to make sure that you design enough storage space for all of this equipment, this new porcelain, on an ongoing basis." Then he went to the facilities group and so on. This systems integration approach is how CSR is now functioning on every issue "whether it's fair-trade or shade grown coffee or recycling or it's any of the pieces of those issues."

Our sustainability integration project with Starbucks is another example of the power of working cross-functionally and thinking systemically. We first met Sue Mecklenburg and Ben Packard at the Specialty Coffee Association of America conference in the spring of 2000 where we were delivering a series of presentations on sustainability and The Natural Step framework, particularly as it applied to analyzing the dynamics of the global coffee industry. At that time, Packard recalls, "What I learned in talking to other companies, like Norm Thompson Outfitters and Nike, was that for those of us who aren't in this sustainability implementation business, The Natural Step framework helps people talk to each other about these issues and gives them a common language across the functional areas in the company."

Packard was looking for a way to focus the company's environmental efforts and to gather some momentum both around that focus and toward measurement. Packard comments, "I had proposed when we became a CSR group that what we needed to do was step back. We had a lot of interesting programs in place. We had already been giving to CARE for eight years. We already had a Conservation International partnership. We had been recycling burlap bags for as long as anybody could remember. We had a Green Team. We had a lot of interesting tactics in place. But what I really wanted to do was to verify that what we are addressing truly represents the relatively large impacts of the business. People inside are getting tired of me saying 'relatively,' but to me that is what is important: that we focus on the right things. As a company, you can have hundreds of environmental impacts and you cannot simultaneously address them all. So you've got to make sure as a leader in this area that you are addressing the big ones."

To identify the highest-leverage focus areas for Starbucks, we worked with a cross-functional project team and developed an eco-audit protocol. During an intensive two-day workshop, we created a sustainability systems map of the company to develop a better picture of potential sustainability impacts using The Natural Step framework as an analytical tool, taking financial, social and environmental areas into consideration. We then jointly identified areas of potential sustainability impact. Together with the Starbucks team we identified the four priority focus areas that the company could move forward and integrate into its strategy and business planning processes:

- Sourcing practices (coffee, tea, milk, and paper)
- Transportation (from source to store)
- Energy and water consumption
- Store design and operation

We developed sample indicators that would be meaningful and measurable, from both a business strategy and a sustainability perspective, to enable Starbucks management to monitor progress in these areas. These indicators were benchmarked against the current best practices across a range of criteria. We then conducted a study that assessed these four focus areas against best practices across a number of different measurements with companies using The Natural Step framework, Interbrand companies, and others that we considered leaders in CSR reporting.

Packard was then able to use the information the team developed, present it to the Starbucks operating council, and make the case about why these particular focus areas could help Starbucks improve its performance as a company and what the benefit would be to doing so, including the fact that these areas are important to Starbucks partners. Starbucks has done research that indicates that although

corporate social responsibility is not necessarily the reason why partners join Starbucks, it is one of the reasons why they stay.

Packard presented the project as "a way to proactively manage our
environmental impacts so that we are not reactive. As a leader in this
area we should not ever be perceived as reactive in environmental
issues. This project is a way of scoping the issues that may be coming
down the line. It is a way to help us manage communication around
these issues and also a way to capture the value in the social responsibility investment community."

ENVIRONMENTAL MISSION STATEMENT

Starbucks is committed to a role of environmental leadership in all
facets of its business. The company fulfills this mission by a commitment to:

- Understanding environmental issues and sharing information with its partners.

- Developing innovative and flexible solutions to bring
  about change.

- Striving to buy, sell and use environmentally-friendly
  products.

- Recognizing that fiscal responsibility is essential to its
  environmental future.

- Instilling environmental responsibility as a corporate
  value.

- Measuring and monitoring progress for each project.

Source: www.starbucks.com

The operating council agreed to roll out the initiative across the
company, and the finance and planning department committed to
integrate the focus areas into the strategic planning process. At the
same time, the board of directors made a commitment that Starbucks
will set the standards for corporate social responsibility and, including
sustainability, made it one of the company's strategic directives.

One marker of the success of this approach to integrating sustainability thinking into business practice occurred in the spring of

2001 while the following year's budgets were being prepared. Packard reports: "A couple of units actually called me in April and said, 'What is this footprint thing? Can you come and talk at our next staff meeting about what this means?' One was the transportation and logistics group, which is clearly an area where we need to strengthen our performance. I presented the footprint and they started nodding and then it was just like boom, boom, boom, with ideas ... so they got it!"

In December 2001, the team conducted a year-end review of the environmental footprint to confirm that the focus areas chosen the year before still represented the highest leverage opportunities to address issues of concern to Starbucks globally and their confidence in the data collected to date. The team identified the obstacles and opportunities to addressing these issues faster, more productively, and more cross-functionally. Based on changes in company structure, international events, and a changed economic outlook, the team proposed a number of modifications to the focus areas and also recommended the next steps that the company should take to improve performance and develop meaningful metrics in these areas. These recommendations will be presented to the company's senior management team in early 2002.

Partnerships

On its website, Starbucks states it is "committed to addressing social and environmental issues in order to help sustain the people and places that produce Starbucks coffees."[18] The company is also clear that its distinctive competence is business and so to address these issues effectively, the company is developing relationships with organizations with experience in them. In this section we will feature some of the more prominent partnerships.

Starbucks' new year-round sustainable coffee offering program reiterates our commitment to our guiding principles, which includes contributing positively to our communities and environment. Our long-term efforts and support of programs in origin countries will continue so that Starbucks may help protect biodiversity and improve the lives of families in coffee farming communities.

— Orin Smith, President & CEO

CARE (Cooperative for Assistance and Relief Everywhere)[19]

Since 1991, Starbucks has donated more that $1.7 million to CARE, making it the largest annual North American cash contributor. Through the projects developed out of this partnership, Starbucks and CARE are able to impact the lives of more than 2.7 million people in Africa, Latin America, and Southeast Asia in countries as diverse as Guatemala, Honduras, Nicaragua, Kenya, Ethiopia, and Indonesia. Projects focus on a range of community needs including training for local groups in organizational planning, financial management, community education and health practices, improving agricultural practices, promotion of education particularly for females, child health and education, alternative income generation, disaster relief, environmental restoration, and conservation management.

The relationship with CARE, started because CARE and Starbucks operated in the same countries, consists primarily of an annual contribution and some cause-related marketing around a CARE sampler of products from each country where the two organizations have projects. The partnership arrangement was based on Starbucks' intention to be involved in the countries where they buy coffee. CARE would choose the kind of projects that were most important.

Part of the new plan that Starbucks is developing with CARE is focused around natural disasters. Mecklenburg explains, "There are always natural disasters in the countries where we source products, and we have historically responded to them on a very ad hoc basis. In response to Hurricane Mitch, we wrote a check for $100,000. When there was an earthquake in Columbia, we took one dollar a pound from the sale of Columbian coffee and gave it to Columbia. It is very uneven."

Starbucks is developing a program with CARE that is similar to their CUP Fund. This approach appreciates that there will be problems, so they set some money aside. They work with CARE as their agent when there are emergencies in the field. Mecklenburg comments, "We're basically going to put the money in CARE's Emergency Response Fund and when countries where we source products apply for it, will direct CARE to distribute this money, but have it set up in such a way that people know that CARE is our disaster agent; so that it becomes not just a response, but it becomes a program, it becomes a plan, a way of doing business. When there's a problem, CARE is there for us."

One of the tigers for me is what the company needs from relationships with non-profit organizations. What we need is to extend our reach into places where we feel we have responsibilities and where our customers and our partners feel we have responsibilities. So, at least from my perspective, a true partnership isn't one where we simply write a check so somebody can do good work, but not work that is relevant to what we're doing. There's certainly plenty of work to be done around the world, but our business also has plenty of impact. I consider our partners as agents in the field, so they have to be operating in the field that we are in.

— Sue Mecklenburg, Vice-President, Business Practice

Conservation International[20]

Conservation International (CI) is a non-profit organization whose mission is "to conserve the Earth's natural heritage and global biodiversity and to demonstrate that human societies are able to live harmoniously with nature." In 1998, Starbucks entered into a three-year partnership with CI around Conservation Coffee.

Conservation Coffee is coffee cultivated in specific ways that help conserve biodiversity. CI has identified the areas of the world with the richest concentrations of life, many claiming plants and animal species found nowhere else, and calls these regions biodiversity hotspots. The hotspots are 25 highly threatened areas that, combined, claim more than 60 percent of total terrestrial diversity in less than two percent of the Earth's land area. CI focuses much of its work on these areas, as well as major tropical wilderness areas, marine ecosystems and select major wetlands.

The way in which coffee is grown can have an impact on plants, animals and entire ecosystems because coffee grows in high altitude tropical areas where much of the world's biodiversity is found. CI's Conservation Coffee program works with coffee farmers in the hotspots and wilderness areas to cultivate coffee without harmful chemicals and in the shade of the forest canopy, helping to protect the forests, streams and wildlife. Coffee that is grown in the shade has a lower impact on its surrounding environment than "sun" coffee, which requires higher chemical input and the removal of forests. Shade coffee can be an important part of an integrated conservation strategy for sensitive ecosystems.

The Starbucks-CI partnership focuses on the El Trufino Biosphere Reserve in Chiapas, Mexico, a mountainous region that is part of the Mesoamerica biodiversity hotspot. This area is also known for producing high-quality coffee in a buffer zone that surrounds the reserve. The project helps farmers protect the biodiversity of this last remaining cloud forest in southern Mexico by promoting organic and traditional shade-growing of coffee plants. Starbucks provides financial support to the Chiapas project for training in agricultural techniques, and offers technical expertise to farmers on raising the quality of their product.

Mecklenburg feels that the CI partnership is a very exciting model that works well because of the way it was set up. They developed a memorandum of agreement that outlined what they wanted to achieve together, bearing in mind what things were within their grasp. In the first year of the project, the issue of purchasing the coffee was completely off the table. Starbucks' part of the agreement was to increase public awareness, provide money, and provide technical assistance — things that the company could control — whereas they couldn't at the outset, guarantee the quality of the coffee. Mecklenburg cautions, "Set yourself up for success, not failure."

Starbucks and CI have completed their three-year partnership agreement on the Chiapas project producing the high-quality coffee that Starbucks needs, which is sold now under the label: *Shade Grown Mexico*. The second phase of the partnership expands the project to five additional sites, the first two being in Columbia and Guatemala. If they succeed, the plan is to replicate them.

Mecklenburg comments: "We always work on the coffee. These are coffee farmers. These are people trying to grow good coffee. But I don't think the project needs to be contingent on whether we buy and sell the coffee. What we are trying to do is to help farmers grow this coffee in an environmentally sensitive way. We've increased the amount of land set aside as forest by 220 percent in the Chiapas project, and, whether or not we bought that coffee, that should happen."

The CI project in Chiapas is reaching its biodiversity goals. There are also other indications of success: farmers' incomes and exports are up and they've learned more about the market. To address the challenge farmers have accessing credit, Starbucks guaranteed $300,000 in loans in Chiapas in 2001. This leads to increased incomes for farmers because the access to credit enables them to sell their coffee to the export market. Mecklenburg elaborates, "We guaranteed loans for the farmers that put money in their pockets by giving them access to credit at good rates. Most of these were pre-harvest loans, money that is difficult for farmers to get because, before harvest, they have no collateral. By our being willing to mitigate that risk, other people were willing to loan to the farmers ahead of their harvest."

Through this partnership, Starbucks is working to strengthen the capacity of a cooperative at the same time as it encourages the farmers to preserve the environment, grow high-quality coffee that brings a higher price, and also to create the market savvy and the linkages so that if Starbucks were to disappear tomorrow this cooperative has a strength that it didn't have before.

> *We started with Chiapas and we had no idea whether it would produce what we wanted. We were concerned because a lot of these programs just don't work. And we were concerned that this product would not meet our quality standards — that our customers would reject it irrespective of whether or not it was a good thing environmentally. But to the contrary, they really got onto it. Our partners really supported it. So it seems to be good for everybody.*
>
> — Orin Smith, President & CEO

During the first phase of their partnership, Starbucks gave CI $150,000 over three years. During the second phase, they are providing CI with $200,000 a year for three years. In addition, Starbucks sponsored a fundraiser that raised an additional $75,000, and they're currently working on another fundraiser for 2002.

Calvert Social Investment Foundation[21]

Starbucks has committed one million dollars in financial support to be directed through the Calvert Social Investment Foundation so coffee farmers can make quality improvements, capital investments, and microenterprise and/or obtain credit at fair rates. This program is intended to enable farmers to improve their standard of living and provide better lives for their families. The Calvert Foundation places capital to provide microcredit, finance small business needs, and fund development for communities in need, in the United States and worldwide.

TransFair USA[22]

Starbucks Coffee Company and TransFair USA, a third-party certification organization, formed an alliance in April 2000 whereby Starbucks committed to promoting and selling Fair Trade Certified coffee through its U.S. retail stores and on-line through Starbucks.com. TransFair USA ensures that farmers who sell Fair Trade Certified products receive a guaranteed minimum price for their harvest. Starbucks began selling Fair Trade Certified coffee in U.S. stores on October 4, 2000. Shortly thereafter, Starbucks began offering Fair Trade Certified coffee to colleges and universities and more recently to hotel, restaurant, hospital and corporate business accounts.

In late 2001, Starbucks announced that they are expanding the Fair Trade Certified coffee program through three initiatives. First, Starbucks made a commitment to purchase, over a 12- to 18-month period, one million pounds of Fair Trade Certified green coffee that meets Starbucks' quality standards. As a result of this purchase, Starbucks is beginning a conversion incentive for college and university accounts to encourage the use of Fair Trade Certified drip coffee as their "core" offering in January 2002. As a part of this specific program, Starbucks plans to continue to sell Fair Trade Certified coffee at no price premium to accounts that have converted.

> *In a time when coffee farmers around the world are struggling to support their families and keep their farms, coffee companies like Starbucks need to take a leadership role in helping to stabilize this unfortunate, and some cases life-threatening, situation in coffee growing regions. Our $1 million investment through Calvert Community Investments and purchase of 1 million pounds of Fair Trade Certified coffee will, we hope, provide much-needed funds for impoverished coffee farming communities.*
>
> — Orin Smith, President & CEO

In addition, Starbucks will offer Fair Trade Certified coffee as Coffee of the Day on the 20th of each month, beginning in the spring of 2002 in all its company-owned stores in the U.S. Fair

Trade Certified coffee is already available in more than 2,900 company-owned stores across the United States, further highlighting the Company's commitment to improving the lives of farmers in origin countries. The offer will be promoted through marketing materials in each location, and retail stores will have adequate inventory of Fair Trade Certified whole bean coffee to support the increased awareness. Finally, Starbucks hopes to begin offering Fair Trade Certified coffee in Canada and other countries in early 2002.

Enterprise Works Worldwide[24]

In 1997, Starbucks entered into a partnership with Appropriate Technology International, now known as Enterprise Works Worldwide, a non-profit organization that fights poverty through self-help economic development programs for the poor in Africa, Asia, and Latin America. The Guatemala Coffee Project is based on Enterprise Works Worldwide's philosophy that "hope for a more inclusive global economy lies in increasing the earning power and income of the world's two billion small producers, building on their own hard work and entrepreneurial drive by enabling them to add commercial value to the goods they're producing and then sell the resulting products on lucrative markets — domestic, regional, and international."

The project financed the construction of two new coffee processing plants that enabled two participating farmers' cooperatives — Las Flores and Los Corteces — to improve their processing capabilities and the quality of their product. Each plant can now produce up to 90,000 pounds of high-quality gourmet coffee a year. The plants also treat wastewater to prevent water contamination, use processing residue as fertilizer to avoid the use of chemical fertilizers, and reduce water use through recycling water. In the spring of 1999, Starbucks purchased all the processed gourmet coffee produced by these two cooperatives in the 1998/99 growing season.

WALKING THE TALK

In addition to these partnerships and the systems approach to corporate social responsibility and sustainability, Starbucks is engaged in several other initiatives that indicate how they are walking the talk, including:

New Coffee Sourcing Guidelines

In November of 2001, Starbucks announced new coffee purchasing guidelines developed in partnership with The Center for Environmental Leadership in Business,[25] a division of Conservation International. By adopting these guidelines, Starbucks hopes to encourage the production of coffee that meets important environmental, social, economic, and quality standards. The guidelines are based on the Conservation Principles for Coffee Production developed jointly by the Consumers Choice Council,[26] Conservation International, the Rainforest Alliance,[27] and the Smithsonian Migratory Bird Center.[28] Mecklenburg comments, "We are working to create a system that promotes sustainability for the people and places that produce coffee. We want a system that recognizes regional differences, provides incentives for improvement, and is flexible and workable. There are many questions we can't answer and problems we can't foresee, so we decided to launch these guidelines as a pilot program for two crop years. During that time, we hope to work with producers and others in the supply chain to modify this system as necessary to meet their needs and our goal of increasing the sustainability of the coffee industry." Glenn Prickett, executive director of The Center for Environmental Leadership in Business remarks, "With these guidelines, Starbucks is taking a leadership role in addressing the environmental and social issues surrounding the global coffee industry. We hope that the success of this program demonstrates to the rest of the coffee industry that they can benefit by producing coffee in a way that protects global biodiversity and improves the livelihoods of coffee farmers."

Organic Composting

Organic residue from Starbucks' coffee roasting and extract operations is processed along with other organic material and made into a commercially viable soil amendment.

Burlap Bag Recycling

Starbucks sorts and ships its burlap coffee bags to a processor that shreds and reuses the material in other products. In 1997 alone, Starbucks recycled more than 320,000 pounds of burlap bags.

New Hot Cup and Reusable Mugs

In a 1996 to 2000 partnership with the Alliance for Environmental Innovation, a project of the Environmental Defense Fund and the

Pew Charitable Trusts, Starbucks conducted research on the development of a more environmentally friendly disposable hot cup and increasing the use of reusable mugs and commuter tumblers by Starbucks customers.

Coffee as Compost

Retail locations recycle coffee grounds when possible, package them, and encourage customers to use the spent grounds at home in their gardens and compost piles.

Retail Store Recycling Services

To help stores address individual recycling challenges, Starbucks has contracted with a national consulting service to work with store partners to establish recycling services for their stores.

The Green Team

Store managers representing each region of North America serve on the Starbucks Green Team to develop and implement strategic environmental initiatives.

Earth Day Activities

Starbucks partners across North America participate in more than 100 environmental cleanups annually in celebration of Earth Day, including beach and park cleanups, tree plantings and Adopt-a-Highway projects.

Store Design

A particularly exciting area that Starbucks has just launched is a program to develop a more sustainable store design that will include environmentally friendly construction materials. Eric Ramsing, Starbucks' corporate architect, is a proponent of sustainable building design and construction, and is working with a team to figure out how to apply these principles to new store construction and renovation. Starbucks is starting by taking one of their store designs and bidding it to confirm the cost. They are then having an independent third party conduct a U.S. Green Building Council LEED[29] appraisal on the store design to see how the current design compares to the LEED scorecard. Ramsing explains, "We don't know where we stand at this point. This benchmarking effort will find out where we stand so that we can take the appropriate action. It may be that we are in the silver range right now, which is our initial goal. If we find that we are at the silver level, then that's just great. If we're not there, then we go back through the design stage and look at what we need to change. Following the redesign, we will redraw and reengineer the store, bid it, and find out what the store would cost. At that point we can compare the two designs side by side and figure out what it's going to cost to do what we propose. Given the clear definition of cost and potential payback, it becomes a business decision whether or not to proceed with building the store." Once the store is built, Starbucks will monitor it for a designated period to see how it performs in comparison to their normal program. They will then use their findings to project what the ultimate savings would be over the course of operating at the LEED standard.

The project that Ramsing spoke about was for new construction projects. Starbucks would also like to do something similar for renovations. He comments further, "We do more tenant improvement work than anything else. Tenant improvement work is where we go into an existing mall and take out whatever was there from the previous tenant and then put in our material." New construction gives Starbucks the opportunity to insert something into the building package that they are less able to do with tenant improvement work. At this point, LEED doesn't have a program for assessing tenant improvement projects. Ramsing reports, "The U.S. Green Building Council recognizes this and they project that they will have a new section of LEED ready for release in 2005 or 2006."

The foregoing discussion of sustainability partnerships and projects provides you with a sense of just a few of the many initiatives that Starbucks has taken on its ongoing voyage to discover the nature of authentic corporate responsibility in the complex, extremely competitive world of global commerce in the early 21st century.

ADVICE ON THE SUSTAINABILITY JOURNEY

We asked some Starbucks partners who have key roles in the successful implementation of sustainable development in the company's operations to share some advice with others on their own journey to sustainability.

Arnie Alger, Director, Strategy and Planning

- I'm a big believer in 'servant leadership.' When you position yourself as a servant, a servant to other individuals, a servant to the environment, then your leadership is basically based on values that you have. If you really believe in that, a lot of good things will come to you, and this work in sustainability is one of those things.

- There is a triangulation principle here. When you want to hit a center point, you triangulate to that center point. You have upper management support as one point of the triangle, finance support as another, and the environment or other sustainability issue as the third point of the triangle. With an integration of these three components, I see some very big wins for the company.

- The timing is right. If you think about it, would you rather shop at a company that is socially responsible or one that doesn't care about these things.

Sue Mecklenburg, Vice-President, Business Practice

- Moving corporate responsibility to the forefront in anybody's daily agenda is the challenge we all face. I came to a company that had social responsibility as part of the value system, so I always have that to fall back on. Having a CEO that's really committed to that makes it a lot easier.

- You need to be persistent, you need to make your case, you need to have a lot of integrity, and you just need to keep at it and show results.

- One of the most effective things that we've done is to sponsor people in other departments to go to places where their peers talk about these issues. If we talk to the architects, they say 'oh that's nice,' but if we pay for an architect to go to a Green Building conference, then that architect comes back and says 'Wow, that is what my peers are saying,' and so we found that one of the most effective ways is not for us to be the agent for information, but let their peers do that. We devote a large piece of our budget for travel and conference fees for other departments.

- Always look for alliances. Find out what's important to people and then approach them in a way that meets their needs too. I'm always asking, 'What are your interests, how can we align our interests?' It's important to make sure that you help to empower them to do what you knew they wanted to do anyway.

- Make a good business case and don't shy away just because it is going to cost money. We make all kinds of decisions that aren't cheap or free. We buy very expensive coffee because we want high quality coffee. We don't just make a business case that we should buy cheaper coffee because we'd save money. So I think that if you're spending money on an environmental issue, that sometimes is just an expense that you decide that you're going to make. I'm just very fortunate to be in a company where you're allowed to make your case based on all of a range of things, you don't have to first make a business case and then tag the rest of those things along with it. The financial case is not the sole driver. Every company makes trade-offs in the decisions they make. These are multifaceted issues that have many implications and you need to consider the whole picture.

Ben Packard, Director, Environmental Affairs

- First ask, 'What is your company's mission statement? What business are you in and who are you as a company?' Don't waste your time trying to implement sustainability until you've talked to the owner of the company and asked those questions.

- If you want to be a leader in corporate social responsibility, the investment community has to recognize it, and one of the ways they recognize it is if they see clear focus and measurement and performance tracking in place as they do on financial measurements.

- At the end of the day, it is about the quality of your relationships with people and that applies whether you're talking to an internal purchasing agent, an activist, or a student. Nothing is sustainable if the personal relationships aren't there. Take time to understand what matters to the other person. It means understanding what motivates other people in the company. For example, on the environmental footprint team, there are twenty different motivations for why people are there. I think my role is to understand who the champions are going to be in the company and what motivates them. You need to be relevant to their concerns and you've got to be relevant to the business. That means you need to understand what's going on in the business.

Dennis Stefanacci, Senior Vice-President, Corporate Social Responsibility

- Look for a company that lives its mission, because everybody is interested in doing good. I doubt if you would run across any company that would say to you, and be sincere about it, that they were interested in not doing good. What makes this company different is that it has made a decision on what it stands for and what its mission is and it doesn't waver from that mission. So start out by looking for a good company. That's a company that will step to the forefront of this area.

- You can't build a company just on the bottom line without having the heart and the dedication to being committed to the environments and the communities in which you're working. You have to be part of those communities, so it has to be more than the bottom line. You also need to work with your investors. I've seen a number of statistics now that show that when investors — whether they're mutual funds or individual investors — look at how they build their funds, 35 percent of that decision is non-financial.

- Sit face to face with your critics. Listen to them. Find out why they are involved with the issues. Look for common ground.

FINAL REFLECTIONS

For more than ten years we have gone out of our way to locate a Starbucks close to the hotels where we stay on our frequent travels. Having that very first latte or mocha of the day from our favorite coffee company brings a delicious familiarity to every morning, even one that begins in a very unfamiliar destination. From London, England, to Atlanta, Georgia, to Kailua, Hawaii, to Melbourne, Australia, we have savored the flavor of our favorite brand. Yet interestingly, in all that time, we had never read any corporate literature, never penetrated beneath the familiar aroma of the shops we love to frequent. We simply continued to enjoy the experience. You can therefore imagine our enormous pleasure to discover the values that pervade the culture of Starbucks and underlie the experience of the customer. We knew Starbucks was doing something right; we just hadn't appreciated how really right in so many ways. So now we know something of the reasons why the *baristas* are almost unfailingly cheerful wherever you go in the Starbucks system, why the beans have so much flavor, and why the taste is so dependable.

Yet until we had the opportunity to learn more, we never knew what lay beneath the experience that we sought, and continue to seek, wherever our travels take us. So in the end, from a commercial perspective, what Starbucks is doing behind the scenes, with generous employee benefits, shade-grown coffee, partnering with non-profit organizations to support countries of origin where it sources coffee, composting coffee grounds, and countless other responsible initiatives, it all amounts to simply good business. Because the totality of what Starbucks is and does continues to draw customers back to the stores, over and over and over. It's what keeps us, and millions more satisfied customers, coming back every day for just one more cup of our favorite brew.

> *This is a values-driven company, and a lot of the satisfaction that people get in working here is because of the kinds of things we say we stand for. If we quit doing that, we would lose a lot of energy, the vitality, the trust that exists in the organization.*
>
> — Orin Smith, President and CEO

Howard Schultz set out to create a different kind of company, one that honors and respects its workers and gives back to society, a company that doesn't leave anyone behind. The company's top leadership shares this vision. It is the guiding light of the company's actions, actions that have created the most flourishing specialty coffee retailer in history. The success of their system and their philosophy speaks for itself. The continuing challenge for Starbucks, as for every company committed to being a good corporate citizen, is how to continue to live those values with authenticity.

CHAPTER 6

WHISTLER
"IT'S OUR NATURE"

*Whistler is committed to being a world leader
in environmental stewardship as we move
towards environmental sustainability.*

—Whistler Environmental Mission Statement[1]

*The Natural Step framework is a key component
of trying to communicate a very complex
question to the community in a very simple,
easy to understand format that reaches
families, business and even our guests.*

— Hugh O'Reilly, Mayor

THOUSANDS OF YEARS before Sir Francis Drake[2] allegedly "discovered" the rugged west coast of that seemingly boundless territory that would eventually become Canada, the Coast Salish people inhabited this area and had a rich, vibrant, and diverse culture. The Squamish people, part of the Coast Salish nation, lived in villages along the Squamish River and its creeks, the Howe Sound area, Burrard Inlet and Indian Arm. They moved with the seasons over a large and abundant territory from the coast to the mountains, gathering food and materials, and visiting their relations. They had a socially and environmentally sustainable society for millennia before the introduction of western society. They were conscious of the direct and immediate relationship between humankind and the rest of the natural world — nature permeated every aspect of their culture.

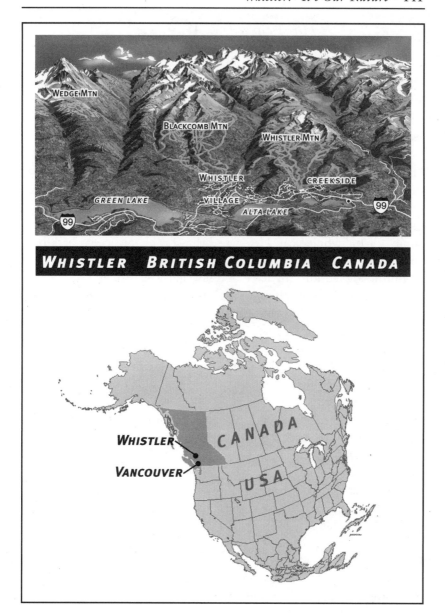

We open the story of Whistler with a legend from the Squamish people; a word of warning from the past that is as relevant today as it was before the days of the European colonization, and is as relevant to the people of the community now known as Whistler, as it is to people all over the world.

The Legend of Wountie[3]

A LONG TIME AGO, even before the time of the great flood, the Cheakamus River provided food for the Squamish people. Each year, at the end of summer, when the salmon came home to spawn, the people would cast their cedar root nets into the water and get enough fish for the winter to come.

One day, a man came to fish for food for his family for the winter. He looked into the river and found that many fish were coming home this year. He said thanks to the spirit of the fish, for giving themselves as food for his family, and cast his net into the river and waited. In time, he drew his nets in, and they were full of fish, enough for his family for the whole year. He packed these away into cedar bark baskets, and prepared to go home.

But he looked into the river, and saw all those fish, and decided to cast his net again, even though he already had sufficient for his family for a whole year. And he did so, and it again filled with fish, which he threw onto the shore.

A third time, he cast his net into the water and waited, even though he now had sufficient for his family for the next two years. This time, when he pulled his net in, it was torn beyond repair by sticks, stumps and branches, which filled the net. To his dismay, the fish on the shore and the fish in the cedar bark baskets were also sticks and branches. He had no fish; his nets were ruined.

It was then he looked up at the mountain, and saw Wountie, the spirit protecting the Cheakamus, who told him that he had broken faith with the river and with nature, by taking more than he needed for himself and his family. And this was the consequence. Now he had nothing.

And so, to this day, as you gaze high on the mountain overlooking the Cheakamus and Paradise Valley, you can see the image of Wountie, protecting the Cheakamus.

The fisherman? Well, his family went hungry and starved, a lesson for all the people in his family. A lesson for all the people.

❋ ❋ ❋

GLOBAL SYSTEMS CONTEXT

The story in this chapter is about a community that is seeking to keep its faith with nature so that all of the families who live in Whistler, and all those who come to enjoy the area's beauty and outdoor recreation, can continue to do so sustainably and without limit. Whistler is not alone in this quest. Resort communities are part of one of the world's most important and fastest growing industries, travel and tourism, which accounts for more than 6 percent of all international trade. Since 1950, total annual expenditure on tourism has risen from $2 billion to annual worldwide revenues of $476 billion in 2000, an increase of 4.5 percent over 1999. This amount exceeds the combined Gross National Product (GNP) of the world's 55 poorest countries.[4]

Today tourism provides approximately 210 million jobs worldwide. By 2011, this is estimated to grow to 260 million jobs, approximately 9 percent of total employment worldwide. Travel and tourism is expected to generate 12.8 percent of total exports ($1.064 trillion) in 2001, growing to $2.58 trillion in 2011. Capital investment in the industry is estimated at $656.7 billion or 9 percent of total investment in 2001. By 2011 this should reach $1.43 trillion or 9.3 percent of total.[5]

The World Tourism Organization's long-term growth forecast *Tourism: 2020 Vision* predicts that the tourism sector will expand by an average of 4.1 percent a year over the next two decades, will surpass a total of one billion international travellers by the year 2010, and will reach 1.6 billion by the year 2020. According to this report, the majority of all tourist expenditure in 1995 came from 20 rich nations (17 European, U.S., Canada and Japan) and accounted for 81.8 percent of all tourist expenditure in that year with five nations (U.S., Japan, Germany, U.K., and France) accounting for over one-half.[6]

Although these numbers are impressive, international tourism is particularly vulnerable to a variety of factors including economic recession, currency crises, political instability, terrorism, disruptions in traffic, transport and communications systems, shifts in tastes, and environmental threats and pollution. It is also a very competitive industry. Travel and tourist destinations must compete on a global scale that transcends season or geographic location. The tourist experience can be satisfied by a vast array of competing offerings. Winter in the northern mountains competes with summer in the southern latitudes as each becomes more accessible and as Internet and other media technologies make the array of offerings more visible and attractive.

Many developing countries and undeveloped regions rely on tourism as a key development strategy because the industry provides significant employment potential.

Mountains, in particular, have long been the destination of travelers, often seeking sanctuary and spiritual renewal. Winter sports, in particular, have been a major driver for the development of mountain tourism with an estimated market of 65 to 70 million people worldwide. Ironically, the same elements that attract tourists, whether for adventure or solitude, to mountain areas — clean, cool air, varied topography, scenic beauty, and diverse natural landscapes — are also the reasons that make mountain areas vulnerable.

Mountains are fragile ecosystems on which more than one-half of the world's population may ultimately rely. "Mountain environments are sensitive, living laboratories for monitoring climate change, of highest significance for biological diversity, and the source of over 80 percent of the world's fresh surface water resources."[7] Increased access means that tourism has become a primary source of revenue for many of these mountain areas as well as a source of environmental stress and often significant environmental degradation.

In addition, tourism generally entails the movement of people from their homes to other destinations, travel that is mainly dependent upon the combustion of fossil fuels. Thus, global tourism is closely linked with climate change. It is estimated that tourism accounts for about 50 percent of traffic movements, and that air traffic alone contributes about 2.5 percent of the human-generated production of carbon dioxide, which results in millions of tons of carbon being added to the atmosphere each year. Tourism is therefore a significant contributor to the increasing concentrations of greenhouse gases in the atmosphere.

Climate change is an important concern for mountain communities and mountain tourism. Their landscapes may be vulnerable to significant alteration as changes in temperature influence natural ecosystems. In most parts of the world, glaciers, an important part of many mountain landscapes, have been retreating in recent decades. This not only may affect the attractiveness of the very terrain of mountain tourist destinations, it also may have important implications for the survivability of mountain communities. For example, as glaciers retreat, water supplies increase in the short term, but as the glaciers shrink and disappear, water shortages will have potentially devastating effects on fragile mountain ecosystems as well as the human systems, the human societies, living downstream.

There is certainly reason to be concerned about the sustainable development of mountain regions, and there are numerous challenges and opportunities in balancing the local conditions of individual mountain communities, valleys, and regions with the demands of tourism.

WHISTLER HISTORY[8]

The area that is now Whistler was used by both the Squamish people and by the Lillooet people, the most westerly group of the Interior Salish people, and the chief intermediaries in coastal trade. The first Europeans, (representatives of the Hudson's Bay Company), began to appear in the area in 1827 looking for a route to move furs to the coast. In 1834, the Hudson's Bay Company began establishing trading posts up and down the west coast of the territory that Drake had claimed for England. But it wasn't until the 1850s that Europeans began to arrive in large numbers during the Fraser gold rush. In 1858, a group of miners established the first town of Pemberton, north of what is now Whistler, on the shores of the Lilloet River. In that same year, the Colony of British Columbia was established and the area now known as Whistler was first surveyed and documented by the Hudson's Bay Company.

It would still be years before the British North America Act (now called the Constitution Act, 1867), created Canada, and four more years before the Colony of British Columbia joined Canada. During that time, the indigenous population, now known as the First Nations people, made up the majority of the population. In the 1860s, British Naval officers and surveyors named the mountain now known as Whistler Mountain, London Mountain. In 1873, a rough trail was cut from Squamish to Pemberton. The valley was used mainly as a traveling route.

John Millar, a trapper who ran a stopping house on the Pemberton Trail, was one of the first settlers in the valley. In 1911, on a trip to Vancouver, Millar convinced Alex and Myrtle Philip to take a fishing trip on a chain of lakes near his cabin. They had moved west from the state of Maine to open a restaurant, with the dream of opening a fishing resort. At that time it took two days to travel from Vancouver to Whistler: a steamer ship from Vancouver to Squamish, overnight in Brackendale, and a hike with pack horses up the rugged Pemberton Trail. In 1913 the Philips purchased ten acres of land on the northwest corner of Alta Lake for Can$700, and by 1914 they had built their lodge.

In the early 1900s, there were a few trappers and prospectors like John Millar and Harry Horstman who settled in the Whistler area via the Pemberton Trail, the only direct route from the coast to the Pemberton Valley. In 1914 the Pacific Great Eastern Railway (PGE), now BC Rail, opened the valley to the outside world. Eventually the Philips expanded their lodge to accommodate 100 people, and it soon became the most popular resort west of Banff and Jasper in Alberta. In 1948, the Philips sold the lodge. It burned down in 1977. The site is now preserved as Rainbow Park. The Philips lived in the area for the rest of their lives. Alex died in 1968 at the age of 86 and Myrtle died in 1986 at the age of 95.

In the early 1960s, a group of Vancouver businessmen and members of Canada's Olympic Committee formed the Garibaldi Olympic Development Association to find and develop a site to host a future Winter Olympic Games. At that time, the area that is now Whistler was basically wilderness. It had no road, no electricity, no water and no sewer system. In 1960, the Garibaldi Lift Company was formed and by the summer of 1965 it had completed a four-person gondola to the mountain's mid-point, a double chairlift to the treeline, and two T-bars on Whistler Glacier, along with a number of cut runs and a day lodge. On August 27, 1965, the name of London Mountain was officially changed to Whistler Mountain, after the whistling sound made by the western hoary marmots that lived there. Skiing began in 1965 and the first ski lift opened in early 1966. Since the turn of the century, the British Columbia provincial government had promised to build a road, but it was not until Whistler was being developed as a ski area in the early 1960s that a rough gravel road was pushed from Squamish through to Alta Lake. The road was extended to Pemberton in 1964, and in 1969 it was finally paved. At this time the permanent population of the Whistler Valley was approximately 25 people.

In 1974, the provincial government — interested in developing tourism — introduced a land freeze and a development study to identify the important community issues in the rapidly growing settlement of Alta Lake. As a result of this study, in September 1975, the Resort Municipality of Whistler (RMOW) was created as the first and only Resort Municipality in Canada, by a special act of the Provincial Legislative Assembly, and granted the powers of local government.

In 1977, the new municipality developed an Official Community Plan (OCP) that visualized and carefully laid out the direction for the community, including a town center where the two mountains, Whistler and Blackcomb, converged. A call was issued for development proposals on Blackcomb Mountain. In January 1978, 53 acres of Crown land was given to the municipality to develop the town center. The Whistler Village Land Company was formed as a subsidiary company with the mandate to manage, develop and sell land within the town center.

Construction for the town site began, in August 1978, on what had previously been the garbage dump for the area. Blackcomb Mountain development was launched and opened for skiing the winter of 1980-81, creating one of the largest ski complexes in North America with the two longest vertical drops. In 1985, Blackcomb Mountain expanded its terrain making it North America's only "Mile High Mountain." By 1991, Whistler was being recognized as North America's Number One Ski Resort by Snow Country Magazine, an honor Whistler has often held since then with many other magazines and travel associations.

The Official Community Plan carefully laid out the direction for future growth of the community. This plan created a unique pedestrian-oriented village, which coordinated the architectural design of the village buildings, and carefully integrated the village into the two principal ski developments on Whistler Mountain and Blackcomb Mountain. This plan concentrated commercial development in the village and the Whistler Creek area, and eliminated the possibility of uncontrolled development throughout the valley.

The transformation of a small wilderness summer recreation community into an award-winning, four-season international resort in just 25 years is unparalleled in ski history. Similarly unparalleled is the equal emphasis that the citizens and government of the Resort Municipality of Whistler place on creating and maintaining a strong four-season destination resort *and* a strong mountain community. In Whistler, there is the realization that one is inextricably linked with the other.

The community's second OCP, adopted in 1982, maintained and reinforced the priorities established in 1976. It expanded on the concept of growth management, requiring phasing of accommodation with the capacities of the infrastructure and the natural environment. A restriction on development was established at 45,000 bed units and public accommodation was encouraged over new private housing. For the first time, an evaluation procedure for new accommodation was established based on capacity analysis, site performance standards, and environmental impact.

In 1989, the third OCP was adopted, expanding on growth management strategies and focusing on the enhancement of more year-round amenities. The plan also made provision for an additional 7,500 bed units, raising the development cap to 52,500. The fourth and current OCP was adopted in 1994, and amended in 1995, to provide for an additional 1,700 affordable residential bed units.

Development continues to be limited under Whistler's growth management strategy. Any proposed amendments to the OCP that would increase the bed unit capacity or significantly increase the commercial, service or light industrial floor space can only be considered under the comprehensive development plan if the proposed development:

- Provides clear and substantial benefits to the community and the resort;

- Is, in the opinion of Council, greatly supported by the community;

- Will not cause unacceptable impacts on the community, resort or environment; and

- Meets all policies of the OCP.

In 1993, Whistler instituted a Community and Resort Monitoring Program to provide the municipality with an accurate measurement of the quality of life and the quality of the environment. A variety of sources provide information on water quality, parking availability, skier visits, school enrollment, and other topics. Changes from year to year are measured and the implications are analyzed. This information enables the resort community to refine its strategies in growth management and guide future planning decisions, as well as respond to changing needs in the community.

Monitoring information also identifies possible needs for changes to RMOW policy, helps the municipality refine its capital program or operations program, and enables the community to establish standards for acceptable ranges of important indicators. Information gathered over the past years in the monitoring program contributed significantly to the development of *Whistler 2002*, the vision for the resort community (this document is described in more detail later in the chapter). The three-volume document also includes the Long-Term Financial Plan and the municipality's Five-Year Business Plan. The

Community and Resort Monitoring Program plays a key ongoing role in realizing the resort community's vision as it monitors progress and measures success.

Whistler's current population, estimated to be 9,600, is projected to grow to 11,000 by 2002 with much the same profile as today — largely youthful (more than 68 percent of the population is under 34 with the average age group 25 to 34 years). The number of seniors and children and families living in Whistler full-time is expected to increase. With second-home owners and guests, the population can swell to a total population between 15,000 and 30,000.

Approximately 14,000 people work full-time or part-time in Whistler, the majority in sales and services. Tax revenues from all levels of government total about Can$375 million annually. The community contributes significantly to regional school and hospital taxes. Whistler's tourism-based economy is estimated to create about 30,000 jobs in the region including the Lower Mainland area around Vancouver, which represents approximately Can$650 million in wages and salaries. It is estimated that Whistler contributes in excess of one billion dollars (Can) to the provincial economy each year.

Whistler/Blackcomb, the largest ski area on the continent, has more than 2,800 hectares (just over 7,000 acres) of skiing area, 33 lifts, more than 200 runs and 12 massive alpine bowls and the most ski-in/ski-out accommodation of any mountain recreation resort in North America. The ski operations at Whistler Mountain (elevation 7,160 feet/2182 meters) and Blackcomb Mountain (elevation 7,494 feet/2284 meters) competed with each other for two decades before merging in the spring of 1997. Competition between the two led to their status in the minds (and hearts) of many skiers and snowboarders as the premier North American winter resorts. Today Whistler/Blackcomb Ski Resort is one of only three resorts in the world with two million skier/boarder visits per winter season and is the only resort in North America with this distinction.

The volume of summer tourism at Whistler now rivals that of winter. Whistler has three championship designer golf courses and three more are within one hour's drive.

WHISTLER 2002: CHARTING A COURSE FOR THE FUTURE

In 1996, Hugh O'Reilly was elected mayor of the Resort Municipality of Whistler and Jim Godfrey was hired to be the chief administrative officer (CAO). O'Reilly recalls "What really got me excited about the opportunity to become Mayor was knowing that Jim was going to be the administrator. I remember that one of Jim's first comments was, 'I've been here a short time and everyone talks about the vision, but nowhere is it articulated. I can't find it written anywhere.' We took it upon ourselves to involve the community in articulating its vision. Within that process the community defined our key values. Moving toward environmental sustainability was 100 percent supported."

THE RESORT COMMUNITY OF WHISTLER VALUES

- A strong, healthy community — where growth and development are managed and controlled, where the needs of its residents are met, where community life and individual well-being are fostered, where the diversity of people is celebrated, and where social interactions, recreation, culture, health services and lifelong learning are accessible to all.

- Our natural environment — and our role as responsible guardians of it, respecting and protecting nature's wealth for ourselves and for future generations.

- A safe community —where residents and guests of all ages are comfortable and secure.

- The people who live, work and play here — our families, children, neighbors, colleagues and friends.

- Our guests — and our desire to provide exceptional service in all we do.

- Our partners — and the positive, cooperative relationship that recognizes the values of all the communities in the Sea-to-Sky corridor.

- Sound fiscal management where a healthy economy is sustainable through thoughtful, long-range financial planning.

Source: Whistler 2002

In 1997, the RMOW embarked on creating a vision that "charts a new course" for the community into the 21st century. Godfrey recalls, "We came up with a clear vision that we would be the *premier mountain resort community.* We wanted to distinguish ourselves from other resorts. There are a lot of great resorts, but we wanted to be a great resort *community.*"

The vision was created through a community consultation process that started with collecting ideas and thoughts from annual town hall meetings, informal workshops and interviews with council, municipal staff, and community partners, as well as through past community surveys. Based on this information, the RMOW prepared a workbook with a draft of the vision, presented it to the annual town hall meeting on December 13, 1997, and followed with a process of community involvement through workshops and presentations to the public, employees, community groups and corporations. Comments and survey questions were tabulated at the Centre for Tourism Policy and Research at Simon Fraser University. From this process the municipality refined the vision that now guides it. The 1999-2002 council reviewed the vision and it is now available in print and electronic form.[9]

Whistler 2002 outlines five priorities of equal importance. These priorities provide the foundation for the community's Vision Statement.

WHISTLER'S VISION STATEMENT

Whistler will be the premier mountain resort community. We will continue to build a thriving resort community that emphasizes the quality of life for its residents and respects the diversity of its people. We will develop and implement long-term growth management programs that move us toward environmental sustainability and help us achieve financial stability. We, and our visitors, will enjoy an optimum mix of world-class recreational opportunities and first-class service in a rugged mountain environment unique to Whistler.

Whistler 2002 states:

> The municipality continues to foster and participate in environmental partnerships, such as the Fisheries Stewardship Group, and is working to improve intergovernmental cooperation in the areas of wildlife management, flood protection and management of surrounding ecosystems.

It is leading by example and has completed an audit of practices and established a municipal energy and materials policy based on the principles of The Natural Step, a framework developed by the international science community to build an ecological and economically sustainable society.

The rest of the resort community is also following environmental management practices based on The Natural Step framework, making us a leader among resorts in environmental sustainability.[10]

The Whistler Environmental Strategy

The Whistler Environmental Strategy (WES) was developed to address the community's priority of moving toward environmental sustainability as expressed in the *Whistler 2002* vision. It is a comprehensive, coordinated approach for improving environmental stewardship throughout the resort community, and provides a detailed planning document for the municipal government. The WES establishes a set of environmental values for the RMOW:

- Local Stewardship — caring for local natural areas and processes;
- Global and regional responsibility — partnering to manage the impact on regional ecosystems and the global ecosphere; and
- The rights of future generations — protecting the rights of future generations so that they can participate in the stewardship of healthy, functioning ecosystems.

A set of environmental operating principles are connected to these environmental values and, based on these values and principles, the WES identifies:

- Directions — general paths to be followed in given environmental topic areas;
- Strategic goals — desirable long-term environmental conditions for each direction;
- Guidelines — recommended environmental criteria for evaluating resort community or municipal tasks;
- Triggers — commitments to take specified actions at a future date in response to certain conditions; and
- Tasks — activities (projects, programs or policies) that support movement toward strategic goals.

Mayor O'Reilly reports that the WES was reviewed independently by a professor at the University of British Columbia, "who said to us that clearly it was one of the better documents he'd ever seen, but he said 'the challenge will be trying to implement it.' That's always the challenge. It's easy to write it, it's hard to do."

While the Whistler Environmental Strategy draft was being completed, Dr. Karl-Henrik Robèrt, founder of The Natural Step, came to Whistler on a snowboarding vacation with his two sons in March, 2000. Robèrt agreed to make three presentations on The Natural Step framework for sustainability to interested members of the community. O'Reilly recalls, "The key breakthrough, in my opinion, was Dr. Robèrt being here. It was the answer to my dilemma. The strategy was a complicated plan that was difficult to communicate. The Natural Step framework really provided the mechanism for delivery: simple to understand, something we *could* communicate. It's not prescriptive, it's not judgmental, and it doesn't in any way tell the business community that everything that they've built is wrong. It does suggest that we need to, and can, do things differently and better."

> *You don't very often see an initiative that gets the kind of support that this one has. The interesting part is that I think we've just barely broken the crust on it.*
>
> — Mayor Hugh O'Reilly, RMOW

Godfrey recalls, "What struck me sitting there and listening to Dr. Robèrt was how engaged the people around the table were; they were riveted to the discussion that was taking place. Then we had the second presentation that involved the Chamber of Commerce, and the Chamber of Commerce was very engaged, more than I'd seen in a lot of other presentations. I thought, this is something that would provide a major vehicle for us to be able to move forward in a very comprehensive way."

Godfrey continues, "A group of us got together and decided we should look at adopting The Natural Step framework as a common language, a common framework that would supplement and complement some of the things that we were already doing. As a result, Whistler's Early Adopters of The Natural Step framework group came together."

The Whistler Early Adopters of The Natural Step Framework

The Whistler Early Adopters of The Natural Step framework consists of a number of key organizations, including the community's largest employers. Members of the group include: the Resort Municipality of Whistler (the municipal government); Whistler/Blackcomb Ski Resorts (the company that owns and operates the ski/snowboarding resort on the two mountains and attendant facilities); the Fairmont Chateau Whistler (Whistler's flagship hotel and a pre-eminent property in the Fairmont chain), Tourism Whistler (the marketing organization for Whistler that represents more than 6,000 members who own, manage or do business on resort lands); Whistler Fotosource (representing small businesses that make up the majority of businesses in Whistler); and the Association of Whistler Area Residents for the Environment (AWARE, a members-based environmental advocacy, watchdog and educational organization). This represents a unique and ground-breaking public/private/non-governmental organization partnership created for the purpose of moving toward sustainability. We feature some of the background and activities of these organizations later in this chapter.

Whistler's Early Adopters of the TNS framework have formed a "learning community" that is working cooperatively using the TNS framework to develop a common mental model of how to understand sustainability; promote a common message about moving toward sustainability in the community; develop common training programs; develop toolkits (manuals and resource materials) to facilitate and guide the implementation of more sustainable practices in households, small and large organizations, and in schools; create a website as a community sustainability resource, and document their shared learning experience. The Early Adopters are, in effect, test pilots for sustainability and, as they follow the TNS framework within their own organizations, they share their learning experiences with other interested Whistler organizations and citizens.

In May 2000, senior representatives of the Early Adopter organizations met and developed the Early Adopters Agreement, a signed memorandum, to formally articulate their commitment. The RMOW committed staff time to support the Early Adopters group. Dave Waldron, a contributor to both *Whistler 2002* and the WES, was made available to provide coordination of the group and its initiatives. The Early Adopters began to explore how to progress collaboratively in this new venture. The Early Adopters agreed to take a joint approach to sustainability education and awareness building in their organizations and to build internal capacity for doing so in each of their organizations. In late November of 2000, we conducted an intensive two-day facilitator workshop for teams from each of the Early Adopter organizations. The purpose of the workshop was to train the facilitation teams so they could develop and conduct sustainability awareness presentations, based on the TNS framework, within their own organizations. During the two months following the workshop, teams developed internal sustainability presentations adapted to the specific cultures and needs of their own organizations, and an implementation plan to provide sustainability awareness sessions to their respective employees.

The Early Adopters of The Natural Step framework also agreed on a common strategy to build awareness about sustainability in the wider Whistler community with the ultimate goal of inviting others in the community — households, businesses, schools, and guests — to learn with them and to help move the community in a more sustainable direction. Toward that end, in early December 2000, the Early Adopters and The Natural Step hosted more than 300 delegates to the first Whistler Sustainability Symposium, held at the Fairmont Chateau Whistler. The Symposium featured leading businesses that are using the TNS framework from Europe and North America. The purpose of the Symposium was "to inform and inspire a growing network of B.C. communities and Whistler organizations about the imperatives and opportunities associated with The Natural Step framework for sustainability."[11]

During the spring of 2001, the Early Adopter teams implemented their presentation plans to lay the foundation of sustainability awareness in their organizations. In the meantime, we continued to work with members of the Whistler community to develop community resource toolkits designed for use in large and small businesses, households and schools. In April, a diverse cross-section of the Whistler community participated in an envisioning workshop conducted and designed by Envisioning & Storytelling, a Vancouver-based communications firm. The workshop was designed to help create an inspiring common message that would engage the community in the purpose of moving toward sustainability.

Paul Smith, founder and president of Envisioning & Storytelling (E&S), was excited at the prospect of working with the Whistler community to articulate this vision of sustainability. When Joe Houssian, founder and head of Intrawest, Whistler/Blackcomb's parent company, was acquiring Blackcomb, he brought in E&S to help the company envision what Blackcomb could be in relationship to Whistler, and what Blackcomb and Whistler could be in combination. That was the first resort project that E&S had accomplished. Since that time E&S has worked in more than 100 resort developments around the world to help them to develop compelling visions of the future and to tell their story. Smith remarks, "The part of storytelling I like is the emotion-based storytelling. I love touching a chord with people. I love telling them the story in such a way that it reaches them at a very, very personal level to the point where you can sometimes see their eyes well up with tears or their faces light up with joy."

Particularly given his experience in many other resort communities and his passion for nature, Smith was intrigued by the Whistler sustainability story and how the community was using The Natural Step framework. He says, "When I first heard the fact that this was a framework that would allow for environmental sustainability, economic sustainability, cultural and social sustainability, that there could be harmony — it is the first example that I have ever heard that accommodates everyone, comfortably accommodates everyone and is so simple — it really got my attention." Out of the envisioning process, E&S produced a "storyline" and a video presentation that is instrumental in helping the community as a whole develop a shared understanding of what sustainability means in a resort community context. Through the work with E&S, the community has adopted *Whistler. It's Our Nature* as the title of the initiative to promote the use of The Natural Step framework in Whistler.

The Natural Step framework has generated a lot of conversation within the valley. People invite each other over for dinner and they talk about TNS; it has had a huge impact. This initiative has helped us develop a network of individuals in the community who are doing the same things. We have a lot of informal conversations and we learn a lot from that as well. There was influence from executives in town talking to other executives here and that does have an impact.

— Allana Hamm, Environmental Coordinator,
Whistler/Blackcomb Ski Resorts

Beginning in July 2001, we conducted an intensive ten-week advanced sustainability facilitator training course for 20 members from the Early Adopter organizations that was designed specifically for the Whistler community. The purpose of this course was to expose internal teams in the Early Adopter organizations to systems thinking; theory and practice in sustainability; The Natural Step framework for sustainability; presentation, facilitation and coaching skills; strategies, tools, and metrics for sustainability; theories and practice of organizational learning and innovation diffusion; and to provide a coaching environment in which they could apply this learning in their own organizations. In addition, the course was designed to strengthen the Early Adopter group as a sustainability learning community. Several participants in the course were trained to serve as community resources to help small and medium-sized businesses, households, and schools in their journey to sustainability.

To provide the community with multiple ways to explore and understand what sustainability is, and how to think about and implement more sustainable practices, a number of initiatives were developed and implemented in late 2001 and are continuing throughout 2002:

- *Whistler. It's Our Nature*[12] invites Whistler residents, second-home owners, and businesses to start their own journey toward sustainability, using the Natural Step framework. The initiative includes workshops, toolkits and opportunities for the entire community to become involved in moving toward sustainability. The toolkits will help all community members focus on issues and challenges specific to their interests, be they business owners, homeowners, school teachers, students, or local government officials.

- Part of the *Whistler. It's Our Nature* program, a speaker series entitled "Leadership Through Sustainable Innovation," brings internationally renowned speakers to share their journey and their lessons with all interested members of the Whistler community. The speaker series is provided as a public service. Early speakers include Dr. Donald Aiken, noted renewable energy expert; Ray Anderson, founder and Chair of Interface, Inc.; Mathis Wackernagel, co-developer of the ecological footprint concept; Janine Benyus, author of *Biomimicry*; and Natural Step founder, Dr. Karl-Henrik Robèrt.

- The creation of the Whistler Centre for Sustainability, home of the *Whistler. It's Our Nature* initiative, where resources and knowledge can be shared both on-line and in person.

- In 2002, the RMOW will draft British Columbia's first Comprehensive Sustainability Plan (CSP), one that will build on The Natural Step framework for sustainability. It will focus on economic, social, and environmental sustainability in order to ensure a prosperous and healthy community in the future. Godfrey remarks, "We want to provide the leadership in terms of initiating the plan and the technical expertise that goes along with developing it. We also want to ensure that we engage the community so that we continue to develop a shared vision of the future."

Sustainability Integration: Step by Step

The rest of this chapter looks at some of the activities that have taken place in the Whistler Early Adopter organizations up to the present.

The Resort Municipality of Whistler (RMOW)

The RMOW, the municipal government that serves the community of Whistler, has five main divisions, employs approximately 350 people, and manages an annual budget of about Can$50 million. In service to, and in coordination with, the community of Whistler, the RMOW has been responsible for developing *Whistler 2002* and the Whistler Environmental Strategy, and has been a leader in bringing together the Whistler Early Adopter group. The RMOW will also take the lead and responsibility for the development of the Comprehensive Sustainability Plan (CSP) for the resort municipality. The RMOW has been involved with environmental initiatives for many years, serving as environmental steward of land use planning, watershed management, water and wastewater management, transportation management, and numerous other areas. For example, an environmental legacy fund created from landfill tipping fees now totals one million dollars (Can). Interest income from this fund supports community projects, such as the development of the *Whistler. It's Our Nature* toolkits. Pesticide-free landscaping is achieved through the use of low-pressure hot water. Naturescaping uses plants naturally found in the Whistler area to minimize maintenance and watering, and to re-establish wildlife habitat. Significant diversion of waste is achieved through extensive materials reuse and recycling programs. Finally, the Whistler Way has become a popular program for taking more environmentally sustainable modes of transportation around Whistler — for example, Whistler's award-winning transit system carries more than two million riders each year, the highest per capita ridership in B.C.

The RMOW has also played a vital leadership and facilitative role in helping the community explore and articulate its shared values and its vision for the future. The RMOW has been diligently working to develop the policies and plans that support bringing these values and vision into being, all the while providing the essential services that are the responsibility of any municipal government.

> *I recognize that there are all sorts of places, communities or organizations that are ahead of us. There is a lot that's being done, so I wouldn't consider ourselves to be a leader at this point in time. I would see ourselves being a community that's on a journey and we're going to move step by step and try and do the right thing and maybe at some time in the future we'll be a leader.*
>
> — Jim Godfrey, CAO, RMOW

The RMOW understands that it plays both a leadership role and a catalyst role with respect to sustainability in the community and beyond. O'Reilly feels that by doing so, Whistler can in turn influence the direction and actions of other communities. "I think Whistler has an incredible reputation. A lot of communities followed our model as a resort. If we can do the sustainability initiative right, then maybe it is something else that people are going to pick up on and follow and that would ultimately be the success that you'd want to have." Godfrey adds to this, "My personal view of the future is that I would like us to be the premier mountain resort community. I'd also like us to be a role model as far as sustainability goes. I'd like people to be extremely comfortable with who we are, what we are, and how we do things, and that we actually walk the talk. I would like that to be more than the corporation of the Resort Municipality of Whistler. I would like that to be Whistler as a whole."

To lead by example and support its strategic initiatives, the RMOW instituted an awareness and implementation program with municipal staff, guided by The Natural Step framework. It focuses on understanding and applying sustainability thinking to day-to-day initiatives that produce demonstrable results. Between February and April of 2001, all RMOW staff had the opportunity to participate in sustainability awareness presentations. RMOW staff then did some initial brainstorming to identify actions they could take. From July through September 2001, four staff members took part in the advanced ten-week sustainability facilitator training course after which they implemented a process of going back to all employees to identify objectives and actions that the RMOW could take to introduce more sustainable practices.

Based on the recommendation of the general managers of the RMOW's functional areas, their staff was organized into 14 groups for sustainability training. Provisions were made to ensure that everyone had the opportunity to participate while municipal services continued uninterrupted. Each session ran for approximately two hours. They started with an introduction and review of The Natural Step framework previously presented to all staff during the spring. The sessions used the four System Conditions as their ultimate sustainability objectives and focused on identifying key environmental impacts in relationship to them; that is, in what ways were RMOW activities, and the activities of specific functions and departments supporting or not supporting each System Condition. The groups engaged in a visioning exercise around how the function, the department or the RMOW would look in a sustainable world; they identified objectives and suggested the first steps on that journey.

The team who designed this brainstorming understood the importance of creating a feedback system so that employees who made suggestions would know what became of their ideas. They learned from previous experience. Dave Waldron recalls a similar process that took place about eight years previously where environmental actions were suggested, and later the participants said they didn't even know what happened to those suggestions. Waldron reports, "In fact, when we went through the list, over one-half of them are done or underway, but nobody reported back and said 'yes, this got done.' They were too busy moving on to the next thing. So communicating back is really important." To ensure that employees knew that all suggestions were valuable and considered, the team divided the suggestions into four categories: actions that could be taken right away with no additional resources, actions that could be taken right away with additional resources, actions that required strategic policy or budgetary consideration and might take one to five years to put into place, and actions designated as "no/because" so that a decision on any action that could not be taken would include the reason why it could not be done. The actions of a more strategic nature were, where possible, incorporated into the WES as potential tasks.

The process was approached as a team-building opportunity, as well as an important step in reinforcing education about sustainability and identifying some of the actions that the RMOW could take to move in that direction. The design team encouraged managers to give a green light to as many of the actions in the first and second categories as were possible. As those actions are implemented, the plan is to evaluate their success and, based on that evaluation, to recommend improvements for future action. Roger Weetman, Program Supervisor, Meadow Park Sports Centre, and a member of the advanced sustainability facilitators team for the RMOW comments, "It was a unique opportunity for all the staff to work together toward a common goal. In each session people were asked to use their knowledge and experience of how things are done in their area to identify the concrete actions that could be taken to meet the sustainability objectives."

In the process, many challenges also emerged. For example, Waldron points out an issue that occurs in most organizations: competing priorities. He comments, "There are so many other priorities in the municipality, and so many big ticket items, and everything is competing at the business plan juncture." Weetman adds, "In order for this to be successful over the next ten years, the municipality's challenge is to influence more of a social behavior change within some departments." Waldron agrees and cautions: "The social change issue, the culture change, takes time, and it happens for different people in different ways." He sees that one of the ways to influence culture change internally is to succeed in the broader community initiative. "When we can say to staff — 'This isn't just municipal staff, this is a bunch of other organizations doing these very progressive things, and we think that we're one of the progressive organizations around and we're proud of that, but there are also some other organizations that are showing us some things that we can learn.' — that inspires people. We think that the simple TNS framework is a very effective way to engage people. Add to that the other things that will happen, the *Whistler. It's Our Nature* toolkits that we're putting together — one goes out to every household — the video that is being produced, the speaker series. All of these things are happening at several levels to keep this in people's minds, this is something that's happening everywhere. It's happening at work, it's happening at home, it's happening all over, and we think that over time it will just be the way we do things."

Whistler/Blackcomb Ski Resorts

In 1986, Intrawest Properties Ltd. (now Intrawest Corporation)[13] purchased Blackcomb and between 1987 and 1991 invested more than $59 million on improvements. In 1997, Intrawest acquired Whistler Mountain and merged the operations of both mountains.

Intrawest is the largest owner and operator of village-centered destination resorts on the North American continent. Headquartered in Vancouver, British Columbia, less than a two-hour drive from Whistler, Intrawest currently owns ten mountain resorts, one warm-weather resort, eighteen golf courses, a premier vacation ownership business (Club Intrawest) and five world-class resort villages at other locations, including one in France. In addition, Intrawest has a significant investment in Compagnie des Alpes, the largest ski company in the world in terms of skier visits, and Alpine Helicopters, owner of Canadian Mountain Holidays, the largest heli-skiing operation in the world. The company is involved with all aspects of resort living including lodging, food and beverage, themed retail, animated operations and real-estate development. It has approximately one billion dollars in revenues and 16,000 employees who manage and serve the company's 6.2 million skier visits and 546,000 golf rounds.

Intrawest prides itself on creating "unique, memorable, ultimately body-and-soul satisfying experiences." Joe Houssian, founder and CEO, comments, "People want to get away to something that is a bit more wholesome, to something they can touch and feel, a bit more earthy. If we ruin the resort environment, from Intrawest's point of view we've essentially ruined our business plan." Houssian's interest in sustainability goes even deeper. Pointing to his son, Joey, 23, who has been working with The Natural Step and the Whistler Early Adopters creating sustainability toolkits, and has taken the advanced sustainability facilitator training, Houssian adds, "The bankers of twenty years from now are him. I would like him as my banker to think that we're leading the world in the stewardship of our planet....I think that one of the very positive things that is happening now is that the younger generation is leading. I think the younger generation has such a positive impact on the older generation, and as they get older and they get more aggressive and smarter and more in positions of power, this thing is going to accelerate very, very rapidly. I think my generation has to get on board or get out of the way."

> *The best of all worlds is where as a business man I can do what I'm supposed to do, which is maximize the wealth that we've created in our company with the resources we're using, and at the same time do something positive for the planet. Isn't that the best of all worlds?*
>
> — Joe Houssian, Founder, President and CEO, Intrawest Corporation

Houssian points out that when he did his MBA he was taught that corporate responsibility was about being profitable. "We were taught to take resources and maximize wealth out of those resources, and then give that back to the community through dividends, taxes, and profit distribution. Let others in society worry about the other goals and objectives." Since then, the environmental impact of resort development has become a fundamental part of due diligence, obtaining permits, and community relations. Houssian admits, "We did it because we had to do it 15 years ago. Now we do it because — I'm not sure I would go as far as to say we do it now because we want to do it — that's probably where we're evolving to. We do it now because it's just smart. It's smart business. It's smart in terms of the community. It's smart in terms of getting our approvals. It's smart in terms of our customer."

Whistler/Blackcomb is still taking early steps in moving toward more sustainable practices. Blackcomb Mountain launched its environmental program in 1993, spearheaded by Arthur DeJong, then Mountain Operations Manager at Blackcomb, and now Mountain Planning & Environmental Resource Manager for Whistler /Blackcomb. Since that time, the environmental program has grown considerably. DeJong admits he knew nothing about environmentalism or stewardship practices in 1993. Then an oil spill occurred on

Blackcomb. He points to that day as a turning point in his life because he felt totally responsible as Mountain Operations Manager. As a result of that incident, DeJong became a student of nature. He explains, "You have to take the best ecological natural life form inventory, understand what its needs are, and a) try to absolutely minimize what you take out of it; b) try to mimic it if you can; and c) if you can see connections that benefit natural life forms, help to enhance it."

Since 1993, Blackcomb, and now Whistler/Blackcomb, has been developing an extensive Environmental Management System (EMS) to identify and more effectively manage operations that impact the environment. In addition, they are working to design and implement a comprehensive environmental strategy that can be a model to other resorts. Whistler/Blackcomb supports the National Ski Area Association's Sustainable Slopes Charter and has aligned its EMS with the Sustainable Slopes guiding principles. The EMS is the main tool used by Whistler/Blackcomb to establish programs in the areas of:

- Fish and wildlife management,
- Forest, soil and watershed management,
- Low impact land use decisions,
- Environmental education,
- Water conservation,
- Energy conservation,
- Solid waste management,
- Fuel and hazardous waste management, and
- Community outreach.

If this industry in the long term is going to succeed, it has to lead conservation. If we follow, others will choose our destiny. We can't wait. We should lead through practicing the best possible ways of managing our landforms with what we know at the time and communicate that. Not brag that we're great environmentalists or anything like that, but we should lead.

— Arthur DeJong, Mountain Planning and Environmental Resource Manager, Whistler/Blackcomb Ski Resorts

The level of commitment to triple bottom line sustainability and stewardship — economics, environment, and community — among the senior leadership team at Whistler/Blackcomb has increased dramatically over the past several years. In its initial stages, the environmental program was the sole responsibility of the Mountain Operations Manager. After the merger of Whistler and Blackcomb Mountains, Doug Forseth, the Vice-President of Operations, created the position of Environmental Coordinator to broaden the scope of the internal program. Allana Hamm now effectively fills that multifaceted role.

In the early stages of the program, the environmental team gained support from the senior leadership team by emphasizing the need for compliance. The program has grown beyond a focus on compliance issues to being highly proactive. The senior leadership team recognizes the ever growing importance of environmental sustainability to their business, community, guests, and generations to come, and is beginning to communicate this both internally and externally.

Whistler/Blackcomb viewed the creation of the Early Adopters group as an important way to participate in a community initiative toward more sustainable practices. DeJong comments, "The biggest thing, with the most impact, that The Natural Step has done is that you've brought everyone together. That is so valuable. Things have changed here." Together with other Early Adopter organizations, a team from Whistler/Blackcomb participated in the awareness presentation facilitator's workshop that we conducted in November 2000, as well as the December Sustainability Symposium. In April 2001, Whistler/Blackcomb's entire senior management team attended our presentation on The Natural Step framework for sustainability, which was then followed by a similar introduction to sustainability for all Whistler/Blackcomb managers.

I think more and more people are recognizing that this planet is a space ship and it's the only one we've got. You've got to be thinking long haul.

— Joe Houssian, Founder, President and CEO,
Intrawest Corporation

Many of Whistler/Blackcomb's employees are seasonal, so there is high turnover. Nonetheless, Whistler/Blackcomb teaches both new and returning staff about its commitment to the community and the environment and about the programs it has established to support this commitment. The training outlines employee responsibilities to the environment and focuses on the stewardship initiatives that are relevant to specific job descriptions. Education also includes how employees can become involved in committees, groups and initiatives in the Whistler Valley. Several tools are used to reinforce this education including:

- Educational materials that outline procedures specific to departments,
- *Whistler. It's Our Nature* household toolkits for use by staff,
- An energy conservation handbook for staff,
- A *Staff Guide to Recycling* that is distributed during recruitment and at all staff housing locations,
- Training sessions with environmental staff at the beginning of each season, as well as staff meetings throughout the season to outline Whistler/Blackcomb's 3Rs (reduce, reuse, recycle) program,
- An Energy Quest education program that promotes energy conservation,
- A bi-weekly environmental section in the *Weekly Messenger* newsletter that talks about 3Rs initiatives and recognizes staff contributions,
- Information on the company recycling program is accessible through shared folders in the e-mail system,
- A Recycling Hotline for staff and guests,
- Regular visits by environmental team staff to all buildings to ensure that they are equipped with containers, signage and clear information on using our recycling system,
- Waste and energy audits of buildings at night and reports.

Two members of Whistler/Blackcomb's environmental team participated in the ten-week advanced sustainability facilitator training course in sustainability that we conducted at Whistler in the summer of 2001. Following the guidelines presented in that course, they are introducing sustainability concepts in the organization through pilot projects. Starting with two departments, they are providing sustainability

> *Whistler/Blackcomb's environmental vision is to contribute to the goal of sustainability by developing, through its Environmental Management System, the highest level of environmental stewardship in the North American mountain resort industry. It is our belief that environmental stewardship is a cornerstone to becoming the best mountain resort experience in the world.*
>
> — Whistler/Blackcomb Ski Resorts

awareness training, applying the concepts to departmental projects and practice, charting progress and financial savings, and using these successes as case examples in other departments. These pilot projects supplement and reinforce several successful initiatives that have already been launched, including the following:

Habitat Improvement Team

Whistler/Blackcomb has established a community based group for those wishing to take a more hands-on approach to helping the environment. The group has been active since the summer of 1998. The Habitat Improvement Team (HIT) runs from May until September and involves people going out into the community to work on projects for local groups. Whistler/Blackcomb provides the tools, transportation, instruction and refreshments after each session. HIT carries out projects for AWARE (Association of Whistler Area Residents for the Environment), the Whistler Fish Stewardship Group, the Municipality, and the Bear Task Team. In August, the Whistler/Blackcomb Streamkeepers tackle a weekend-long project for the Whistler Fish Stewardship Group.

Whistler/Blackcomb Environmental Fund

The Whistler/Blackcomb Environmental Fund was established in January 2001 to fund community environmental projects in Whistler. The fund is supported by staff donations that are matched by the Whistler/Blackcomb Foundation. A volunteer board of staff members manages the Environmental Fund. The board identifies key projects in the Whistler Valley which can be funded from start to finish and then sees that they are carried out. Staff members not wishing to support the fund financially can still get involved by participating in the projects.

Energy Quest

Whistler/Blackcomb has initiated an on-mountain energy conservation program called Energy Quest. The program goal is to reduce the consumption of fuel and electricity by 15 to 20 percent. They are looking at sustainable alternative energy sources and currently working with BC Hydro to conduct a comprehensive audit of facilities and operations and to design an effective conservation strategy.

Bear Family Sponsorship Program

This program raised funds for local bear researcher Michael Allen. The funds were used to purchase a scale that weighs bears without needing to handle them. Knowing the bears' weights can help determine which habitats in the ski area produce the most weight gain for a bear. Six Whistler/Blackcomb departments sponsored black bear families. Sponsors were given a large mounted photo of their bear family and information about its history and activities. In fact, the health of the bear community on Whistler/Blackcomb is a source of real pride and great interest in the Whistler community. There are currently nine black bear families totaling 28 individual bears inhabiting the 7,000 acres of forest lands and mountain meadows under Whistler/Blackcomb stewardship.

Forest, Soil and Watershed Management

Whistler/Blackcomb's Master Plan aims to establish recreational designs with the least amount of environmental impact. Avoidance of wetlands and riparian zones, use of natural contours versus cut and fills, and developing glades and narrower trails are part of the plan.

Operation Green Up

Whistler and Blackcomb mountains represent a network of slopes, streams, lakes and forested areas. Whistler/Blackcomb is looking at this natural system and designing enhancement and restoration projects. This program, Operation Green Up, will span five years at a cost of Can$1.5 million. Its primary objectives are to protect drinking water and fish habitat values, apply planting strategies and seed mixes which will enhance wildlife, plant native species whenever possible, enhance visual appeal and protect recreational assets.

> *The Natural Step has given us a sustainability framework to subscribe to, to refer to, and to guide us. I think people can all understand the theory and the logic of The Natural Step framework.*
>
> — Doug Forseth, Vice-President, Resort Operations, Whistler/Blackcomb

The Environmental Side of Lift Expansion

Two new quad chairs were added to Whistler Mountain during the summer of 1999. Original estimates stated that 10,000 cubic meters of timber would be removed to accommodate these lifts. Through environmentally minded planning and design, Whistler/Blackcomb reduced this considerably to 3,200 cubic meters. This was achieved by:

- Narrowing lift lines,
- Substituting gladed runs for conventional ski trail design, and
- Wherever possible, transplanting juvenile or smaller trees into riparian zones rather than destroying them.

All employees participated in a mandatory watershed best practices training session. To limit siltation in adjacent streams containment ponds, barriers and silt fences were put in place. Buildup of silt was constantly removed and fences and barriers were replaced, significantly reducing the material entering the watercourse.

Gladed Runs

Over the last several years, the trend in skiing and snowboarding has moved toward more challenging terrain. In an effort to merge environmental stewardship with recreational design, Whistler/Blackcomb has moved away from conventional trail design and created many gladed runs on both Whistler and Blackcomb. Glading involves selectively cutting some of the forest but leaving the majority intact, rather than clearing everything as in conventional practice. Gladed runs have a positive influence on wildlife, increasing bear and deer populations on the mountains. Thinning the tree canopy opens up the area to more sunshine and allows the undergrowth to flourish, which results in an increase in the grasses and berries that provide food for wildlife.

Waste Management

Whistler/Blackcomb is working to reduce waste at the source, to reuse goods and materials, and to recycle all materials accepted in the Sea-to-Sky Corridor. In 1996, they carried out a waste audit for all buildings on Blackcomb. Using data from this audit they constructed a Waste Reduction Workplan, which suggests ways of reducing waste in all facets of their operation. In 2000, the recycling program at Whistler/Blackcomb

- recycled over 540,000 beverage containers, recouping over $37,000 that was turned back into the recycling program; and

- employed one full-time environmental assistant and several full-time sorters.

Whistler/Blackcomb is conducting waste audits at all of their larger facilities to compare results from earlier audits and find opportunities for further waste reduction. They have also created a clearinghouse for reusable items called Mountain Materials Exchange. Staff donate items such as desks and other furniture, ski equipment, office equipment and clothing. Each week a list of these items is printed in the staff newsletter and staff can arrange to pick these up for reuse. The company saves money by reducing tipping fees and by reusing items instead of purchasing new ones.

Everyone involved with the movement to greater corporate responsibility and environmental stewardship at Whistler/Blackcomb will tell you first, that they are in the very early stages and, second, that they are committed to making more progress. They know there is much more to learn and a long way to go. Doug Forseth, Vice-President, Resort Operations for Whistler/Blackcomb, points out that when they began in 1993, they didn't know what it would take to become environmental stewards. He comments, "We got started on a small step and it's gotten bigger and it's grown better and it's become a greater part of our culture and how we think and act. But there's no doubt in my mind that we've got a long way to go to be great stewards." To which Joe Houssian adds: "I want to get the company to focus on it because, to the extent we're going to create a legacy, we can do it in the whole sustainability field. I see that perhaps a role model is being created here at Whistler that can then be rolled out to other resorts."

Fairmont Chateau Whistler[14]

The Fairmont Chateau Whistler (FCW) is part of Fairmont Hotels and Resorts, a North American hotel management company that resulted from the merger between Fairmont Hotels and Canadian Pacific Hotels. Back in the 19th century, Canadian Pacific Hotels began with a vision to build "dining stations" along the newly constructed trans-Canada railway. The first hotel opened in the Rocky Mountains in 1886, and others followed from Victoria, British Columbia to St. John's, Newfoundland. These include such famous Canadian landmarks as the Banff Springs Hotel, Jasper Park Lodge, Chateau Lake Louise, Chateau Laurier, and Le Chateau Frontenac. The chain now has significant properties throughout Canada, the U.S., Mexico, Bermuda and Barbados.

Prior to the merger in 1999, Canadian Pacific Hotels had become an industry leader and catalyst in greening hotel operations. In 1990, the corporate office surveyed all employees to find out if they would support an environmental program. An overwhelming 91 percent of staff surveyed strongly supported more environmentally responsible practices within their hotels. In response, a corporate greening program called the Green Partnership was launched across the chain. Over the years, this program evolved from an environmental guidebook to a more comprehensive incentive and monitoring program that is administered by a corporate environmental office. From its inception, the FCW has actively participated in this program.

> *We all have the power of one. Each one of us can begin to make a difference, and collectively, a lot of individuals can move mountains (or save them)... and corporations can make single decisions to shift policy that in time will produce major cultural and behavioral change.*
>
> — David Roberts, General Manager, Fairmont Chateau Whistler

An elegant chateau-style building that is one of the most beautiful and substantial resort hotels in the world, the Fairmont Chateau Whistler is an all-season hotel resort that has attained a top ranking in the Top 100 Hotels of the World. It has 560 guest rooms and employs over 600 staff, depending on the season. Its guest rooms are complemented with 28,000 square feet of function space, six independent meeting rooms, three major ballrooms, a number of hospitality suites, and a rooftop garden terrace. FCW's facilities also include two restaurants, a bar, a health club, spa, staff housing and an 18-hole golf course.

Fairmont Chateau Whistler Resort
SUSTAINABILITY POLICY

Our Commitment

The Fairmont Chateau Whistler is a four-season luxury resort in Whistler, British Columbia, with a vision to provide cherished guest and employee experiences long into the future.

We believe that sustaining natural life-support systems and contributing to a vibrant, healthy society is necessary for sustained economic success and global human progress. We therefore commit to continual improvement in developing our operations to become environmental sustainability leaders in the Fairmont chain and in the hospitality industry.

To do this, we will meet or exceed all relevant regulations and build on our current commitments, which include the Fairmont Green Partnership Program, the golf course Audubon Cooperative Sanctuary System certification, and the Sustainable Whistler Project.

We define sustainability using the following basic rules, or System Conditions, and endeavour to prioritize our actions using The Natural Step framework:

"In a sustainable society, nature is not subject to systematically increasing:

1. concentrations of substances extracted from the Earth's crust;

2. concentrations of substances produced by society;

3. degradation by physical means;

and, in that society,

4. human needs are met worldwide.

Environmental stewardship has been an important part of FCW values and operations since the hotel opened in 1989 under the leadership of the hotel's chief executive, General Manager, David Roberts. Some early initiatives of the FCW include:

- An active Green Team since the hotel opened,
- Leading the Whistler community in a comprehensive recycling program, before it was financially viable,
- Taking the initiative to find alternatives for disposing organic waste in bear country, where traditional composting was not possible, and
- Other initiatives that contributed to being two-time winner of the corporate Environmental Hotel of the Year Award. These initiatives include an organic terrace herb garden, sheet and towel reuse policies, golf course Audubon Cooperative Sanctuary System certification, and local partnerships to donate amenities, furniture and other hotel products.

When The Natural Step founder Dr. Robèrt visited Whistler in March of 2000, David Roberts invited him to address his senior staff at the hotel on The Natural Step framework, and then Robèrt and Roberts spent the evening over dinner at the Chateau discussing sustainability. After that, Roberts became one of the leaders in organizing the Early Adopter group. A team from the FCW participated in the awareness presentation facilitator workshop in November 2000. To involve and inspire the leadership team, all FCW managers participated in the Whistler Sustainability Symposium held at the FCW in December 2000. In early 2001, the FCW trainers who had attended the November workshop developed a sustainability awareness program that was delivered to each department. TNS-based awareness training was also integrated into new employees' orientation programs.

Together with developing and implementing internal training, the FCW's sustainability program began with a preliminary environmental review to gain a better understanding of current resource flows and practices. From this review, many areas presented opportunities for improvement, four of which were chosen for immediate focus. These were waste management, energy management, community philanthropy, and development of more sustainable services. Supply chain management was also prioritized as an important strategy to reduce environmental impacts.

Solution Teams were formed for each of these areas, to identify and prioritize problems and actions. Team members are those employees who have the knowledge and position to implement change, such as the chief engineer, and other enthusiastic staff. To ensure resources and accountability, each of the Solution Teams is led by an Executive Team member. Once the teams were formed, they participated in Ideas to Action workshops, where they reviewed the current reality of the FCW's operations and envisioned an ideal, sustainable future. Based on the difference between this vision and the current reality, each team set its own measurable objectives for 2001. Projects to reach these objectives were then brainstormed, prioritized and selected. These projects continue to gain momentum and have been successful because member buy-in was established when the teams defined their own objectives, and projects are grounded because the members are the experts from their areas of operations. The team members are also from different departments, so they learn to consider the challenges across all divisions rather than just in their own.

The teams review their progress on an ongoing basis, and the measurements are communicated to the rest of the operation. Since the success of many of these initiatives depends directly on the participation of all employees, it is important that staff is constantly updated on progress. The executive management team reviews the process and outcomes of the program annually at strategic retreat sessions.

The four focus areas were refined for 2002 to reinforce these desired outcomes within the organization. Dan Wilson, Environmental Coordinator, explains, "We've come up with four directions: instead of energy, we are focusing on sustainable energy; instead of waste, we are focusing on sustainable material flows, so it's not just waste; it's also procurement, the way we do our purchasing and how materials move through our organization. The next area is communication and capacity, which includes building knowledge of The Natural Step framework and sustainability in the organization and with our stakeholders, our suppliers and our customers, and the fourth area is how to meet society's basic needs, which we are doing through the Foundation."

FAIRMONT CHATEAU WHISTLER RESORT
SUSTAINABILITY POLICY

Our Strategy

More specifically, our commitment to sustaining natural life support systems is guided by continuous improvement in:

- eliminating waste toward closed loop operations;
- increasing eco-efficiency by optimizing resource use;
- stimulating and using innovation, emerging technologies and alternative, renewable resources;
- developing innovative and lower impact 'resort services';
- eliminating the use of environmentally destructive substances (we will avoid using products when we are unsure of their environmental implications, as outlined by the precautionary principle); and
- reinvesting in natural capital, where possible.

Our commitment to fostering a healthy and vibrant society is guided by fair and respectful treatment of our employees, guests and community neighbours. More specifically, we will:

- make economic contributions to the development of our community through the Fairmont Chateau Whistler Charity Foundation, corporate programs, and in-kind donations.
- contribute to building general community capacity through proactive support of community learning, volunteerism, and internal skill development.
- work with the Whistler community and other Fairmont properties to share sustainability learning and to help create demand for more sustainable resort products.

This policy applies to all resort operations and, as possible, extends to supplier and business partner operations where we can exert influence.

The management team will review this policy and sustainability goals on an annual basis, and ensure that annual action plans are completed. Our internal measurement of progress will develop to include financial, environmental and social indicators, as possible.

This sustainability policy will be documented, implemented and communicated to both internal and external constituents.

Through ongoing empowerment, education and incentive we will build the capacity of our staff to embrace this policy, guided by principles of respect, accountability, balance, empathy, passion and integrity.

> *Working towards sustainability makes sense for business. By demonstrating the benefits of our successes, we will be able to tell our story to other businesses and encourage them to also take steps toward sustainability.*
>
> — Sonya Hwang, Director of Communications, Fairmont Chateau Whistler

In addition, the FCW has undertaken:

- The formation of a 'sustainability consortium' by the Golf Club manager with two other Whistler golf courses, and

- A survey of their suppliers to identify environmental best practices and opportunities; information that will be shared with all Fairmont hotels and Whistler businesses.

Tourism Whistler

Tourism Whistler is the organization responsible for marketing Whistler as a four-season resort destination in target markets around the world. With more than 6000 members who own property or operate businesses in Whistler, Tourism Whistler is looked upon as a leader in the business community. As such, they are expected to provide vision and strategies that will enable Whistler's remarkable success to continue. Tourism Whistler also operates a central reservation booking service, activity and information centre, the Whistler Conference Centre, and the Whistler Golf Club. In peak season, Tourism Whistler employs approximately 140 staff, with average year-round staff of about 105 and a turnover rate of about 22 percent annually. Total revenue for 2000 was approximately $8 million including membership assessments, sales and marketing, golf course revenues and conference center revenues.

> *Tourism Whistler as an organization is committed to working together with the Whistler community in moving towards environmental sustainability. It's good for business — it's good for the future of Whistler.*
>
> — Suzanne Denbak, President, Tourism Whistler

Suzanne Denbak, president and CEO of Tourism Whistler, has been a consistent champion of the Whistler Early Adopters, and the vision of creating a Whistler experience associated with stewarding and restoring the natural environment as well as nurturing the human spirit. In October 2001, Tourism Whistler's Board of Directors adopted a new mission that begins to reflect this commitment: "To be a leader and a catalyst in promoting the sustainable economic well-being of the resort community through the development and execution of well-planned, customer-driven sales and marketing strategies and the effective management of the Whistler Conference Centre, the Whistler Golf Club, and Whistler Central Reservations."

With that leadership comes the responsibility to study and understand trends in tourism as well as trends that will affect tourism. Denbak comments:

> While scanning current business trends and divining their meaning for Whistler, one trend has become increasingly apparent — there is a growing social consciousness in the world today — a growing concern for the environment. This trend has clear and immediate implications for the tourism industry. No longer will we sit on the sidelines and watch leading environmental and consumer organizations target resource based industries like logging and mining for their effect on the environment. Tourism is next — because it also affects the environment and often not in positive ways.
>
> Already ski resorts are being rated based on their environmental record. Lawsuits have been launched against tourism marketing organizations that spend government funds to attract incremental visitors who in turn impact the environment. The tourism industry can pretend this isn't happening and be hit by this oncoming train, or we can step forward and proactively plan and strategize to respond to this trend. Tourism Whistler has opted for this proactive stance.

Tourism Whistler creates strategic partnerships that grow the resort's business and enhance the guest experience. The organization is committed to:

- Positioning Whistler as a preferred resort destination in all target markets,
- Successfully growing the business,
- Continuously improving the value we provide to its stakeholders, and
- Creating a climate for the growth and development of its staff

Tourism Whistler, together with the RMOW and the FCW, hosted the first presentation that The Natural Step founder Dr. Robèrt gave in Whistler, and was one of the first organizations to suggest the formation of a group of Early Adopters of The Natural Step framework. Tourism Whistler staff participated in the awareness presentation facilitator's course in November, 2000, after which the awareness presentation team designed, scripted and participated in the production of a training video featuring The Natural Step four System Conditions. In January 2001, we facilitated a sustainability vision and mission session with senior management, which generated the following statements:

Sustainability Vision: We will change the world by touching every heart and soul who experiences Whistler.

Sustainability Mission: We will be caretakers of the Whistler experience. We will change the face of tourism so that it restores and protects the natural world for all the children of all the species. We will redefine success to enhance the lives of our employees, members and guests.

> *The environment is our product — it's what we sell and it's what makes the Whistler experience unique and special. We have an authentic wilderness experience that is now very rare in the world today. Our visitors have told us this is one of the most important reasons for choosing Whistler over another destination. If we protect the environment, we protect our product. If we protect our product, we protect our profits — even if our personal values didn't tell us to do this, our business sense certainly does.*
>
> — Suzanne Denbak, President, Tourism Whistler

During the course of 2001, the awareness training team set out to provide sustainability awareness education to all Tourism Whistler staff. In each awareness session, the team did a visioning process with the staff. They started the process by having staff brainstorm key words that captured their personal visions for the organization. Then they shared the vision and mission statements that had been generated by the senior management team. Shannon Story, Manager of Member and Guest Experience, reports, "Every time we have done it, it has fit in well. All the key words that come up are reflected in the vision and mission. There has been a lot of staff buy-in into the vision and mission."

Three Tourism Whistler staff members participated in the ten-week advanced sustainability facilitator training course and are leading the organization through a sustainability baseline audit process. The team wanted to use this process as an opportunity to involve more staff, so they introduced the baseline audit at one of their quarterly staff meetings, beginning with a review of the funnel and the System Conditions from the awareness training sessions. This was followed by a game that tested employees' knowledge of the System Conditions while competing for prizes. They then organized the audit into categories based on the four System Conditions, one group for each System Condition, and called for volunteers to participate in each group, based on the area of sustainability they were most interested in learning more about. After the staff meeting, they sent out a web-link so that volunteers could sign up. They had a great response, which led to launching the audit at the end of 2001.

> *The Natural Step framework has provided Tourism Whistler with a simple yet robust compass for decision-making. It's based in irrefutable science. It works with root causes and it's non-prescriptive in nature — there are no lists of dos and don'ts. Rather each business is respected for its own knowledge of its processes and is taught to use the four System Conditions when making decisions. The combination of rigid science and flexible application to unique business circumstances ensures that The Natural Step framework can be applied successfully in any business circumstance.*
>
> — Suzanne Denbak, President, Tourism Whistler

After the baseline audit is completed, Tourism Whistler will produce a systems map to help them identify high leverage areas for sustainability improvement. They will set out objectives and identify appropriate performance indicators.

While the awareness training is being conducted and the baseline audit information is being gathered, Tourism Whistler has moved forward on a number of important areas. They have begun examining their practices at the golf course: experimenting with different pesticides and working with other Whistler groups on the stream that is part of the golf course. The operations manager has become part of a supply group that is looking at alternative purchasing solutions. They have integrated sustainability into the business planning process so that the necessary time and resources are allocated for developing more sustainable practices. Michelle Comeau-Thompson, Manager of Media Relations, reports that this is "very exciting because our business plan is very action-oriented and everything that we do is measured against that."

With respect to Whistler embracing a commitment to sustainability, Denbak comments, "This needn't be a frightening future for the industry — because consumer choice is not just about boycott, it is also about the millions of individual decisions made, decisions that will be made increasingly in line with personal values. In the tourism business, consumers will choose vacation destinations with a view not just to hotels, amenities and activities, but also to their environmental record."

Association of Whistler Area Residents for the Environment (AWARE)

AWARE is a volunteer membership-based organization that exists to improve the quality of life in the Whistler community by protecting the natural heritage and moving toward environmental sustainablility. For AWARE the only option for Whistler is a sensible balanced approach to environmental sustainability from both an environmental and economic point of view.

Mitch Rhodes, president of AWARE comments:

> AWARE was organized in 1988 to initiate a recycling program for the Whistler community. Out of that success, the organization became the environmental conscience of Whistler. Many of the environmental issues that faced the community came to AWARE and the organization often found itself at odds with local government and business. The classic confrontation

between urban development versus habitat protection ensued. During Whistler's rapid expansion in the early 1990s, AWARE was often the lone advocate on the habitat protection side of the debate or issue.

Today AWARE continues its work on recycling by working to remove organic materials from the waste stream through planning for a community composting program. In the fall of 2001, AWARE started the first stages of implementing a demonstration unit and will also be installing worm composters in classrooms. However, AWARE's sphere of interest ranges far beyond this arena. For example, AWARE members were very involved in the community consultation process that led to the production of *Whistler 2002*. Members have also participated in the review groups for the Whistler Environmental Strategy. AWARE members sit on numerous advisory groups in the community dealing with transportation issues and are actively pursuing alternate strategies for transportation both in the valley and in the highway corridor between Vancouver and Whistler.

> *Even if Whistler achieves sustainability, or rather as close to sustainable as a community can be, there is still a problem. It will be as if Whistler has a first class cabin on the Titanic. I believe Whistler has an opportunity and perhaps even a responsibility to provide a sustainable message and model to the world. I also believe the people of Whistler are up to the task. I feel privileged to be a participant in the "Whistler. It's Our Nature" initiative.*
>
> — Mitch Rhodes, President, AWARE

Conservation and protection of key wilderness in the south Coast Mountains is a priority for AWARE. The organization educates the public and advocates for protection of vanishing wilderness values. With other organizations, AWARE is working toward protecting a viable wilderness network in the Sea-to-Sky Corridor, which is shared with the neighboring communities in the Squamish and Lillooet Forest Districts. Rhodes observes:

> Over the years AWARE became, what I have coined, "the environmental sink" for Whistler — a place for most environmental issues, large or small, to accumulate. The task of dealing with over one hundred issues

that flowed from the community into AWARE's environmental sink became unmanageable and overwhelmed the organization due to its volunteer nature and limited financial resources.

AWARE serves as a community watchdog in the land use planning process in the Whistler Valley ensuring that the provincial park system is not compromised by encroaching development and inappropriate uses. As Whistler's pace of growth slows and the community approaches the maximum development allowed under the community plan, AWARE is providing input as the community develops a final Protected Area Network Plan. AWARE is also active in "on the ground" habitat restoration. When Rhodes joined the AWARE board in 2000, he found an organization that was overwhelmed with too many issues and too few resources to address them. Having limited experience with environmental issues, he focused his business skills on helping AWARE develop a strategic plan. Before the strategic planning process began, Rhodes attended one of Dr. Robèrt's presentations in March, 2000. He remarks:

> The principles of The Natural Step framework and its significance for AWARE were immediate, and AWARE signed on as an Early Adopter. The era of hardened adversarial positioning among local government, business, and AWARE was ending with various municipal documents such as *Whistler 2002* and *The Whistler Environmental Strategy*. The signing of the Early Adopters agreement sealed that trend and began an era of cooperation and common vision.

Members of AWARE participated in the November presentation facilitator's workshop; AWARE co-sponsored and participated in the December Sustainability Forum; and they were involved in the workshop on the mapping of current reality. Three members of AWARE also participated in the ten-week advanced sustainability facilitator training course and bring this knowledge and experience to the wider community, particularly to households, small businesses and schools. AWARE has been an important contributor to the development and production of the community sustainability toolkits and will continue to play a vital role in engaging wider community involvement.

The "down stream" consequences of unsustainable activity continue to flow into AWARE's environmental sink. From a strategic planning perspective, the sustainability initiative in Whistler provided AWARE with an opportunity to focus on high leverage points from which to plan, operate and effect change. In the process of helping to move the community toward sustainability using The Natural Step framework, AWARE moved their effort "upstream." The more sustainable Whistler becomes, the emptier AWARE's environmental sink will be.

— Mitch Rhodes, President, AWARE

ADVICE ON THE SUSTAINABILITY JOURNEY

From the Whistler Early Adopters of The Natural Step Framework

Hugh O'Reilly, Mayor, Resort Municipality of Whistler

- Having an overall vision is extremely powerful. From that you can generate key directions that people can clearly understand. Everyone has got to have something that they can focus on and use as their point of reference. I think that you have to have that otherwise it's really easy to derail the program, to have short-term problems supercede long-term solutions and visions. I think sustainability has to be such a high priority that it meets your vision and everything else is secondary.

Jim Godfrey, Chief Administrative Officer, Resort Municipality of Whistler

- If you follow The Natural Step model, really take the time to plan for it, take the time to envision what you really want to be, and then work back from there. Be strategic. Don't underestimate the resources required to move forward effectively with a major sustainability initiative. Don't underestimate the value associated with it. Take the time to build support. Don't underestimate the power of working with other community partners.

Mike Purcell, Director of Planning, Resort Municipality of Whistler

- I think what really triggered this community to start working on this issue was the presentation that Dr. Robèrt gave to a group of local business people, the mayor and council members and some senior staff members at municipal hall. When we walked out of that presentation, I think there wasn't a doubt in anyone's mind about what we needed to do. I heard a number of people make statements like "it's brilliant in its simplicity" and "it's a great tool to help guide us in what we need to do" and there was so much excitement about it that it didn't stop, it just snowballed from that point onwards. It was amazing. So my advice: do the same thing.

Dave Waldron, Resort Municipality of Whistler, Coordinator, Whistler Early Adopter Initiative

- Coming from a technical background, I've always focused on the technical side, making sure all the pieces are in place, that you've really thought it through, it's intellectually tight, it's got a solid foundation, and the intellectual appeal. The thing that I learned and the thing that I think is really important is the emotional inspiration; that is so valuable. What inspires people? That's one thing. Then you need to bring the two together. You need both because if you just inspire people and get them all excited and then there's confusion and they say 'What can we do? Who do I talk to?' Without answers they get frustrated and the inspiration is lost. So bring those two together and manage the relationship between the two.

Arthur DeJong, Mountain Planning and Environmental Resource Manager, Whistler/Blackcomb Ski Resorts

- Don't go on your own initiative or your own intuition first. Go to your community. Find out what matters most to your community because if you don't you might end up doing things that aren't going to be supported and it will just fall flat. So find out what really matters in your community or, as I like to say, in your neighbor's house as well as your own and start from that. From that point you can empower yourself to become part of the solution as opposed to the problem and the people around you that may have questioned you and challenged you, and maybe have said "no" to developing your mountain may turn around and actually look to you for advice and expertise in how to safeguard their interest.

Allana Hamm, Environmental Coordinator, Whistler/Blackcomb Ski Resorts

- Develop incentives for people to think long-term rather than just the fiscal period. Be strategic so you can be proactive rather than reactive. Although you may be enthusiastic and want to run out and start doing something, remember to create baselines so you really track your progress and tell the story about what you did. You can be very successful with the programs you set out to do, but if you haven't created the baseline, you aren't able to tell the story effectively.

> *The momentum of using the TNS framework in the community has had a huge impact on us because it is more pressure from the outside. So the environmental department is pushing it from the inside and now the community is saying 'we are expecting you to come on board because it is important to all of us.' We are very concerned with making sure that we are a strong part of the community and that the community sees us in a positive light.*
>
> — Allana Hamm, Environmental Coordinator,
> Whistler/Blackcomb Ski Resorts

Jane Wong, Project Manager, Whistler/Blackcomb Ski Resorts

- The Natural Step provides a framework, but the people in the organization are the experts, they have to figure out what to do. People look for the list of dos and don'ts. The value of this framework is that you have to figure out what those dos and don'ts are within your own organization, how you operate.

Sonya Hwang, Director of Communications, Fairmont Chateau Whistler

- Communication is vitally important. For example, communicating to our employees why it is so important to recycle. Why it is important to turn off things, such as lights. Communicating to the guests so they understand why we are doing what we're doing. Communication is what is really going to drive this forward. You need to focus on communication and building relationships. As a PR person I'm proud to say what I'm doing in this program is really important.

Dan Wilson, Sustainability Coordinator, Fairmont Chateau Whistler

- When you start a sustainability project in an organization, there are keen people who have high expectations of being able to change everything right away. Unfortunately there are also people who resist change. To keep the keen people from getting too frustrated with the challenges of change, it is important to be strategic and manage their expectations. To help accelerate change, take time and devote resources to share knowledge with managers so they have a better understanding of sustainability and The Natural Step framework before it percolates to the front lines. You really need to get the top people on board.

Joey Houssian, Research Associate, Whistler Sustainability Initiative

- The biggest thing that I've learned is there is no silver bullet. You can't just do it overnight. How do you get started? There's not just one thing. Make the commitment, give permission and unleash the creativity. Start with little things, things that you can control and build from there.

FINAL REFLECTIONS

The Whistler Early Adopters of The Natural Step framework for sustainability represent a truly unique public/private/non-profit partnership. How often have you seen examples of municipal government plus big business and small business plus environmental activists enthusiastically and genuinely collaborating for their common good — their common well-being, their common journey to sustainability? It usually takes a disaster. Not at Whister, not this time. The sustainability initiative is coming when Whistler is absolutely at the top of its game, at the top of the international resort ratings. That alone ought to give us hope for the future.

Perhaps Whistler's greatest source of strength in this process is that the foundation of its wealth — the beauty of the mountains, the purity of the air and water, the unspoiled wilderness — is staring everyone squarely in the face every single day of the year. It draws skiers, boarders, and other enthusiasts throughout the winter and hikers, campers, mountain bikers, and climbers during the summer. This is why people from all over the world come to Whistler. It's still beautiful. It's not spoiled. So the community has a real shot at this thing called sustainability.

However, it is said that trust is easy until you face uncertainty, and then that trust is put to the test. Perhaps that is the same for sustainability. Will Whistler stand by its commitments to forge a sustainable path to a better future if there is a major economic slowdown? Another test will arrive shortly as the community reaches build-out, the maximum development allowed under the community plan. Will Whistler stand by its principles to protect its most valuable asset, a pristine natural environment, or will it bow to the pressure for more and more developments so typical of successful resorts? Will it find a satisfactory solution to the ongoing issue of affordable housing for people working and making a life in the community? Other resorts and other towns have shown what happens if a community abandons its principles for the expedient, short-term solutions. These are just a few of the challenges inherent in the desire to be both sustainable and a resort community.

Just like the fisherman in the old Squamish legend, the community of Whistler is planning for its future under the watchful eye of Wountie. Whistler's challenge is to keep faith with nature for the future well-being of its many interested stakeholders and community members. The real opportunity is what it can contribute to the world as a first-class destination resort in the midst of a rugged and beautiful wilderness — as a model for other resort communities — and to future generations. Whistler's role as steward of this beautiful area is to ensure that the generations of our children and grandchildren will have the possibility of enjoying tomorrow what we have the privilege of enjoying today.

What gives us hope is the depth of the commitment and the passion that we see in so many people in Whistler today. The quest for authentic community sustainability is already embodied in hundreds of people in every aspect of the community and at every level, from senior executives to seasonal workers. In truth, those who live, work, and play in Whistler want Whistler to work for the long-term. The Whistler sustainability initiative has given expression to the hope, the passion, the goodwill, and the intelligence of a growing number of very talented people. Whistler has recently adopted a new slogan that came out of the sustainability initiative — *Whistler. It's Our Nature.* It suggests the story Whistler wants to tell: a story about stewarding the beauty and health of the natural setting upon which its success is established; a story about harnessing the wisdom, collaboration and shared vision of the community to secure its future and share what it learns in the process; and a story about the possibility that in the future, decisions and actions that support a sustainable and vibrant society will become second nature to us all. Wountie may be smiling after all.

CHAPTER 7

CH2M HILL

"RESPONSIBLE SOLUTIONS FOR A SUSTAINABLE FUTURE."

*The concept of sustainable development does,
in my view, provide the best basis and rallying theme
for the transition to a more secure, sustainable,
and equitable future for humankind.*

— Ralph Peterson, President & CEO, CH2M HILL

THE ENGINEER'S ROLE is often filled with dynamic tension. We call upon engineers to transform scientific insights into marvelous new technologies that enhance our lives. At the same time we hold them responsible for our safety and sense of security. We expect engineers to make sure our water is uncontaminated, our lights stay on, our bridges don't collapse, and that the infrastructure holding our society together works and remains intact. Between these two poles — the domain of the engineering profession — is a dynamic tension between promise and disaster. So as the profession continuously moves toward the promise of new insights, technologies, and processes, it must also keep itself solidly anchored on terra firma, maintaining a secure foothold on what it knows works.

Engineering shapes the way we live, the way we work, and practically everything that we do. We are surrounded everyday by engineering achievements that would have been considered miraculous, science fiction or just plain impossible only a few years ago. Many of these we take for granted as basic requirements for living in the 21st century.

Today the Earth itself is increasingly a product of human engineering. As Brad Allenby, AT&T's Research Vice-President of Technology and Environment, observes, "A myriad of economic and engineering decisions, evaluated and taken as if independent, are in reality tightly coupled both to each other and to underlying natural systems. Anthropogenic climate change; loss of biodiversity and critical habitat; degradation of soil, water, and air resources; dispersion of toxic metals and organics — these are the fruits of human engineering just as surely as the computer, the automobile, and the highway infrastructure."[1] Although unintended, many of these effects are the direct and indirect result of the same human ingenuity, design, decisions and activities that provide what we have come to expect as essential to our standard of living. The systemic impacts of human engineering are bringing us new and unprecedented challenges.

The role that engineering and related technical professions play in moving society toward sustainability cannot be overstated. As scientific evidence increasingly links our unsustainable lifestyles to the depletion of life-support systems on our planet, what is the role and responsibility toward sustainability of engineering and related professions?

Engineers are asking this same question. In 2000, the theme of the annual conference of the International Federation of Consulting Engineers (FIDIC) was *Sustainability: The Challenge of the New Millennium*. José Medem Sanjuán, president of the World Federation of Engineering Organizations (WFEO), a non-governmental organization that brings together national engineering organizations from over 80 countries and represents some eight million engineers, asserted:

> As engineers, we must support sustainable development, having in mind that human beings are at the center of concern for sustainability. We must work to promote public recognition and understanding of the need for sustainable development and the policies and technology required to achieve an ecologically sustainable world for future generations, applying the values of the scientific and technological community to build sustainability.[2]

Medem suggests that engineers must view environmental, technological, economic and social development as "interdependent concepts in which industrial development and ecological sustainability are addressed as complementary aspects of a common goal."[3]

Sustainable development, Medem posits, demands that engineers take on new roles, "The concepts and principles of sustainable development place a burden on the engineer. A burden to change the way we do business."[4]

Carrying this burden makes for an interesting dance. One of the tigers that professional service firms dance with is that their work is driven by client demand and client perceptions of what is relevant, important and cost-effective. The successful firms are those that listen carefully to their clients and deliver what their clients want. In general, engineering, planning and design professionals work in a very competitive field, and their clients operate within time, policy, regulatory, and budgetary constraints. If clients do not ask for sustainability-oriented solutions, or if they reject the relevance or importance of sustainability considerations in their projects, it doesn't matter how good a firm is in that regard, it risks losing the job or not being able to apply the best solutions from a sustainability perspective.

Another tiger that engineers dance with is the "siloed" structure of the engineering, planning and design professions. Knowledge and expertise have become very specialized. Engineers, planners and designers are educated and trained to focus on a specific problem and to solve that problem. They are generally not educated, trained, or hired to view that problem from a total systems perspective.

At the same time as professional service firms are dancing with these tigers, the responsible and successful firms must also be attuned to the needs and solutions that clients will ask for in the future. This requires being skilled in analyzing and synthesizing data on future trends that will drive and affect future client and societal needs. It also demands building the internal knowledge and competence to meet those needs and the ability to communicate with and educate clients and potential clients about needs and solutions they may not yet see as relevant to their concerns. So how does a professional services firm dance with these very real and often contradictory tigers?

The story of engineering for sustainability can find no more appropriate venue than in CH2M HILL. Headquartered in Denver, Colorado, with more than 12,000 staff worldwide, including approximately 9,500 with professional designations, and over $2 billion in annual revenues, CH2M HILL has evolved into one of the world's great professional service firms.

The Client is King... or Queen

The origins of CH2M HILL can be traced to a classroom in the engineering faculty of Oregon State College in the mid-1930s with three students, Holly Cornell, James Howland, and T. Burke Hayes and their civil engineering professor, Fred Merryfield. After they graduated, Hayes, Howland and Cornell moved east to attend graduate school. Although all four joined the armed services during World War II, they kept the dream of opening their own firm in Oregon when the war ended.

After the war, Merryfield returned to teaching at Oregon State, and his extensive network of contacts began offering him project work. He began referring some clients to Cornell who had returned from the European front in October of 1945. By January 1946, Howland and Hayes had also returned home. The four long-time friends quickly formed Cornell, Howland, Hayes & Merryfield and moved into office space over a downtown hardware store.

The timing was outstanding. Little construction had taken place during the Depression or during World War II. So in 1946 a backlog of demand translated into tremendous opportunity. The new firm, Cornell, Howland, Hayes & Merryfield, quickly established a reputation for excellent quality work. They instituted a consensus management style that invited everyone to contribute to decisions, and then to share the responsibility those decisions carried with them. Just as members of the organization shared responsibility, they also shared earnings. The idea of employee ownership emerged in 1949. That same year the firm had completed 200 projects, built a new office in Corvallis, and became known as C-H-2-M. Some say a client coined the abbreviation because the name of the firm was too long, others remember it resulting from a word game. Whatever the source, the name stuck.

In 1953, with 500 projects under their belts, CH2M designed and introduced an automatic variable speed pump that could accommodate daily fluctuations and seasonal variations in sewerage flow common to the Pacific Northwest as a result of the region's dry summers and wet winters. The resulting product was called FLOmatcher. While FLOmatcher became a successful product for the young firm, it was another CH2M innovation, MicroFLOC, that became a springboard catapulting CH2M from a regional consulting firm to a national operation. Developed mainly by Archie Rice, MicroFLOC was an advanced technology for economically treating drinking water. Once MicroFLOC was developed, Ralph Roderick pushed to use the new technology for advanced wastewater treatment.

In 1965, CH2M teamed with Clair A. Hill & Associates to use MicroFLOC to design the world's first major advanced wastewater treatment plant at Lake Tahoe. The highly successful project received the American Consulting Engineers Council (ACEC) Grand Award and brought the firm national recognition that led to more work nationwide. The success at Lake Tahoe also stimulated the 1971 merger of CH2M and Clair A. Hill & Associates of Redding, California. The newly blended firm was awarded a series of high-visibility water and wastewater treatment projects and gained a national reputation for high quality, innovative results.

In 1966, when CH2M HILL became incorporated, the company kept a sense of partnership where rewards flowed to the shareholders who did project work. This basic incentive structure is still in place today. In the 1970s, rewards became shared more broadly with the adoption of an Employee Stock Ownership Plan that extended ownership benefits to all qualified employees.

CH2M HILL evolved as revenues and staff numbers grew. Gaining a strong reputation as a water, wastewater and environmental firm, it continued to provide a full suite of services to a broad range of clients. The firm also developed its first matrix management system that decentralized project management and client relations and centralized the direction of technical expertise.

Jim Howland led the firm for nearly 30 years in a variety of roles that included managing partner, president and board chairman. One of the most lasting legacies that he created during that time is a 12-page booklet. Illustrated with cartoons, Jim's "little yellow book" outlines many values that are still embraced by the company today. One of the most lasting is, "The client is king... or queen. Each one is important."

Today CH2M HILL is a family of companies that, at any given moment, has approximately 15,000 projects underway around the world. The firm's environmental practice experienced explosive growth over the past 20 years, moving from approximately $10 million in revenues in 1981 to approximately $1 billion in 2001 so that it now accounts for approximately one-half of CH2M HILL's revenues. Now only 60 percent of the firm's approximately 12,000 professional staff are engineers, the rest include architects, landscape designers, municipal planners, chemists, physicists, and economists. CH2M HILL has evolved from being an engineering firm to being a global project delivery firm that provides complete program management, planning, engineering design, technology, construction, financing and project development services to private industry and public sector clients around the world.

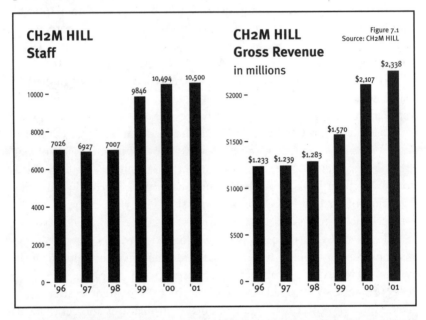

Figure 7.1
Source: CH2M HILL

In the early 21st century, given the depth of its resources and the diversity of both its professional staff and its capabilities, CH2M HILL is able to take any industrial or public works project from concept through planning, financing, design, construction, operations and maintenance. Through a global network of 370 permanent and project offices, the firm provides local professional advice and global resources from more than 41 countries on six continents. The firm's main business groups include Water (focusing on water resources and treatment), Transportation (including aviation, ports and intermodal, transit, and highways), Energy & Environmental Systems (including energy, environment, telecommunications, nuclear, facility management, and services for the U.S. Departments of Energy and Defense), and Industry (focusing on electronics, pharmaceuticals, food, and consumer products). In addition, CH2M HILL provides contract operations and management services infrastructure facilities, through

Operations Management International (OMI), a CH2M HILL company, created in 1980, that serves municipal and industrial clients worldwide. In 2001, OMI was awarded the Malcolm Baldridge National Quality Award. Alongside these established areas of business, from time to time a new area of practice will emerge within the firm. One early stage practice group that has emerged in the firm during the past decade is that of Sustainable Development.

SUSTAINABILITY. IT'S A JOURNEY . . .

Emerge —v.i. (1) to appear out of or from behind something. (2) to come out of an experience, condition, or situation, especially a difficult one. (3) to become known or apparent.[5]

As we have come to understand something of the internal workings of CH2M HILL, it is clear that the concept of innovation diffusion, as described in chapter 3, could have been developed in the learning laboratory that is the organizational life and culture of the firm. The leadership style in CH2M HILL provides encouragement to staff with new ideas, then puts the responsibility on the staff to develop the idea, enroll the support of others, build a mass of interested professionals, and demonstrate that the idea can be of use to clients and will provide a locus of revenue. The emergence of sustainability within the firm over the past decade is following the pattern that has led to highly successful practices in other areas. The practice of environmental engineering, for example, followed that pattern, developing slowly yet progressively during the late 1960s and 1970s, then exploding in the 1980s and 1990s to become one of the core areas of expertise and revenues for the firm at the beginning of the new millennium. Given CH2M HILL's enormous strength in both water and environment, and with rapidly growing energy and transportation practices, the firm has tremendous potential to be a vital sustainability solutions provider. Exploring that potential and how it has been developing so far is the subject of the balance of this chapter.

In many respects, CH2M HILL's primary product is knowledge. That knowledge resides in its people. It is no surprise then that the journey toward integrating sustainability thinking into practice at CH2M HILL arose from the passion, interests, curiosity, concerns and knowledge of its professional staff. Furthermore, and consistent with CH2M HILL's culture, the movement toward sustainability was not driven from the top down. Although it has enjoyed the support and encouragement of CH2M HILL's president and CEO, Ralph R. Peterson, from the beginning, it has emerged from within the company. The professionals at CH2M HILL work in areas that are directly related to human impacts and dependence on the environment, whether it is designing the built environment or in providing clean water, treating wastewater, building a transit system, preventing or mitigating pollution or handling contaminated and hazardous waste sites. A considerable amount of this work is dealing with environmental problems resulting from human activities.

Some individuals in the firm began to feel that addressing these issues, albeit extremely important, failed to get at the real root of the problems. They also felt that there were ways of viewing, and potentially solving, some of these problems that weren't being addressed by the traditional engineering approach. To achieve long-term solutions to societal problems, the focus was often too narrow and too short-term, and the solutions were not really integrating the knowledge that could be brought to bear across disciplines.

One of the tigers standing in the path of a more sustainable approach is the fact that engineering solutions are generally sought, and therefore delivered, within specialized disciplines. Problems and solutions are conventionally viewed as discrete issues: solid waste, energy, transportation, water, and so on. Legislation has been passed and regulatory agencies have been established around these issues. Because of this segmentation, clients often do not request that analyses or solutions be viewed or delivered from a total systems perspective.

In the early 1990s, Linda Morse, now head of the CH2M HILL Sustainable Development Practice Group, was working on integrated waste management and other environmental issues when a number of books, articles and conversations piqued her interest in sustainable development. She was becoming increasingly aware that the issues she was dealing with could be viewed more systemically. At the same time, she began to recognize the importance of the larger global issues that were explained in professional literature and in the media. She began to recognize that there was a tremendous need for alternative ways of addressing these issues and that CH2M HILL had the potential to make a difference in these complex realms. Morse explains:

> Being in an engineering company during this period, I
> was acutely aware of what an enormous impact a firm
> like CH2M HILL has on the built environment and on

the natural environment. In many cases the impact is a positive one; whether it's providing clean water or cleaning up past mistakes at hazardous waste sites and contaminated ground water, there's a large element that is positive in an environmental sense. But I also recognized that as a company, we had often not explored the overall effects in a more holistic sense.

Morse found that there were others in CH2M HILL who shared her concerns and interests:

There were indeed people around the company who were thinking in the same terms and were recognizing that this was an important concept and trend that could be very important to what CH2M HILL is as a company, our business practices, and our clients.

A group of like-minded professionals within the firm began to exchange phone calls, emails, articles, and ideas and eventually formed an informal "skunk works" group around their interest in sustainable development. Morse recalls:

During the early days, there was a lot of exchanging information about how sustainable development could be relevant to CH2M HILL. We asked big questions in the process. 'How do we make it relevant to what we do?' We intuitively know that it is. When we talk with other people who haven't heard the concepts or may even have a negative impression, how do we engage them in the conversation, in the dialogue? At the beginning, we were on a steep learning curve, as we were refining our own thoughts and values and how they related to CH2M HILL's values and the services we offer.

In these early days, there wasn't any formal targeted investment for exploring sustainability by the company. The skunk works was a voluntary group that purposely kept a low profile while they built their own capabilities and understanding about how sustainability applied to CH2M HILL's business. They became more visible as some members began talking with more of the middle and upper-level managers in the company and received, in some cases, a very positive response, interest and some hard questions, particularly about how the concepts add value to their clients. The skunk works continued to receive

Peterson's encouragement, although not yet any financial or resources commitment. Over time the skunk works grew into an internal network that met periodically to share and apply new knowledge.

In 1997, CH2M HILL corporately sponsored Morse's participation in an intensive weeklong sustainability workshop conducted by The Natural Step organization that took place in Santa Fe, New Mexico. Morse recalls:

> Santa Fe was a very important experience, not only to learn about The Natural Step framework for sustainability in a very focused and extended fashion, but also to be with people who were all interested and involved in learning, who understand how they could bring these ideas and principles back to their own enterprise, whether that was a corporation, or other consulting firms, or non-profits or public agencies. It was a great experience to be exposed to some of the leading thinkers in sustainability. It really was a seminal event for me.

She took this knowledge back to CH2M HILL and to her colleagues and began giving presentations internally, as well as externally to a limited number of interested clients. Morse comments, "We always go back to what the client needs are. That's the driver that underlies so many of the decisions we make." Sustainability had to become relevant to client needs.

In 1998, a formal Sustainable Development Practice Group was formed within CH2M HILL, signaling that the firm considered this to be an emerging area of practice, either because of market trends and client demand, or because it is a potential business driver. Developing a practice group meant that sustainability was seen as something that the company should foster and nurture. It also meant a commitment of financial support to develop capabilities internally and to help clarify how sustainability concepts could apply to client projects and address client needs.

There were two main focus areas during the early part of the sustainability practice. The first was to demonstrate the relevance of sustainability concepts to actual projects, either by initiating projects with a distinct sustainability focus or by bringing this perspective into the normal course of the company's business such as wastewater treatment plants, designing a berth at a new port facility, environmental cleanup, or industrial process work for companies.

The second focus area was on education and training in sustainability. Morse comments:

> We knew that without doing that, we were going to always be in the backwater. People would hear about sustainable development and not really know what it was, might even have a negative reaction, not know what value it was to clients. We recognized that education and training were important to the practice, and that led us into various vehicles for education: brown bag luncheon presentations, training within the context of business development and project implementation, and net meetings conducted remotely. A national sustainability training program has recently been developed using The Natural Step framework for sustainability and various implementation strategies and tools, and hands-on application in real projects.

Increased knowledge and practice led to sustainability tool development. By working specifically within projects to determine how best to apply sustainability concepts in a given area, staff developed tools that were transferable to other projects in that area or to other processes. Progress was made step by practical step.

For example, an opportunity emerged — a $200 million real estate development project — to develop an innovative process of bringing sustainability concepts into project thinking and decision-making. With support from CH2M HILL and support from the client, a group of sustainable development specialists developed an extensive process that brought together staff experts in a wide range of disciplines, such as water, waste water, energy, air quality, transportation, human communities, solid and hazardous waste, building systems, and materials. These experts adopted a common framework for sustainability and then applied that and their expertise in an integrated way to the project. Morse reports, "We used The Natural Step framework for sustainability, and built a process by which we applied TNS principles to the evaluation technologies. We were able to take away from that project a tremendous learning and the development of a tool that continues to be a model for us internally." (Figure 7.2).

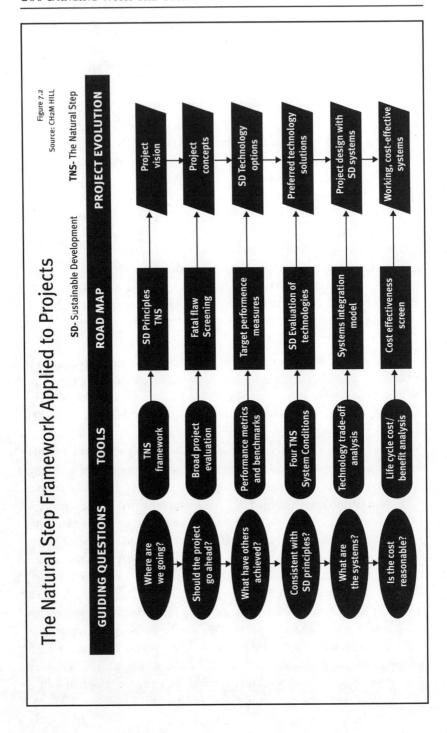

The Natural Step Framework Applied to Projects

SD- Sustainable Development   TNS- The Natural Step

Figure 7.2
Source: CH2M HILL

GUIDING QUESTIONS	TOOLS	ROAD MAP	PROJECT EVOLUTION
Where are we going?	TNS framework	SD Principles TNS	Project vision
Should the project go ahead?	Broad project evaluation	Fatal flaw Screening	Project concepts
What have others achieved?	Performance metrics and benchmarks	Target performance measures	SD Technology options
Consistent with SD principles?	Four TNS System Conditions	SD Evaluation of technologies	Preferred technology solutions
What are the systems?	Technology trade-off analysis	Systems integration model	Project design with SD systems
Is the cost reasonable?	Life cycle cost / benefit analysis	Cost effectiveness screen	Working, cost-effective systems

In 1999, CH2M HILL made two strategic hires that had implications for the firm's evolving journey to sustainability: Nicholas Sonntag and Stephanie Foster. Sonntag, a sustainable development expert with an international reputation and a background in engineering physics and operations research, was hired as the new president for CH2M HILL's Canadian firm. Sonntag came to the company from his position as executive director of the Stockholm Environment Institute, an internationally renowned, independent policy research and implementation organization that provides up-to-date knowledge to decision-makers in business and government to further global action supportive of sustainable development.

CH2M HILL's interest in hiring Sonntag was both to build their business in Canada and to add depth in sustainable development that would benefit the firm overall. Sonntag comments:

> There is a deep personal commitment to sustainability in the senior leadership at CH2M HILL, so the feeling was that Canada would be a great place to test sustainable development (SD) in our business, and evaluate how far can we take the concept in the firm. Since we operate as a Canadian corporation within the CH2M HILL group of companies, we are able to experiment in Canada with how SD could be applied in our specific projects. This is one critical element of the support I have from the CH2M HILL organization — namely that our Canadian operations serve as an SD case study for the firm. The second aspect of support was the belief that sustainable development would be a good differentiator in the market. In Canada we are a midsize firm, with about 375 employees in seven offices, so we have a workable number of staff to train and projects of a modest size. Thus, our mandate is to aggressively grow the business in Canada in all of our business lines, water, transport and environmental services and so on, and to identify ways of introducing the concepts of sustainability into our projects. Then we can see how our clients respond, how our staff respond, and ultimately assess how sustainable development differentiates us in the marketplace, while providing increased value to our clients.

And the results for the first two years? Sonntag reports:

> So far we're getting good response. Our clients are often surprised to find what they think of as an engineering design firm with this kind of awareness and interest in sustainability, and we are now competing for work that we probably wouldn't have considered two years ago. We are having conversations with clients on topics like sustainable development, smart growth, Agenda 21,[6] and all the various aspects that encircle this topic in The Natural Step framework. Two years ago we wouldn't have had those conversations with our clients. It doesn't mean that we weren't already doing some of these things. For example, we always looked for ways to save energy and recycle water. Those objectives have always been there. Now, however, we more fully realize that these are all elements of the overall integrated, or if you like, systems solution.

At the same time, Stephanie Foster joined the firm. She currently serves as director of Strategic Initiatives and International Business Development for CH2M HILL Canada. She is also the executive director of the Earth Council Institute, Canada, responsible for Canadian activities and global programs in the areas of climate change and greenhouse gas emissions trading, economic incentives for sustainable development, and greening of games and sports facilities. Under Foster's direction, CH2M HILL Canada instituted a national sustainability education program designed and conducted in collaboration with The Natural Step. This continuing education process lays the groundwork for a two-pronged approach toward sustainability: "walking the talk" internally and integrating sustainability thinking into client services.

As part of this process, an internal Sustainable Development Task Force was established to help with the transition. Foster explains:

> The Task Force was chartered by the Regional Management Team 'to develop a plan and detailed set of recommendations for action that will enable CH2M HILL Canada to realize its goal of having sustainability principles integrated into our business.' This group of senior staff recommended a variety of actions related to project delivery, design and construction, internal

greening, marketing and communications, human resources, and education. Most of those initiatives are now underway and the Task Force still stands as an advisory group and resource for staff and senior management on sustainability issues.

SUSTAINABILITY INTEGRATION STEP BY STEP

We provide a brief overview of some of the areas where CH2M HILL is integrating sustainability as a principle to guide its business and as a practice area: leadership commitment and support, education, partnerships, walking the talk internally, and integrating sustainability into client services.

Leadership Commitment and Support

CH2M HILL's leadership commitment to sustainability is consistent with the firm's cultural approach to building capacity in vital competencies that provide value to the client. Morse remembers that, as interest in sustainability concepts began to emerge within CH2M HILL in the early 1990s, CEO Ralph Peterson was among the first to talk about it. Jo Danko, a member of the skunk works group and now Operations and Project Delivery Director for the Energy and Industrial Systems business unit, recalls attending meetings with Peterson in the early 90s and being moved and impressed with the depth of his awareness and passion around sustainable development.

Peterson comments:

> I am an optimist when it comes to developing a sustainable future for our planet. I wholeheartedly believe that we hold the power to deliver a world of shared promise to our children and generations that follow us on this globe. Delivering on that promise will not be easy. It requires an active approach to sustainable development. Each of us must see to it that we run our businesses, build our communities, and lead our personal lives in ways that sustain the vital resources and natural systems that enable us to live on this planet. CH2M HILL has embarked on its own journey toward sustainability, and our people are doing all they can to help our business partners and clients realize the sustainable future they hope to achieve.

Despite his personal belief in the global necessity of sustainable development, and the importance of it to the future of his firm, Peterson knows that he cannot get too far ahead of either his professional colleagues within CH2M HILL or their clients. Accordingly, his style over the past decade has been to encourage the emergence of sustainability as a focus within the firm but not to try to force it. He expects the initiative and energy around sustainability to emerge from within the firm and to drive its development.

Mike Kennedy, president of Regional Operations for CH2M HILL and one of the senior leaders of the firm, emphasizes the importance of appreciating how the firm's culture influences the way new ideas emerge:

> Culturally we are both a federation of practitioners and a highly aligned mission focused business. We are a collection of practices, and a relatively eclectic collection, and that's what we tend to nurture, that's what we like. One of the many ways we instill organizational change around here, the way it's worked culturally and historically, is that we listen to our own people, and they listen to our clients, and watch for things that look like trends, indicators, directions and signals from the market place. Today we have an environmental business that's a billion dollars a year. In 1981, it was less than a ten million dollar business. Basically, it was driven by people who said, 'We've got all these regulations coming out, we have clients not knowing what to do, and there's a market emerging. Let's see if we can get good at this.'
>
> The fundamental cultural underpinnings of the firm are founded on making the world a better place. Most of the people in leadership positions are here because of that fundamental belief that this firm and our people can actually make the world a better place.

One of the ways that CH2M HILL helps make the world a better place is to understand what types of challenges their current and future clients will be facing. Kennedy observes that client demands have moved through a progressive set of eras focused on public health concerns, regulatory concerns, and more recently cost-efficiency concerns. A new era is emerging: one focused on sustainable development concerns.

However not all clients are moving into that era at the same pace or the same time. Kennedy explains:

> That's where I think we're headed and where the firm is. We have clients that are in all those places. We have clients who still have public health issues. We have work that is driven by growth and regulation. We have 15,000 projects at any one time, and the client behind each one of those projects is in a different place in this spectrum. So it's a little hard to characterize the firm as being in any one place if you look at our work. If you look at the intellectual leadership of the firm, we are definitely looking forward and saying 'Look, the work we are going to be doing in the future is going to be sustainable, it's going to be driven by sustainable principles.'

A grounded, non-judgmental, non-blaming attitude — the essence of true professionalism — has contributed to the firm's continued growth and success. It is well articulated by Jo Danko:

> Every one of our clients is on the road to sustainability. They're just all in different places. Each of our clients has a different organizational culture, a different business philosophy, and a different perspective on sustainable development. Each of them is valid. Recognizing that each client's perspective is valid is the essence of diversity. As professionals, we try to connect with people on the level they are at and work with them to develop solutions.
>
> Sustainability as a word doesn't even need to come up. To make progress with a client, we must first understand their current business challenge or opportunity from their perspective and then help shape it by incorporating sustainable principles on a level that is relevant to their situation. Focus and respect for a client and their needs generates long-lasting, sustainable solutions.

CH2M HILL's Sustainability Policy Statement[7]

In order to signal the growing and still emerging belief that sustainability is the way of the future, the leadership of the firm has adopted a policy statement helping to set that direction. CH2M HILL expresses its mission as making "technology work to help our clients build a better world." In addition to that, the firm's policy now includes the following:

> CH2M HILL remains committed to improving the economic and social quality of human life and the preservation of the carrying capacity of nature for future generations. We embrace this commitment in the context of our core belief that our long-term success requires that we create value for our clients, owner-employees and the communities in which we live. We recognize that fulfilling our commitment is a journey with many uncertainties rather than a known end point. To this end, we strive to adhere to the following principles.

In the service of our clients we will:

- Provide the best counsel available on the application of sustainable practice to help our clients meet their objectives;

- Commit ourselves to the pursuit of continual learning and mastery of new technologies and methods to make sustainable solutions feasible and practical; and

- Partner with clients, wherever possible, to share with others the learning gained from new sustainable solutions to the difficult challenges they face.

In the operation of our firm we will:

- Seek economically feasible opportunities to apply sustainable development concepts to do more with less, reduce the use of toxic materials, conserve natural resources, and minimize waste and emissions;

- Encourage the adoption of sustainable practices by our suppliers and seek partnerships with those suppliers who share our objectives;

- Create workplaces for our employees that are safe, healthy, and functional, and that embody sustainability principles to the highest practicable degree;

- Periodically seek out the views of experts and others

outside the company to gain additional perspectives on our quest to conduct business sustainability; and

- Develop, adopt and continuously improve metrics to measure and monitor our progress in achieving our goals.

In participation with other stakeholders we will:

- Seek opportunities to work with communities, governments, and non-governmental and professional organizations to help articulate, teach, and advance the principles of sustainability.

- Let our journey on the pathway to a sustainable world be its own reward.

In Canada, CH2M HILL has developed the following statements:

Our Vision: Responsible solutions for a sustainable future.

Our Mission: To make technology work to help our clients build a better world in a sustainable way.

For CH2M HILL, educating clients and the marketplace to consider and demand sustainability solutions is a primary ingredient of developing a successful and innovative practice. This requires careful attention to how the firm's sustainability competence is communicated to external stakeholders.

External Communication of the Commitment to Sustainability

CH2M HILL is also conveying its ability to help clients create more sustainable solutions and implement more sustainable practices.

From CH2M HILL in Canada:

> With the combined resources of more than 375 employees Canada-wide, CH2M HILL offers a complete range of environmental services and technologies to our clients across Canada and in the global market. The CH2M HILL team of engineers, planners, architects, hydrogeologists, scientists, and technical specialists is committed to being a leader in the pursuit of a sustainable future for Canada and the planet. By

working proactively with our clients, we seek to provide them with integrated, practical low-maintenance solutions that demonstrate an innovative level of sustainability.

As a firm, CH2M HILL aspires to add value to the communities in which people live and work. CH2M HILL is a company that appreciates the value of the natural environment and considers the environment a priority in all that we do; this is reflected in our ongoing development of environmentally-restorative and pollution-preventative engineering solutions.

From the U.S.:

For several decades we have helped hundreds of clients develop and implement programs to mitigate environmental impacts, prevent pollution, enhance reuse and recycling, and use energy and resources more efficiently — all elements of sustainable development. We leverage more than 55 years of experience to aid our clients in integrating the concepts of sustainable development into their ongoing business strategies, balancing the sometimes competing needs of the Earth, the economy, and the community.

As forerunners of the sustainable development movement, we are creating models by which sustainability can be understood and applied. We are using these models to help clients around the world meet their sustainability goals.

Internal Education

When the skunk works group formed in the early 1990s, they set education as a high priority. They evolved into a practice group and continued their commitment to education. Every SD practice group member has made presentations at numerous brown bag luncheons throughout the firm. This is still one of the important ways that informal education takes place around sustainability, together with project-specific education and intranet-based remote education.

In 2000, we collaborated with CH2M HILL Canada to launch a national sustainability education program that involved a series of two- to three-day intensive workshops starting with senior managers in the Regional Management Team and extending to staff at all levels of the firm. A similar program was initiated in the United States. The Canadian operations have also launched an educational program for a sustainable work environment. This program provides employees with advice on ways to implement sound and sustainable office practices that reduce waste and conserve resources. This program, along with the CH2M HILL corporate sustainability policy, is intended to help employees maintain and nourish the environment in which they work as well as inspire those who visit CH2M HILL offices. An internal office greening program has been initiated in both the Canadian and the U.S. firms. In addition, CH2M HILL has developed mechanisms to provide educational opportunities to clients and to the general public, including a speaker series in Toronto where they are invited to hear and meet prominent thinkers in sustainability. These speaker events have become very popular and have stimulated greater interest in sustainability among CH2M HILL Canada clients and allied organizations.

Partnerships

Beginning with the Rio Earth Summit of 1992, CH2M HILL has participated in many sustainability efforts around the world, and has helped to shape the dialogue on the subject. CH2M HILL was an early member of the World Business Council for Sustainable Development and continues to play a very active role. It is very involved with the U.S. Green Building Council (and many other organizations stemming from the Rio Summit), Business for Social Responsibility, and the World Resources Institute. Maurice F. Strong, the internationally prominent Canadian (at last count he had been awarded 47 honorary doctorates from universities around the world) who was the Secretary General and architect of the UN Earth Summit, continues to be a valuable advisor to the company's board of directors on international matters. Staff at all levels of CH2M HILL participate in numerous organizations and committees to further the understanding and benefits of sustainable development across a range of sectors.

Walking the Talk

CH2M HILL starts its commitment to sustainability at home. In Canada, the in-house greening program is billed as a "company-wide common sense approach" to improving the quality of employees' lives both at work and at home. To implement the program, CH2M HILL is carrying out a comprehensive effort that spans all business groups, administrative support functions, and offices throughout Canada.

Staff volunteers across Canada are working to minimize the environmental footprint of CH2M HILL operations by improving efficiencies and monitoring the use of resources. They have developed an internal corporate "Guide to a Sustainable Work Environment" outlining a range of actions that the company is taking to accomplish its goals. They have set goals to minimize their paper use and divert waste from the landfill. They are increasing the use of certified green products in their offices through green procurement and supply chain management. By tracking the greenhouse gas (GHG) emissions that are a by-product of their business travel, they are measuring their GHG impact and are working to offset these emissions through tree-planting programs. Company volunteers also support a variety of social and environmental programs in their communities including Earth Day activities, working with local schools, and contributing to the fundraising activities of local non-governmental organizations.

CH2M HILL Canada created a unique on-line achievements program, GREEN! Leaf (Growing Real Environmental Efforts Now!), that encourages and recognizes employees' participation in environmentally and socially responsible activities. Each of the seven Canadian offices has a GREEN! Team that promotes internal sustainable development. Financial incentives are also available to staff who show leadership in demonstrating practical applications of sustainability principles in their work or at home.

Firmwide, CH2M HILL has adopted a greening initiative that is complementary to the one adopted in Canada. A pilot project created by Andrea Ramage, Organizational Greening Manager in the Northwest Region of the U.S., has evolved into a national internal office greening program aiming to raise awareness about sustainable practices among employees, decrease the company's consumption of natural resources, reduce its environmental footprint, and reap cost savings and revenue-generating benefits. Working with the firm's management team, more than 200 staff have participated in the pilot greening activities and have been the impetus behind the creation of the more than 30 greening projects now underway. Initiated in early 2000, the program is already returning encouraging results such as:

- Saving a client $30,000 by delivering 700 copies of a bulky environmental impact statement on 500 CDs (at $5 each) and in 200 paper copies (at $65 each), instead of all in paper;

- Improving indoor air quality, reducing long-term maintenance costs, and realizing $178,800 in life-cycle cost savings by installing non-offgassing, recyclable carpet tiles in the renovation of a 90,000 square foot office. As the carpet becomes worn, they selectively replace carpet tiles in high-traffic areas (i.e., approximately 20 percent of the total carpeted area). Non-VOC paint was also used as part of the same office renovation; and

- Changing invoicing procedures to reduce paper copies with an estimated savings of $12,000 per year.

In addition, CH2M HILL recently demonstrated its support of renewable energy through a three-year, $15,000 purchase of the environmental benefits of new wind energy from the Bonneville Environmental Foundation (BEF). BEF will use the revenues to develop new wind energy that will displace, on behalf of CH2M HILL, 950 tons of carbon dioxide (CO_2) emissions over three years. With BEF's "green tag" energy product, the customer's annual payment to the foundation goes to pay that share of the cost of new wind energy that exceeds the market price of conventional power. The actual output is then sold as conventional power at market prices, while the contributor, such as CH2M HILL, earns credit for the environmental benefits.

INTEGRATING SUSTAINABILITY INTO CLIENT SERVICES

CH2M HILL is leveraging its significant knowledge and experience in environmental issues to become one of the leaders in the "how to" of sustainable development. This requires integrating knowledge, talents and resources that have been traditionally dispersed or focused on other priorities into an approach that is better designed for sustainability. The company increasingly sees sustainability as a method of planning positively for the future, as opposed to reacting to existing problems. It is also a filter through which growth and development options may be usefully viewed to make more effective decisions with long-term implications.

Because the nature of CH2M HILL's traditional work is so integrally connected to many aspects of sustainability, there are countless projects we could feature to demonstrate how the company contributes to a more sustainable society. The company's basic approach is to view sustainability as a framework for decision-making that is dynamic and adaptable. A sampling of CH2M HILL's projects include their work with Nike, (particularly around manufacturing), with U.S. Marine Corps Base Camp Lejeune, North Carolina, with a new sustainably designed community in Burnaby, near Vancouver, B.C., and a community-based water program in the Ukraine.

NIKE, Oregon and Overseas

CH2M HILL has worked closely with Nike since 1998 to integrate sustainability into many aspects of Nike's far-flung operations, helping Nike's sub-contract manufacturers reduce pollution, petroleum-based solvents, solid waste, and water use, as well as helping the company with sustainable product designs. Most of the petroleum-based solvents have been replaced with more benign water-based chemicals that are equal in quality and, in some cases, cheaper to use. CH2M HILL has provided expertise on green chemistry issues and tracking the use of PVC in Nike's products. The firm has also consulted on confidential processes and material analyses to achieve the goal of a closed-loop product life cycle. In Nike footwear sub-contractors' operations in 45 factories in six countries, a CH2M HILL study identified short- and long-term opportunities to reduce pollution and save operating costs. Significantly, this study confirmed the linkage between pollution prevention and improved business performance.

CH2M HILL continues to perform valuable global environmental data management, analysis, and reporting functions for Nike. This work has been critical to our success in defining significant environmental aspects within our subcontractor factories' Environmental Management System programs. It has also been a key component in baselining and measuring continuous environmental improvement in those factories.

— Phil Berry, Technical Director,
Footwear Sustainability, Nike

CH2M HILL has been Nike's global water use and wastewater consultant since 1998. The firm is working on a water quality initiative to ensure that the wastewater from several hundred of Nike's apparel and textile sub-contractors is treated and discharged in a responsible manner. This includes setting global quality standards for wastewater discharge. CH2M HILL is also providing worldwide training to Nike staff and textile vendors on water conservation and water quality. The firm is working to optimize water usage in Nike footwear sub-contractors' factory operations and to coordinate the installation of wastewater treatment systems in several dozen factories in Asia. Most recently, CH2M HILL has been working with Nike on the creation of their Responsibility Reports, including the development of sustainability indicators.

U.S. Marine Corps Base Camp Lejeune, North Carolina

CH2M HILL is currently working with U.S. Marine Corps Base Camp Lejeune, and the Marine Corps Air Station New River, in North Carolina, together referred to as Camp Lejeune, to promote environmental sustainability in the day-to-day operations of the bases. This project includes the development of an Environmental Sustainability Guidance Manual (ESGM) and training video for department managers to aid in planning, developing and implementing environmentally sustainable future operations both locally and abroad. Camp Lejeune, one of the largest marine bases in the world, provides specialized training to prepare troops for amphibious and land combat operations. The 153,000-acre base supports 144,000 marines, sailors, including approximately 40,000 battle-ready war fighters, and their families. The base has 6,800 buildings, 450 miles of roads, a municipal solid waste landfill, five water treatment plants, and one wastewater treatment plant. The perimeter of the base includes 14 miles of Atlantic Ocean frontage.

Allen Davis, project manager for CH2M HILL recalls that Bob Warren, then Assistant Chief of Staff for Environmental Management at the base with an environmental staff of approximately 100 people, was one of the driving and visionary forces behind the development of the ESGM. Warren had spent thirty years working on the environmental engineering aspects of controlling, preventing and cleaning up the effects of pollution as well as in programs for the protection and enhancement of plant and animal species and their habitats.

'Make no little plans, they have no magic to stir men's blood' To take on sustainability initiatives one must have commitment. It's hard to be committed to something unless you truly understand it. Therefore an incursion into sustainability requires an investment in learning. That means lots of reading and study. It's more than just work. An old friend once introduced me to the metaphor, 'Work is sweat, commitment is blood.' I think sustainability has to get into your blood. You have to think bigger than you ever thought before. Sustainability is a new paradigm. It has been said that when a paradigm shift occurs everything goes back to zero and past successes mean nothing. That's what it means to launch into sustainability. Daniel Burnham, considered to be the father of modern planning said, 'Make no little plans, they have no magic to stir men's blood.' So not only does sustainability have to get into your blood, you have to be bold enough to propose solutions that will stir the blood of others.

— Bob Warren, former Assistant Chief of Staff
for Environmental Affairs,
MCB Camp Lejeune

In 1997, Warren was managing the substantial environmental program for Camp Lejeune. Governor Jim Hunt of North Carolina invited heads of industry, academia and the military to a summit on "Sustainability and Smart Growth." As the Assistant Chief of Staff for Environmental Management, Warren had the opportunity to accompany Maj. Gen. Ray Smith, then Commanding General of the Marine Corps Base, Camp Lejeune, to the Summit.

Ray Anderson, CEO of Interface, Inc., a leader in sustainable business, was the keynote speaker. He presented several excerpts from his book *Mid Course Correction* and closed with the reading of the poem, "Tomorrow's Child." Warren remembers:

> When it was over, I had tears in my eyes, like many others. While I didn't understand what had happened in that hour, my conception of life and our role in the destiny of Planet Earth was changed forever. In his closing remarks, Governor Hunt challenged each of the participants to go back to their work places and seek ways to

make their impacts on the environment more sustainable. On the trip back to Camp Lejeune, General Smith asked me what I thought we could do at Camp Lejeune to contribute to the governor's goal for a more sustainable North Carolina. I told him I would like to think about it for a couple of days. After ruminating for several days and a couple of late-night brainstorming sessions, we conceived the idea of a Marine Corps Sustainable Base of the Future.

The thought was to look beyond the traditional military five-year planning period and imagine what could be accomplished if the goals were set for twenty-five or fifty years.

Working with CH2M HILL, Warren and his team set about examining all the operations on the installation, many of which had never been included in the traditional environmental compliances processes. Warren comments:

By including every aspect and impact of base operations, we were able to include functions such as energy and water conservation, green building design, alternative fuel sources such as photovoltaics and hydrogen fuel cells, recycling of treated wastewater to reduce groundwater withdrawals, affirmative procurement, lease versus purchase of durable goods and certain textiles, and alternative fuel vehicles including the hydrogen fuel cell hyper-car.

As a result of his very focused attention on the issues of sustainability over many years, Warren offers some astute advice:

I would caution not to be satisfied with half solutions. At Camp Lejeune we built a state-of-the art activated sludge wastewater treatment plant with biological nutrient removal, sand filtration, and ultraviolet disinfection. The effluent from that plant met North Carolina shellfish sanitation standards and was arguably drinkable. And yet, the base was dumping eight million gallons of this treated wastewater each day into the New River while at the same time withdrawing another eight million gallons a day for treatment under the Safe

Drinking Water Act, a throughput of sixteen million gallons a day. Under a more traditional Environmental Management System, it would have been easy to set a goal of simply meeting the state's discharge standards. That would have completed the conventional linear path to compliance and met all former standards. Instead, we set as a goal the ultimate recycling of 100 percent of the treated wastewater for flushing, vehicle washing, irrigation and other non-potable purposes with zero discharge to the New River. This is not something you undertake lightly and certainly not something you accomplish in a two- to five-year period. The biggest contributions to future sustainability will come from those who diligently apply knowledge through unfettered minds.

Just prior to Warren's retirement from the Marines in 2002, we conducted a three-day workshop in sustainable development for him and his staff at Camp Lejeune, coordinating that work with CH2M HILL's Allen Davis. Warren comments:

Another bright spot in the process came just prior to my departure from Camp Lejeune when we undertook training for the environmental staff in The Natural Step framework for sustainability. The Natural Step really helped us to gain an understanding of how we fit into a very complex planetary scheme and how small actions even at military installations can contribute to the global cause.

Since leaving Camp Lejeune in 2000, Warren has continued to promote greening of the government and environmental sustainability. In traveling to military installations across the country, Warren has sensed a heightened awareness of the need for better ways of doing business and an interest in testing solutions that leave less of a mark on the resources of the planet.

Davis believes that the U.S. Department of Defense (DOD) plays a clear leadership role in moving society in a more sustainable direction. He comments:

Over the next five to ten years, I see the government, mainly in the DOD sector, leading the charge in developing sustainable concepts in energy, green buildings and transportation alternatives. As these technologies are developed and integrated within the DOD, I just see them catapulting out into industry on the commercial side.

Camp Lejeune has played an important sustainability leadership role within the military. Davis notes: "I can probably name ten facilities or installations where they have looked at Camp Lejeune and said 'Hey we need to start catching up to them.'"

Burnaby Mountain Project, British Columbia

On the opposite coast of North America from Camp Lejeune, atop Burnaby Mountain, (roughly 15 miles/24 km from downtown Vancouver, British Columbia, and approximately 100 miles/160 km north of Seattle, Washington), plans are developing for a new sustainable community with "green infrastructure" to be built on and next to the campus of Simon Fraser University, one of Canada's leading universities.

At the CH2M HILL Canada office in Vancouver, Kim Stephens, vice-president and project manager, Water Group, working with an interdisciplinary team of consultants led by Hotson-Bakker Architects, is planning a world-class sustainable community where virtually every aspect of this model development will address environmental issues. The project includes 4,500 Earth-friendly residential homes and a variety of retail stores, restaurants and schools. The lower portion of the mountain will remain in its natural state as a permanent conservation area.

> *The Pacific Northwest is a part of North America acutely sensitive to environmental issues. And with the 'salmon crisis' being such a dominant issue, people want action rather than more talk. There is a commitment by all those involved in the Burnaby Mountain project to leave a legacy for the next generation.*
>
> — Kim Stephens, Vice-President & Project Manager, Water Group, CH2M HILL Canada

The new community will be highly urban, with densities ranging from townhouse up to ten-story towers. It will include a main street commercial area, new university buildings, and extensive underground parking. This density of development will involve extensive modifications to the land, including the realignment of several intermittent and disturbed headwater streams, as well as daylighting of existing piped watercourse. The density transfer of the project is one of its sustainability objectives. Rather than creating a single-family housing development that would cover the entire hillside, the density transfer accommodates about the same number of units on 20 percent of the land area, saving 80 percent of the land for conservation purposes.

The second sustainability objective is to create a compact and complete community, integrated with the university campus, that will be walking and transit oriented, reducing the need for single-occupancy vehicle use by up to 40 percent compared with a more traditional single-family development.

The third sustainability objective is to plan for performance monitoring and adaptive management.[8] The Burnaby Mountain Community will be implemented in stages over a 25-year period. This will create opportunities for constant improvement in successive phases of the stormwater and watercourse management plan.

One of the team's responsibilities is to develop an achievable storm water management strategy, a key component of the overall design. The concept design reflects an integrated approach to storm water and riparian corridor management that is holistic in selecting on-site runoff control measures that will protect the downstream fish habitat in Stoney Creek, one of the few remaining high-quality fish-bearing tributaries in the Brunette River Basin. The over-arching watershed protection strategy for Stoney Creek was developed during 1998 and 1999 by CH2M HILL's Stephens and his Seattle-based colleague, Bill Derry.

Over the past four years, through a cross-border sharing of knowledge to advance storm water management, Stephens and Derry have had a major impact in influencing discussion and thinking in British Columbia and Washington State regarding the practical applications of science-based approaches. They pioneered the concept of "integrated storm water management" to fully integrate the engineering, planning and ecological perspectives. The Burnaby Mountain project provides the opportunity to translate the Stoney Creek watershed strategy into a set of practical principles and achievable targets that will guide the detailed site planning for land development.

Municipal Water System, Ukraine

In the Ukraine, citizen involvement has become vital to meeting the challenge of providing fresh water at an affordable price. As the old infrastructure in the region deteriorated, a new approach was required to make the transition from a centralized model to a customer-focused process in which consumers pay for services that were formerly heavily subsidized by the government. It was an approach that involved members of the local community in planning and funding new water systems. This was a radical concept in the newly independent nation facing complex economic and political changes.

The project was led by CH2M HILL, which, for more than 50 years, has successfully applied technology to deliver clean water to people while protecting natural systems throughout the world. Funded by the U.S. Agency for International Development, the project involved several Ukrainian cities. In addition to the basic equipment to analyze systems, Kris Buros, Project Manager, Water Group, CH2M HILL International, and his team are providing Ukrainian water utilities with on-site training on how to involve the public in planning and decision-making.

A major part of the program involves ascertaining people's opinions through the use of focus groups, surveys and face-to-face discussions. The information is used to develop media outreach and public education programs. Final planning by the utilities focuses on customer needs and incorporates public hearings. Virtually the entire project is carried out by local Ukrainian citizens. As a result, even with the end of CH2M HILL's involvement, the concept of engaging people in decisions on infrastructure planning and funding will remain in place to ensure that the achievements are sustainable.

It is rewarding to watch the way that the Ukrainians from all backgrounds and ages have taken to public participation in the rehabilitation of the water system. A positive attitude and involvement by the citizens is crucial to achieve a system that is socially, economically and environmentally sustainable.

— Kris Buros, Project Manager, Water Group,
CH2M HILL International

Ultimately the project does much more than improve the delivery of water to meet basic needs: it helps to create a human infrastructure that empowers people by involving them in their own future.

Advice on the Sustainability Journey from CH2M HILL Practitioners

In terms of intentionally creating the kind of future that we all want to inhabit, and that we earnestly envision for our grandchildren and their grandchildren to inherit, the men and women of CH2M HILL have decades of experience in not only thinking about the important issues of our time but also being responsible for acting on them. In the research and writing of this book, and in working on several joint projects together, we have spent hundreds of hours with these deeply committed, caring, and talented professional people, collecting their advice on how to engage more effectively in sustainable development in various kinds of milieu. It is our privilege to be able to share this hard-won and heartfelt sustainability advice from CH2M HILL.

Dan Arvizu, Senior Vice-President, Technology Fellow, Energy, Environment and Systems

Arvizu heads up CH2M HILL's Energy and Industrial Systems business unit, and is the Director of Technology for the entire Energy, Environment and Systems business group. He came to the firm after 25 years at the Sandia National Laboratories where he ran all the energy programs — clean energy, energy efficiency and advanced energy technologies.

- In the area of sustainability we tend to work with the early adopters. They are the ones out doing things, the Nikes and BPs, they are out doing sustainability because they see this as a differentiator in the marketplace. They want to be known for these kinds of ideals and so it's very easy to work with them.

- We work with the ones on the other end of the spectrum too. If we can help them make a little baby step with sustainability progress, we're certainly going to do that. That's the role of the professional, to enlighten and move companies along, to try to induce them a little bit, but at their pace, so that overall progress can be made. To isolate them and to have them retrench is not in anyone's best interest.

- To the young professional, I would say that sustainability is a noble cause and one that has a place in the business world. It will be a growing priority as time goes on. The problems that we have as a society, as a nation, as a world, are only going to get more pronounced as time goes on. This is an area that's not going to diminish with time.

- The tie-in between sustainability and security is now becoming more apparent in the public mind. Energy independence, economic competitiveness, and environmental quality are all needed and go together. The whole concept of sustainability and improving the national infrastructure requires a major sustained effort. It is important to recognize that we need both the will and the means to make progress. It takes commitment and it takes resources to make some of the desired initiatives take hold. You have to trust that at the end of this investment there's a payoff, and the payoff will be beyond our wildest imagination — because the alternative is unthinkable.

Bill Blosser, Director, Department of Land Conservation Management, State of Oregon

Blosser began his career with CH2M HILL thirty years ago as an urban planner and has been involved in a wide variety of complex planning issues. He was one of the original participants in the CH2M HILL sustainability skunk works. At the end of 2001, Blosser was on secondment to the State of Oregon as the Director of the Department of Land Conservation Management.

- Sustainability gives you an effective approach to working on complex planning issues where you don't want to solve one problem and create another. You need an intellectual framework to approach complex issues and sustainability gives you that.

- The great innovations in large organizations usually come up serendipitously from people with a passion to do it whether or not they have any initial endorsement from the top. Once you get the thing going, then seek endorsement. All you need is the energy of a small group of passionate people that doesn't get shut down by upper management. Our initiative would have died if the first thing we had to do was get the board of directors to endorse a sustainability policy. Having both energy from the bottom and encouragement from the top works best.

Jo Danko, Operations and Project Delivery Director, Energy and Industrial Systems

Danko was trained in chemical engineering with a special interest in environmental engineering and alternative energy engineering. He started with CH2M HILL when he graduated with his master's degree in 1985. Danko recalls that as long as he can remember he wanted to have a positive impact on the built world. Someone told him that he should get into engineering.

- Gaining knowledge is a fundamental cornerstone. Increase awareness. Read *The Natural Step for Business* and *The Ecology of Commerce* and much more, just so you can contemplate sustainability in your own mind and in your own internal consciousness, does this make sense? Test it yourself. Look at the world. Read different and contrary opinions, and then if your conclusion is that the principles of sustainability make sense, try to incorporate them into your own world, your own business and personal life.

- Continue to move forward creatively in your own world with sustainability, and seek the counsel of an expanded network that exists in your organization and in every community. The synergy of multiple humans, a community, enables you to participate in the formation of more robust solutions that will take you much further than you alone could do it.

- Know how the decision makers in the organization make their decisions. What are the critical issues that they are going to need to have addressed before they can proceed with investments in more sustainable practices? It's important to understand how the decision maker in that company is going to be evaluated and valued. Until you understand that, you don't know how to respond to help them move forward.

- It's a dance. It's a matter of knowing what steps you can take, what dance it is that decision makers really can do, which ones can't they do. Are they even on the dance floor yet? If not, can you help them find it?

Jan Dell, Director of Sustainable Manufacturing, Energy and Industrial Systems

Jan Dell has been working in the field of environmental engineering for approximately 20 years. She began her career as a chemical engineer in the most traditional sense, working for a major oil company researching ways to enhance oil recovery. She migrated towards multi-national manufacturing and has been working on projects in Asia since 1986. Today she is involved in many aspects of corporate responsibility and sustainable engineering for a range of multi-national businesses. She has worked with Nike and its Asian contract manufacturers since 1998.

- A sustainable business is ultimately everybody's goal. The concepts of sustainable business — sustainable profit, sustainable production, and sustainable consumption — are logical and make good business sense. They are basic to a business's long-term success.

- Get out in the world of corporate responsibility/sustainability, listen to people, go to conferences, and read books. Listen to companies tell their stories. Develop relationships with those companies, non-governmental organizations, or with consultants that have done work with those companies, and learn from others.

- Understand and respect the culture of each organization. Most companies have a desire to be responsible corporations, but the approach that is taken depends on the company's culture. There are many good ways to implement sustainable business practices. A diversity of approaches should be considered.

Mike Kennedy, President of Regional Operations

Mike Kennedy has spent his entire thirty-year professional career at CH2M HILL. He is one of the firm's senior leaders.

- Start with your own company and your own staff. Every company internally has people who care about the issue of sustainability. Find those people, give them a voice, enable their voice to be heard, support them, and focus some of your internal operations around this.

- Then listen to the environment that you work in, to the marketplace, see who is out there, find places you can hook into the movements that are at work in our society.

Linda Morse, Director, Sustainable Development Practice Group

Morse, a professional at CH2M HILL in the San Francisco Bay area, has a master's degree in environmental planning. She was an original member of the sustainability skunk works and has helped it evolve into the Sustainability Practice Group that she now directs.

- The first thing to understand is that sustainability is a journey. This is not something that is going to happen overnight. Some new technologies arrive on the scene and there is an immediate adoption. But it is usually a discrete technology and not a shift in the way of thinking. At a personal level, anyone who gets engaged in this kind of work needs to understand that the victories may be small and over a long time. Some of them may be large, and that's great. But people just have to continue to work away at it because change may not be as dramatic as you may want to see it.

- Second, in helping other people move in this direction emphasize specific practical applications and relevant instances that are familiar to them. Theory is also important, but people want to know how to apply sustainability. Many people want to hear a little theory but then they want to know how to do it.

- Finally, from our point of view as a service provider and consulting firm, understanding and being able to articulate the business case for sustainability is extremely important. Understand how sustainability can be relevant and valuable to your clients, understand your client's needs, and understand how the two connect.

Andrea Ramage, Organizational Greening Manager

Ramage started her career as a geotechnical engineer. Developing a broader interest in the environment, she initiated a pilot program creating a green team in the Portland office of CH2M HILL to bring more environmentally sustainable practices into the office. She was also a member of the sustainability skunk works and has helped that group evolve into the Sustainability Practice Group. She is now spearheading a national office greening initiative for the firm.

- It's important to recognize that greening your company is an organizational change effort. It's not just a dissemination of technical knowledge. It is definitely an organizational change effort where you are appealing to people's hearts and minds and inspiring them to action. Take time to educate yourself about what makes such efforts succeed or fail.

- Spend time up front building leadership support, and begin to work throughout the organization to build leadership support using informal champions to help you. Many folks who are not used to being in a leadership position look up for their direction, and if they don't see the environmental stewardship message delivered very often they start to question whether it is truly a direction the company wants to go. Help your leaders be vocal and visible.

- I've learned to allow my idealism and my sense of what's right to provide me with the energy to keep pushing for changes, and I've also learned to express what needs to be done in language that people will understand. In other words, in CH2M HILL and other businesses, what people are going to understand is business value, so I've learned to express the benefits of sustainable and green approaches in terms of business value.

Nicholas Sonntag, President, CH2M HILL Canada

Nicholas Sonntag graduated with a degree in engineering physics 30 years ago at the University of British Columbia, co-founded and built a Canadian-based international environmental consulting firm, took on a series of increasingly responsible roles internationally in the field of sustainable development, and then joined CH2M HILL in 2000 as the president of the Canadian firm.

- The movement toward sustainability definitely cannot be top down. It can't be the president of a company telling everybody 'thou shall now think of things this way and only do work following the principles of SD.' It has to be a shared process of learning. It has to be a continuing dialogue. It has to be a path of discovery. The staff has to discover the value of the concepts, the various methodologies, and the process. They have to have their own personal awareness and insight as to the value of sustainable development otherwise it becomes very superficial and doesn't go deep enough.

- An understanding and appreciation of sustainability is something that happens over time and requires the kind of dialogue that we have established at CH2M HILL. We have put our staff through an intensive training to facilitate exploration of different aspects of sustainability. It is critical that they discover the weaknesses as well as the strengths, and have an opportunity to expand their understanding. Ultimately, they eliminate key uncertainties and approach SD from a position of commitment.

- It is critical to work proactively with clients. We don't manufacture and sell them products off-the-shelf. Rather we offer a service, a very sophisticated service, which takes advantage of the expertise of our staff, our awareness of innovative technologies, and ultimately our ability to bring key technologies, people, and processes to the table. As a result, we respond to our clients' needs and we are, to a great extent, driven by our clients' objectives. We do, however, have an opportunity to shape those objectives by working proactively with our clients and helping them appreciate there are different options, some of which are in line with SD principles. They are challenged to find a solution that is more benign or more respectful of the social and natural environment while still providing the same service and benefit. So in a sense we follow as well as lead, as in a true partnership. This way, we can work proactively with our clients, and move together, step by step, toward sustainability.

Bill Wallace, Senior Vice-President, New Markets and Technology Director

Bill Wallace is currently the firm's representative on the World Business Council for Sustainable Development (WBCSD), which is an organization of approximately 150 of the world's largest corporations and professional service firms.

- I think the first thing you need to do is to understand 'sustainability' and define it in terms that the company understands. Unless the company can understand sustainability on its own terms, in its own language, you're not going to get anywhere.

- Once you can make that translation and say, 'How am I going to benefit from this change? What do I have to do to be prepared for this? How do I have to deal with it?' you can then begin to influence the whole enterprise, and the competitive strategy of the firm, because if you understand and can translate sustainability into the organization's own terms, then the next question is: 'What kind of a firm do we want to be if the trends in society continue the way they seem to be going?'

- Ultimately, you will need to be able to compete in that world, and so the next step is to ask how that changes your competitive strategy: You ask, 'How am I going to compete in a world where sustainability is important?'

FINAL REFLECTIONS

In our view, CH2M HILL is the sleeping giant of sustainability. And this giant is gently awakening to its own strength, capacity, and potential in the arena of sustainable development. As is obvious from the preceding description, this is an organization whose technical strengths are exactly those required for a sustainable global population that now numbers in the billions. Clean water, waste water, environmental remediation, energy — the list of the firm's capabilities continues as does the similar list of the skills necessary to create the sustainable society.

The emergence of sustainability within CH2M HILL is practically a textbook example of innovation diffusion. From the insights and passion of a handful of sustainability innovators dispersed across the firm, spreading to more and more early adopters, attaining sufficient institutional buy-in and credibility to be formally recognized as an actual practice group, becoming part of the firm's official policy, and moving toward becoming part of the way the practice is conducted, sustainability as a social construct is growing stronger within the culture and worldview of CH2M HILL.

It would now seem that the only real tiger standing in the path of the full integration of sustainability into CH2M HILL's practice worldwide is the learning and experience required to demonstrate value to the client. This too is underway. Increasing examples of financially and technically successful projects that integrate sustainability are emerging within the firm's global practice. As more clients understand the negative implications of unsustainable trends, more client early adopters are asking for sustainability expertise and services from the firm. As more and more sophisticated clients learn of the long-term financial and operational advantages of sustainability to their projects, they are more and more requesting — and expecting — this expertise from the firm.

The senior leaders of CH2M HILL recognize the importance of sustainability both to the world and to the future of the firm. That is very clear. However, they are wise enough and astute enough to also recognize that this innovation, like all others before it, has to be embraced by the firm and its professional culture in the time-honored way that has become a source of great strength to the firm and great security to its clients.

CHAPTER 8

DANCING LESSONS

*So, I think I would say, enjoy the process of learning to
dance. The process of our profession, and not its final
achievement, is the heart and soul of dance.*

— Jacques d'Amboise[1]

*Ballet technique is arbitrary and very difficult.
It never becomes easy — It becomes possible.*

— Agnes de Mille[2]

LEARNING THE STEPS

WHERE DO WE BEGIN in this dance of sustainability? What can we
learn from the steps taken by other innovative performers and
choreographers? One of the first lessons we learn is that sustainability
is a journey, not a destination. The process, not the final achievement,
is the heart and soul of this dance. Sustainable development consists
of countless decisions and actions taken day-to-day by individuals,
teams, organizations, communities, nations and international bodies.
Sustainability is the emergent property of these countless parts and
their relationships in the global system.

Our challenge is to determine how to contribute to the greater
likelihood that sustainability, rather than unsustainability, will prevail.
We need to figure out how our individual and organizational decisions
and actions are currently contributing to the unsustainable direction
of the system so that we can make better decisions and engage in more
effective actions that contribute to both local and global well-being.
All of the organizations featured in this book are still learning the early
steps of this evolutionary dance. However, they are far enough along
so that we can learn a great deal from their experience.

In *The Natural Step for Business*, we presented a wide array of tools and methodologies linked to eight aspects that are important for sustainability change initiatives in organizations: leadership; vision and strategy; training, education and coaching; employee involvement; practical application and innovation; feedback and measurement; influence; and business function integration. Our work with the organizations that are featured in this book validates those aspects, tools and methodologies. Rather than repeat them here, we refer you to our companion book.[3]

In this chapter, we focus on six themes that have emerged from our work with the organizations featured in this book as well as those in *The Natural Step for Business*. We then explore four dynamics that we have observed which influence both the velocity and trajectory of change in organizations. Finally, we provide examples of steps that some innovative organizations are taking toward instituting more sustainable practices. To reinforce the fact that this sustainability dance can take place on every level and in every sector, these additional case examples are drawn from small, medium and large organizations and from the financial profit, social profit (otherwise known as non-profit) and governmental sectors.

In our work with numerous organizations, six themes, or areas to consider, have emerged:

1. Know the tigers you are inviting to dance and understand the nature of the dance.

2. Take the time to learn what you can about the issues around sustainability and social responsibility and then articulate why these issues are important to your organization.

3. Think in systems.

4. Look for leverage points in your system.

5. Stay focused.

6. Link sustainability thinking to the institutional lifeblood of the organization.

1. Know the tigers you are inviting to dance and understand the nature of the dance.

The first place to start with any change initiative is to know something about the nature of the change you seek to make and the context within which it must occur. One of the first challenges attached to change around sustainability is that our households, businesses and communities are deeply entrenched in systems that currently contribute to an unsustainable trajectory for global society. Consider, for example, the degree to which the production and delivery of goods and services is so dependent upon fossil fuel-based production systems and transportation. Seriously introducing meaningful sustainability-oriented practices and processes means that we may need to question, and most likely change, some of these systems. So we are talking about transforming systems, not simply making adjustments in the existing systems.

Donella Meadows wrote a valuable article entitled "Places to Intervene in a System,"[4] which explores how to most effectively find leverage, or places where small changes can have big effects, when dealing with systems change. One of the most powerful and effective places to intervene when seeking to advance change in a system is at the level of the worldview we hold, the paradigm we believe in. A paradigm is constructed from the great, unstated assumptions that constitute an individual's or a society's deepest set of beliefs about how the world works; in other words, the stories we tell ourselves about what is true in the world. "Paradigms are the sources of systems. From them come goals, information flows, feedbacks, stocks, flows."[5] Meadows comments, "There's nothing physical or expensive or even slow about paradigm change. In a single individual it can happen in a millisecond. All it takes is a click in the mind, a new way of seeing."[6] Nonetheless, individuals and societies resist challenges to their paradigms harder than they resist any other kind of change. So although a paradigm shift may be called for when dealing with sustainability, and you may have experienced such a paradigm shift yourself, the best you may be able to do is to influence the system through other less powerful or transformative, albeit still effective, means.

Besides understanding the nature of the change introduced by sustainability thinking, you need to know the context within which that change must occur. Every organization is a system with a unique culture and purpose. You should understand the system's structure as well as its goals — the policies and procedures for communications, assessment, change management, maintenance, and the rules that govern, reward or punish behavior in the system. As a leader or a change agent, you should be aware of the culture's power over the pace, direction and strategy for the change you seek to influence.

An additional challenge is that the concept "sustainability" often seems difficult to define in practical, concrete terms. We often hear that sustainability, as a concept, is too abstract to convert into action. This viewpoint is understandable given that sustainability does not manifest on the level of the individual, organization or community; it manifests on the level of the global system. Thus sustainability may seem like an abstract concept because *it manifests at a more complex systems level than the level where most of us operate*. Yet the sustainability of society globally depends upon the decisions and actions we take at the individual, organizational and community levels. Therefore it is appropriate for us to focus on concrete practical actions at these levels. Our challenge as individuals, organizations and communities is to understand what needs to happen on the global system level so our decisions and actions are most likely to contribute to success on that level. This is not really such a foreign concept. We create visions and missions for our organizations. We then align a vast array of decisions and actions so the parts of the organization contribute to achieving them.

This is where The Natural Step framework for sustainability provides important value. It helps clarify what needs to happen on a global level if society is to operate in harmony with the rest of nature, based on four minimum conditions for sustainability in that system. This provides a compass, a true north. Individuals, organizations and communities still need to decide how they can operate in alignment with those conditions, how they will steer toward true north, how their participation in the larger system will contribute to a sustainable global society. Happily there are a growing number of guidance systems that can assist in this process such as zero waste strategies, design for environment strategies and tools, environmental and sustainability management systems, comprehensive sustainability plans, and radical resource productivity strategies.

2. Take the time to learn what you can about the issues around sustainability and social responsibility and then articulate why these issues are important to your organization.

A consistent theme that emerges in the featured organizations is the fundamental importance of learning and education. Bob Warren, former Assistant Chief of Staff for Environmental Affairs, Marine Corps Base, Camp Lejeune points out, "If you take on anything new in life, you have to have enough commitment to be able to learn to understand it. You have to be willing to make an investment in knowledge."

Even if the concept of sustainability seems abstract, it is possible to study and understand the implications of continued unsustainable practices and trends on a global level, and to extrapolate the meaning of these implications to a personal and organizational level. We are surrounded by well-documented evidence about the symptoms of unsustainable behavior, as pointed out in chapter 2. It is also possible to study and understand how behaviors that we take for granted today contribute so significantly to the unsustainable direction of society. Making this knowledge accessible is one of the strengths of The Natural Step framework for sustainability.

One of the challenges around serious education about sustainability and social responsibility issues is that the information and knowledge can be overwhelming, particularly when people are exposed to it in a systematic way for the first time. It is a challenging and delicate balancing act to provide an honest picture of the current state of the world so that people can understand the urgency and necessity to take action and change and yet to not overwhelm people with "gloom and doom" such that they feel powerless to make a difference. In our view, education about sustainability needs to lead to a better understanding of the trends that will affect and influence our future actions and possibilities. With that understanding, we can make wiser and better-informed decisions in the present. The point of education is not to paralyze but to empower. That being said, the power of education depends on our ability to make an honest assessment of the reality we are dealing with. We need to be realistic about where we are if we are going to be wise about where we are going.

As important as it is to explore the consequences and implications of unsustainability, it is equally essential to explore real solutions. One way is to look at the experiences of other organizations and communities in their quest to develop more sustainable practices. It helps to integrate case studies into the educational process and to hear directly from practitioners in organizations that are further along in their journey. Nike, for example, brought in some of the leading thinkers and practitioners in the field of sustainable development, and from other companies, to meet with their internal sustainability champions.

CH2M HILL brought in external guest presenters from corporations such as Interface and Nike, and also from the Resort Municipality of Whistler, as part of their internal educational process. Nike brings sustainability and corporate responsibility experts to Portland, Oregon, to advise the company, and then participate in a speaker series, provided free to the public. These talks are videotaped and made available for continued internal education. The Early Adopters of The Natural Step framework in Whistler have instituted a sustainability speaker series, also provided as a public service, as an educational opportunity for all members of the community. These talks are taped and shown on the local cable channel. In this way, the diffusion of the innovation of sustainability gets continued repetition and reinforcement in ever-widening circles.

Who should be engaged in this educational process? Practitioners in every organization that we work with confirm that it is essential for the organization's top leadership to participate in an educational process. If the senior leadership understands the connections and implications of these issues to the organization's mission, purpose and future success, and views action toward more sustainable practices as an organizational priority, they pave the way for others to act.

Ultimately, for real innovation and change to take place, it is valuable to provide education for everyone in the organization. How this is accomplished varies. Nike began with 100 change agents across their global organization. CH2M HILL began by developing a pilot project in Canada. Each organization among the Early Adopters in Whistler has developed a team of facilitators who participated in two levels of sustainability facilitation education. These teams then work within their own organizations to train and coach others in sustainability thinking and action. Although turnover in the resort community is high (as much as 80 percent on a seasonal basis in some organizations), the Whistler Early Adopter organizations have set goals to train all employees and to integrate sustainability education into the orientation for all new employees. In this way, not only are permanent staff becoming more skilled in sustainability thought and practice, thousands of others are exposed to the concepts of sustainability and will take this with them, to some degree, wherever they go.

In Rejuvenation, Inc. of Portland, Oregon (see page 256), education about sustainability using The Natural Step framework is being systematically and strategically disseminated throughout the organization, starting with a core group of managers and branching out to supervisors, master craftsmen, and ultimately to line employees. All Rejuvenation, Inc. managers, a group of 15 to 20 individuals, received a one-hour briefing by the Oregon Natural Step Network and then attended either a full-day or half-day introductory workshop offered by the Network. In the first two years, Rejuvenation, Inc. focused on training personnel in the manufacturing side of the business, as that is where the greatest environmental impacts occur. In the third year, education is being extended to the retail side. In Norm Thompson Outfitters, also of Portland (see page 251), all full-time associates receive a four-hour training session in The Natural Step framework. It is important to remember, however, that education, albeit a fundamental platform for action, is not enough. The concepts and trends around sustainability need to be linked in a meaningful way to the culture, concerns, language, and realities of the organization.

3. Think in systems.

How does an individual, team, organization or community begin to think and act from a systems perspective? One approach that we have found helpful in our work with teams and organizations is to create a map of their systems so that important patterns of connections become more evident. We include not only the conventional elements of the organization's value chain — suppliers, investors, employees, clients, customers — but also the fundamental connections and relationships that the entire value chain has with natural and social systems. Including the biosphere, the lithosphere and the social sphere in a systems map enables a team or organization to see a more complete picture of its operations. They are able to more clearly understand the ecological, social and financial relationships, impacts, and consequences of their operations, and to identify leverage areas where actions and decisions can make the biggest difference.

Ray Anderson, founder and chairman of Interface, Inc., provides an excellent example of this type of systems mapping in his book, *Mid-Course Correction*,[7] and on the Interface website.[8] This map goes beyond the usual picture of a company's relationships with its suppliers and customers and extends the picture to the company's relationship with the Earth's crust (lithosphere), a primary source of its material input, and the region of the Earth's living systems (biosphere), a primary recipient of direct and indirect waste. The map accounts for material and energy inputs and wastes that not only result from the company's direct operations and processes, but also occur during the entire life cycle of its products. The map also depicts the impacts and influence that the company's existence has on human communities (social sphere), directly and indirectly. It places the organization and its actions within the wider context of system relationships. Nike, Starbucks, and several of the Early Adopter organizations in Whistler have used this kind of systems mapping to help identify key focus areas needing more sustainable practices.

When mapping your system or otherwise seeking to bring a systems perspective to the understanding of your operations, it is valuable to create a microcosm of your system by working with internal cross-functional teams. So often, organizations have specialized "silos" that focus specifically on their part of the system and seldom communicate with or take into account the dynamics that occur in other "silos." Whenever possible, we like to help form and work with cross-functional teams on sustainability issues because they broaden people's understanding of their organization's operations and of their role in it. Usually being part of a cross-functional group, while often met with skepticism initially ("we're the experts in our part of the business"), generates new and useful insights. Dennis Stefanacci, Senior Vice-President of Corporate Responsibility for Starbucks Coffee Company, views his role from a systems perspective. Whenever there is a significant issue, Stefanacci brings together a cross-functional team to look at it so that any decisions made will benefit from viewpoints from across the Starbucks system.

In addition to operating with internal cross-functional teams, you can develop a better systems perspective by inviting key external stakeholders to help you "see" and better understand the issues and trends. Such stakeholder input is also valuable in helping you see and understand the real and perceived impacts and influence your organization has on ecological and social systems. One of the ways to achieve meaningful stakeholder input is to build strong partnerships with key external stakeholder groups.

4. Look for the best leverage points in your system.

As described in chapter 3, every individual and organization operates within varying spheres of concern, influence and control. Although sustainability on a global systems level has become a common concern for many of them, genuine actions that will contribute to such sustainability must take place within their actual spheres of control and influence.

After you have drawn a systems map of major relationships, you can determine what on the map falls within the organization's sphere of concern, its sphere of influence and its sphere of control. Then you examine where opportunities exist to find the highest leverage toward change in the direction of more sustainable practices. The right leverage points allow an organization to use its resources to greatest advantage and with greatest efficiency for the purpose of meeting its objectives. In our work with Starbucks, for example, the objectives were to understand the company's global ecological footprint and make meaningful progress toward reducing it. By mapping the Starbucks system, a cross-functional team was able to identify areas where action would have both business and sustainability impact. Although the team's sphere of concern embraces the global system, sustainability and the future, to focus their efforts on meaningful action, they needed to identify areas where the company has real control or influence.

5. Stay focused.

Just as our sphere of concern may extend far beyond the things we can control or influence, so too we must also be realistic about how much we can accomplish with the time and other resources at our disposal, and with the other demands that compete for our attention. We can't do everything we would like to do, so we need to focus our energies and resources on decisions and actions that are meaningful both from a sustainability perspective and the more traditional business perspective of the organization. In our experience, it is beneficial to develop a limited set of sustainability focus areas initially; the organization can essentially put its "stakes in the ground." This facilitates the internal and external communication of the organization's plans and the development of clear and meaningful goals and performance indicators to assess progress. Finally, by focusing on just a few areas, the organization learns from its own experience and develops greater competence in sustainable development. Starbucks, for example, in 2000, determined that it could initially commit firmwide to four key sustainability focus areas. A tremendous lift was given to these initiatives when they became part of the company's business planning process, making all departments accountable for sustainability factors in these areas.

6. Link sustainability thinking to the institutional lifeblood of the organization.

Once the visions, focus areas, goals and objectives have been set, how do they enter the institutional lifeblood of the organization? To answer this question, we must return to the first theme listed in this chapter. You need to know how the organization works. What is its culture? How do individuals within the organization set their priorities? For what results do people get rewarded? How do they know what, among the many things that call for their attention, should actually receive it? Some of the answers to these questions can be found in the institutional systems and processes that are already well-established in the organization such as strategic planning processes, business planning systems, incentive systems, personal goal-setting systems, and management systems.

An organization's lifeblood is enhanced when it links sustainability goals to business accountability and performance. For example, the Starbucks team first identified four key focus areas which were then benchmarked against industry best practices. These focus areas were then presented to and approved by the company's operating council; then the finance and planning department integrated these focus areas into the business planning process. Accountability for sustainability performance is being introduced as a factor in each business plan that is created in the company.

Environmental or sustainability management systems (EMS or SMS)[9] are another important tool for moving sustainability thinking into practice. What we have found is that combining a framework for sustainability with the discipline of an environmental management system is an effective way to integrate sustainability thinking into practice.

Headquartered in Victoria, B.C., British Columbia Buildings Corporation (BCBC), one of the largest real estate owners and managers in North America and a leader in corporate responsibility, took this approach in the creation of the organization's environmental management system. The BCBC team reports:

> We began several years ago to implement a formal Environmental Management System and to seek ISO 14001 registration. One of the things required by ISO is that you set objectives and targets for dealing with your significant environmental aspects, or impacts. In order to get buy-in to the resulting targets, we gathered

together a cross-functional group of staff in a workshop setting to develop those objectives and targets. We set the stage in the workshop with introductions from the president and vice-president in order to stress the importance of the exercise, and we also brought in a consultant with expertise in sustainability as it relates to buildings in order to put the issues in perspective. We then introduced The Natural Step framework and used the A-B-C-D analysis in breakout groups to develop objectives and targets, and then consolidated these targets in the larger group. The Natural Step framework was enormously helpful in bringing everyone to a common understanding of the importance and urgency of the issues. Everybody got it, and the resulting objectives and targets were far more ambitious than we had expected or dared to hope when we were setting up the workshop. There is still the hard work of developing the indicators, the programs and following through with the detailed implementation, but as a result of The Natural Step framework and the inclusive process we are not starting with the bar set too low.

Nike's Footwear Business Unit has defined four long-term goals:

1. Zero waste. Eliminate the concept of waste in product, process, material and energy in any resource that cannot be readily recycled, renewed or reabsorbed into nature.

2. Zero toxic substances. Eliminate substances known/suspected to be harmful to human health or the health of biological systems.

3. 100 percent closed-loop business. Take 100 percent responsibility for products at all stages of product and process life cycle, including end of life.

4. Sustainable growth and profitability. Creating an economy the planet is capable of sustaining indefinitely.

Yet another important vehicle for moving sustainability thinking into the heart of an organization is to conduct transparent reporting — internally and externally — on your goals and your performance.

There is a growing trend for organizations to produce sustainability or corporate social responsibility reports. Such a report should clearly articulate the organization's sustainability game plan with well-defined and measurable goals for moving towards sustainability in the economic, social and environmental dimensions of its operations. The report provides an opportunity for the organization to place its sustainability or corporate responsibility objectives and operating impacts in the context of the geographic, ecosystem and socioeconomic context in which it operates. This helps stakeholders understand how the organization perceives that its actions relate to achieving sustainability on a societal level.

Norm Thompson Outfitters: Sustainability Objectives

We've set what we feel are measurable, significant goals to guide us as we chart our course toward sustainability. Over the next five years, we're committing ourselves to addressing these environmental concerns:

1. **Global warming**
   We shall hold ourselves to a zero net greenhouse gas impact. Toward this goal, we are:

   * Pledging to the Clean Energy Challenge by purchasing green power for our facilities, and encouraging the development of a renewable energy market

   * Analyzing how our products are made and distributed, and minimizing their negative impacts—especially in their transportation

   * Offering alternative commuting incentives to our associates

2. **Toxics**
   We shall reduce or eliminate all identified restricted substances from our products and processes. Toward this goal, we are:

   * Phasing in organic cotton

   * Phasing out PVC

   * Specifying and constantly updating the toxic substances we won't allow in our products

3. Habitat destruction
We shall hold ourselves to a zero negative forestry impact. Toward this goal, we are:

* Developing the market for greener catalogs

* Mailing smarter and preventing waste

* Supporting sustainable forestry

4. Waste
We shall hold ourselves to zero net waste in our facilities. Toward this goal, we are:

* Reducing the amount of office supplies we purchase

* Reusing as much as we can. For example, we take the packaging materials from our inbound vendor shipments and use them again in our outbound shipments, or donate them to organizations who reuse them

* Recycling everything else!

Source: www.normthompson.com

Organizations are just beginning to understand what to report and how to report on environmental and social sustainability aspects of their performance and how to link them to conventional measures of accountability. For leading examples of sustainability and corporate responsibility reports, we refer you to the Nike, Starbucks and Interface websites.[10]

UNDERSTANDING THE DYNAMICS OF THE DANCE

We have observed four fundamental dynamics that influence the direction and speed of change in the dance of sustainability: leadership, participation, partnership and communication.

1. Leadership

What does it mean to be a leader in this ever challenging, often uncertain, essential domain of human endeavor called sustainability? Darcy Winslow of Nike recalls her experience as a choreographer and applies it to the challenge of leadership in this field:

> When leading a group through a dance, the choreographer/teacher always needs to cue the next step four to

eight beats ahead. Without this, you have a group of individuals in chaos, and over time they become frustrated with their 'clumsiness' and move on to other, more pleasant pastimes. Any further ahead than this, you lose your audience with information overload. The goal is to have everyone moving together effortlessly, and if not in similar patterns, then in complementary patterns. Ultimately, they should be having fun and always returning for more and new challenges!

Leadership takes many forms, and different leaders have different leadership styles. In many organizations, the CEO or president embodies the dynamic of leadership. In municipal governments, it is often the mayor or the chief administrative officer. These are the individuals who people, internally and externally, look to for indications of which directions are important and should receive priority within the organization or community. Of course there are also several other leaders within any organization. These are also people that employees look to for direction and approval. Naturally, with any new approach to doing business, such as sustainability or corporate social responsibility, the overt support of the organization's leaders is paramount if the approach is going to receive serious consideration and focus, and more importantly, if precious resources are to be allocated to it.

Each of our four case chapters includes statements that demonstrate leadership commitment to sustainability and social responsibility. We have observed an interesting phenomenon, however. No matter how strong a leader's statements may be about his or her commitment to social responsibility or sustainability, the message has to be delivered consistently and often, and it has to be accompanied by action. It is not enough to say that an organization is committed to a certain direction; the message has to be communicated over and over again, in different venues and media, particularly in contexts that are important for the organization, in the same manner that any other new or important priority or objective for the organization is communicated.

However, statements alone are not enough. Without other evidence of leadership support, leadership statements can leave both internal and external stakeholders doubting the leadership's depth of commitment or sincerity, which can then lead to disillusionment and pushback. Therefore overt statements of commitment and support are necessary but not sufficient to demonstrate leadership commitment.

Other actions, such as Nike's creation of a board level corporate responsibility committee, can effectively communicate serious leadership commitment.

> *The board's creation of this committee reaffirms Nike's commitment to corporate responsibility at every level of our business. The key to a sustainable business, from our perspective, is keeping in mind that we are accountable not only for our financial results, but also for the overall footprint we leave behind, both environmental and social.*
>
> — Phil Knight, CEO & Co-Founder, Nike

Leadership is also demonstrated through the creation of clear organizational policies that set out guiding principles for the organization, and through strategies and objectives that reinforce leadership statements. Several examples of these have been included throughout this book. Leaders need to support their statements, policies and objectives with tangible resources: financial and human. For example, how many staff positions are committed to sustainability and social responsibility? At what level and with what authority in the organization do these positions operate? What kind of budgets do these functions command? What level of financial resources are committed to educate employees? What degree of permission and support do people have to experiment with more sustainable practices? The leaders in all of our case organizations have made commitments in these areas. This support enables the translation of abstract concepts around sustainability and social responsibility to be transformed into concrete actions and practical applications.

Naturally, when we look at leadership we think about the top executives of an organization. However, as Darcy Winslow of Nike reminds us "The domain of leadership is open to all of us. Look for leadership in unconventional places. Look to many parts of the business. A drop here, a drop there, and soon you have a waterfall." Seeking commitment and assurance from the organization's leaders in conventional terms is an important dynamic in this dance of sustainability. What we have observed, however, is that power and leadership also emerge from the middle and grassroots of the organization. For example, Nike's movement toward sustainability emerged from the interests and concerns of the employees. Sarah Severn, a driving force behind the Sustainability Initiative, although not one of Nike's senior executives, became a vital Nike leader in bringing sustainability to the level of a core corporate value. In CH2M HILL, interest around sustainability began with a skunk works of interested employees who met on a voluntary basis. Just as each of us is either part of the problem or part of the solution, we can each be leaders in our own spheres of control and influence.

2. Participation

As we noted in the first chapter, this dance is not a solo performance. Leaders can have great visions and set them out in compelling statements, but it takes empowerment and actual participation for these to become real. Leaders need to enroll and empower the people in their organizations to make a difference. Individuals need to enroll and empower themselves and each other to make a difference. Sometimes this dynamic occurs within an organization and sometimes it is stimulated from outside sources.

The Oregon Natural Step Network (ONSN), a project of the Northwest Earth Institute, provides an excellent example of a nonprofit organization that has played an important role in stimulating interest in sustainability, enrolling people into action, and helping them empower themselves and each other to make a difference in the world. The ONSN has played a vital role in raising awareness about sustainability in the Portland area and throughout Oregon. Through conferences, talks, breakfast meetings, and an effective and active network, the ONSN is not only introducing individuals and organizations to the concepts of sustainability, it is also building a sustainability learning community where best practices can be explored and shared.

One of the goals of the Early Adopter initiative in Whistler is to invite and enroll the entire community in both the vision and the reality of planning, operating, and living in ways to create a more sustainable society. The speaker series, video, toolkits, and workshops are designed to inspire, invite and empower individuals and organizations to make a difference. The Sustainability Initiative at Nike was designed to enroll and empower change agents across the company so they, in turn, could enroll and invite others in their teams to think differently and to begin integrating sustainability principles into their designs, processes, and jobs. Norm Thompson Outfitters is training its employees to identify areas requiring sustainability improvement.

The City of Seattle created the Office of Sustainability and Environment (OSE) to integrate sustainability into its operations. It is exploring ways to most effectively engage the city's 23 departments and approximately 10,000 employees. Appreciating the challenges and opportunities connected to the diffusion of sustainability thinking and practices in this complex social system, the OSE is complementing the development of a sustainability management system with the implementation of targeted and relevant communications and engagement strategies. As a result, the OSE can identify and support early adopters within the government in establishing, strengthening, and communicating best sustainability practices.

Victor Innovatex has started to educate their employees about sustainability, its relationship to their goal of producing high-end commercial textiles, and the ecological and social effects of these products and manufacturing processes. Victor Innovatex recognizes it can achieve this goal most effectively if everyone — the president, sales and marketing staff, and line employees — is engaged in making sustainability operational across all business functions.

These examples show that the locus of action, innovation, leadership and responsibility resides in all those who are enrolled and empowered to participate in the dance. One of the most important dynamics of moving from the abstract notion of sustainability to concrete actions is to enroll, educate and empower everyone so they can participate effectively.

3. Partnerships

It is also important to find the right dancing partners among external stakeholders. We see a growing trend among organizations to seek out and form new partnerships to understand their sustainability impacts better and to address them more effectively. The Early Adopter group at Whistler provides an excellent example from a community perspective. It is a unique governmental/business/non-proft partnership. Starbucks has formed partnerships with Conservation International, CARE and the Calvert Foundation. Nike has formed partnerships with the Global Alliance, Global Compact, the Fair Labor Association, and others to help it become more socially and environmentally responsible. CH2M HILL is working with the World Business Council for Sustainable Development as well as numerous engineering associations. Many of these organizations are members of Business for Social Responsibility.

Victor Innovatex and Nike are each partnering with McDonough Braungart Design Chemistry. Nike and CH2M HILL are also learning together how to advance sustainability objectives. The Natural Step organization itself is engaged in sustainability learning and implementation with hundreds of organizations around the world. Sharing insights, dancing together, collectively we enhance the evolutionary possibilities of the human race and, in so doing, other species as well.

4. Communication

Effective communication is essential to positively influence the velocity and trajectory of change. Sonya Hwang at the Fairmont Chateau Whistler reminds us that the success of any initiative is "about building relationships — it is about communication, communication, communication." As pointed out in chapter 3, communication is *the* vital dynamic that drives the spread of new ideas. If they are not effectively communicated, they go nowhere. Leadership, participation, and partnerships are all built and dependent upon effective communication. Leadership commitment needs to be communicated to inspire. Communication invites and rewards participation and is the lifeblood of partnerships. We learn and teach what is vital and possible through our stories, materials, collateral, books, speeches, reports, videos, conversations, and educational examples.

Be Patient and Practice: step by step by step...

A final word of advice, based on the experience of numerous organizations, is that the integration of sustainability into practice is a long-term process. Although we seek and can usually find significant early wins, it takes time to integrate this new approach to thinking and doing business into operations. It takes time to educate, experiment, communicate, build partnerships, seek and test solutions, measure and assess progress, and confirm or change directions. It takes time to enroll, inspire and involve people. It takes time to learn and master a new choreography and perform with skill and confidence. Across the board, the advice is clear: be patient.

SUSTAINABILITY DANCERS

While you exercise patience in your expectations, it is important that you assertively and proactively put sustainability plans into actual practice in all aspects of organizational and community operations. In this final section we offer brief profiles on the steps some organizations and individuals are taking.

British Columbia Buildings Corporation[11]

British Columbia Buildings Corporation (BCBC) is a unique hybrid organization: operated on business principles, having the public good as part of its mandate, its sole shareholder is the Province of British Columbia. BCBC is what is known in Canada as a Crown corporation — a corporation owned by the provincial or federal government — and was established in 1977 to provide accommodation and real estate services to the provincial government of British Columbia. In 1997, provincial legislation was passed to expand BCBC's mandate to enable the corporation to provide its services to the broader public sector. BCBC, the largest real estate organization in the province and one of the largest real estate owners and managers in North America, has a portfolio of more than 4,000 properties in 260 communities including all the buildings used by the government: office buildings, legislative buildings, hospitals, courthouses and others. Almost 2,400 are owned, more than 1,200 are leased, and the rest are facilities that the corporation maintains. The buildings BCBC manages account for 2.3 million square meters (approximately 23 million square feet) of space, put Can$1.3 million per day into the economy and have an annual energy bill of Can$20 million. To service this real estate, BCBC has approximately 7,000 suppliers across British Columbia.

> *When I first joined BC Buildings Corporation, I was really impressed with the business principles that drove the energy management decisions. This was really brought home to me when I met with the President and requested what I thought was a relatively large budget. I established a foundation for my request by stating that the funding would be used for projects with under a three-year simple payback. The simple answer was to not budget for it! If I could find projects with that good a return he didn't want to establish a budget; he wanted to do the projects and would find the funding immediately.*
>
> — Jack Meredith, Director, Technical Value Department and Green Buildings B.C., BCBC

BCBC's environmental programs have evolved from a focus on energy management and the management of contaminated sites to the establishment of an integrated environmental management system (EMS). The corporation recognizes that buildings make a significant contribution to today's unsustainable consumption of materials and energy. More importantly, BCBC recognizes that there is significant room for improvement and that more environmentally-benign buildings, or "green buildings" as they are often called, are an important part of the solution as society strives for effective environmental stewardship and a sustainable future. In the area of energy, Jack Meredith, Director, Technical Value Department and Green Buildings B.C., reports, "BCBC established an aggressive energy management program in 1978 with a goal to reduce its energy consumption by 25 percent. This goal was achieved within the first five years and more than doubled within ten years when the energy was reduced by 55 percent. The annual energy cost savings due to the program is now over Can\$7 million dollars and by 2001 the accumulated energy cost savings were over Can\$130 million."

> BCBC is using The Natural Step framework as 'a thinking tool' that shapes the organization's shared mental model and provides people with a framework for grappling with sustainability issues.
>
> — Dennis Truss, President & CEO, BCBC

BCBC's strategic plan for 2000 to 2003 includes the introduction and implementation of a rigorous environmental management plan. Using the ISO 14001 EMS framework and principles from The Natural Step framework, BCBC is developing environmental programs that include measurable targets, training, reports, and the involvement of clients and other stakeholders. BCBC recently became the first major public sector organization in Canada to be certified under the ISO 14001 standard.

To help BCBC progress towards sustainable development, the corporation initiated an Organizational Environmental Alignment Project that combines the spheres of leadership, management systems and a shared understanding of sustainability. The resulting Environmental Stewardship Plan incorporates all BCBC's environmental sustainability activities. In this plan, BCBC uses The Natural Step framework to provide the vision that will ensure the future success of strategic planning and environmental management. Meredith comments, "The Natural

Step framework is an amazing tool to focus discussion around what the ideal future state for a situation or project must be. People 'get it' right away and are able to set a vision that leap frogs the barriers that normally stop them when they are looking for incremental improvements."

I have had, ever since I can remember, a deep and spiritual connection with the wilderness and belief in the need to keep as much of it as we can for the physical and mental health of us all. Certainly my annual sea kayak trips on the wilderness of B.C.'s coast keep me grounded and sane. I am terribly afraid that unless we radically change direction as a society, our current unsustainable practices mean that there will be no wilderness for me in the future, let alone my grandchildren's grandchildren. Of all the sustainability issues facing humankind right now, I believe that climate change is the most urgent and the one that relates most closely to what I know and can do something about. Buildings are a huge contributor to the climate change problem but that means they are also part of the solution. That's what motivates me.

— Alex Zimmerman, Environment Manager, BCBC

Although buildings are often invisible on the environmental radar, they have significant environmental impacts. Globally, buildings account for 25 percent of wood harvest, 40 percent of material and energy use, and 17 percent of freshwater use. In Canada, building construction and operation accounts for 39 percent of CO_2 emissions. BCBC sees these environmental impacts as opportunities for improvement, particularly through gains in efficiency and modifying common practices. The international Green Building Challenge, initiated in Canada, helps define what constitutes a "green building." Using a rating system that includes resource consumption, loading (emissions), quality of service, indoor air quality, economics and pre-operation management, this international competition and collaboration inspires lasting changes in building technology and management.

Through B.C.'s Climate Change Business Plan,[12] BCBC has been given the mandate, and Can$1.2 million over three years, to accelerate the adoption of green building principles, practices and technologies in all provincially funded facilities. BCBC has two programs, one for retrofits and one for new buildings, aimed to reduce the environmental impact of provincially funded buildings while fostering growth of the province's environment industry.

Have you ever found yourself sitting at your desk wondering about what the real meaning or purpose of your work is? It's probably a feeling that we have all had at one time or another in our careers, but I can truly state that here in my position at BCBC that sensation has seldom washed over me. The primary reason why I can make a statement like this is that I work in a company where environmental stewardship is not something that is considered after other decisions have been made. As a matter of fact, our mission makes explicit reference to contributing to the sustainability of communities and our environment, and social and environmental responsibility are among our most coveted core values. Whatever the issue has been, be it the introduction of a province wide paper recycling program in the early 1990s or unconditional support for our comprehensive Environmental Stewardship Plan introduced in 2001, decision makers in this company have consistently supported the 'big hairy audacious goals' that have been put forth by myself or my colleagues over the years. This support and commitment has meant a great deal to me as I just don't question what the real meaning or purpose of my work is. I'm here to do my part to protect and preserve our most cherished resource, Mother Earth, and BCBC supports me in this quest.

— Michael Masson, Senior Technical Advisor (Environment), BCBC

The retrofit program targets efficiency improvements at educational and health facilities. It is a voluntary program where projects are designed to be self-financing through reducing energy consumption and maintenance costs. BCBC delivers this program by providing a range of free support services. The new buildings program incorporates green building principles into the design of new facilities. The goal of the program is to develop government facilities requiring less energy to operate, making better use of resources in keeping with the concept of responsible and sustainable development.

The development of a green building, whether new or a retrofit, requires an integrated design process using a team approach. BCBC and its Office of Green Building Technologies develops partnerships across all sectors. The resulting green building projects have evoked enthusiasm from clients and contractors alike. BCBC and its partners have completed successful projects under a variety of budgetary, schedule and climatic constraints. Despite these challenges, BCBC has been able to design green buildings that meet the needs of its clients in a cost-effective, efficient manner while reducing consumption, waste, and operating costs, and providing comfortable, healthy spaces.

> *Environmental stewardship in BC Buildings Corporation is more like a game than like a job. It is like solving a series of complicated puzzles. There are always alternative ways to get the job done. The challenge is to find ways that lessen the environmental impact and save money too. It continues to amaze me how when you get back to basic principles and look at all of the costs that the right environmental solution is not more expensive. Environmental stewardship is addictive. Once you have experienced the feeling of doing the right thing environmentally and at a lower cost, it is hard not to look at every task and ask yourself how can I do this better.*
>
> — Jack Meredith, Director, Technical Value Department and Green Buildings B.C., BCBC

Norm Thompson Outfitters[13]

Norm Thompson Outfitters, Inc. is a 53-year-old privately-held consumer specialty retailer of high-quality clothing, food and gifts headquartered in Hillsboro, Oregon, near Portland. The majority of the company's $200 million annual sales is produced from 80 million catalogues the company distributes nationally, as well as through retail stores in Oregon, and through the company's website. CEO John Emrick has been with the company for 37 years. When the company headquarters were relocated, John and his wife, Jane worked to ensure that the new building had minimal impacts on the environment. Located on a protected wetland, it was the first commercial building to meet Portland General Electric's Earth Smart Gold Standards. It earned a Portland BEST Business Award for innovation in energy efficiency and an American Institute of Architects award for energy and design.

The building:

- Maximizes the use of natural light,

- Features a computerized, efficient energy system that reduces energy use by 35 percent,

- Conserves water with native landscaping, drip irrigation and bioswale,[14]
- Promotes high air quality through operable windows, low VOC paints and glues, and formaldehyde-free underlayment, and
- Incorporates recycled building materials.

Carefully screened and recycled building materials and sustainably harvested products were widely used. Southern exposure and careful design reduced energy needs for light and heat by 35 percent, resulting in annual energy savings of approximately $22,000. Mature trees and a natural wetland were preserved on the building site, and native plants were used for landscaping. Storm water runoff from the company parking lot is now channeled through a bioswale, and back to the wetland, rather than entering the city water system.

Emrick recalls, "When Jane and I had completed our green building, I was so pleased about what we had done and I wanted to let people know about it and why it made sense. Jane said 'You don't just stop with a green building. We need to take a look at our whole business.' We didn't know what to do as far as practices and enlisting all employees to work towards sustainability. The building was just the beginning."

It's going to be a long journey. I think an early adopter of anything runs the risk of burning out before it actually happens. The responsibility that one has to have, when you become aware of what is right, is not to become cynical, not to become discouraged, and not to create walls around people who don't understand. The hardest thing is not to become discouraged. The more you know, the more you know we have a problem – but we will get there. We have to get there.

— John Emrick, CEO, Norm Thompson Outfitters, Inc.

Jane helped to develop a half-day training session, using The Natural Step framework, for Norm Thompson employees. Over a period of nine months, all 400 employees were trained. After the sessions, employees were invited to a brown bag lunch. The lunchroom was divided into four corners for different topics. Employees broke into four groups which groups rotated every 15 minutes and brainstormed possible improvements in specific business functions. By the end of the hour, 192 suggestions had been made. Jane recalls, "They weren't all little ideas. Some were huge." They decided they needed to hire someone full-time to manage sustainability initiatives. Emrick wanted to signal the importance of that position and did so by having it be one of two positions that report directly to him. The other is the president. Derek Smith, the new Corporate Sustainability Manager comments, "The most important point to understand is that corporate responsibility is more about change management than environmental management. The cultural component is the key to actually getting anything done, not understanding all your impacts and setting up the strategy and determining which reductions need to take place. I mean that's all very important, but if you don't have the cultural piece it doesn't matter."

To facilitate that process, they set up an internal advisory board that was hierarchical and cross-functional, representing the whole organization. The task of the advisory board was to answer the question: "What will it take culturally to make this work?" They arrived at several conclusions. Smith recalls, "One was that we needed a roadmap, and so we developed what's called the Sustainability Action Plan. Each department in the company is accountable for goals that are measurable. The action plan is rolled out by the vice-presidents; it is something that they have accountability for." One important advance that Norm Thompson Outfitters has made is the recent conversion of all their catalogues to recycled paper. Emrick comments, "We had the industry leaders meet after we had the test results for the last year and a half, to prove that there was no reduction in sales results from using recycled paper, because of the quality of the paper today. We are trying to influence the industry so that we all change. It is still playing out, but if we're successful in marketing this thought to our peers in industry we will have made an enormous contribution." Emrick says, "I'm proud that we've been an early adopter, somewhat under the radar screen, just doing what we think is right for us. It is great to realize that people are hearing about us and want us to tell our story. One of our goals is to influence others to move in a more sustainable direction."

Some of the other steps that Norm Thompson Outfitters is taking:

Developing the market for greener catalogues: Norm Thompson Outfitters is working with the Alliance for Environmental Innovation, a project of the Environmental Defense Fund[15] and the Pew Charitable Trusts,[16] that works cooperatively with private companies to reduce waste and build environmental considerations into their decisions, creating solutions that make both environmental and business sense. The company's goal is to become a model for their industry.

Supporting sustainable forestry: To ensure long-term forest health, Norm Thompson Outfitters is actively supporting the Certified Forest Products Council,[17] whose mission is to promote responsible buying practices of forest products throughout North America, in an effort to improve the management of forests worldwide.

Organic cotton: Norm Thompson Outfitters is committed to converting all the cotton they sell from conventional to organic by the spring of 2006. They are working with farmers, vendors and other companies to prove demand and to build capacity for organic cotton.

PVC-free: The company is committed to eliminating polyvinyl chloride (PVC) from their product lines by the spring of 2006. They are working with their vendors to substitute less toxic alternatives to PVC that perform just as well and cost no more.

Norm Thompson Outfitters has accepted the National Recycling Challenge, an initiative of the White House Council of Environmental Quality, that is being led by the Federal Environmental Executive, Chair of the White House Task Force on Recycling. In accepting the National Recycling Challenge, the company is currently testing packaging that is recyclable, biodegradable and manufactured from recycled content — while still providing the best protection for its merchandise.

The company donates five percent of pre-tax profits to social and environmental programs in their local community and throughout the world. They have developed a partnership with ABLE Inc., a non-profit organization that makes and sells goods made from fabric scraps. The company also has an on-site organic garden and has instituted awards to associates who initiate the integration of sustainability into their jobs.

In 2000 and 2001, Norm Thompson Outfitters was recognized as the "Rodale Environmental Mailer of the Year," an award presented by the Direct Marketing Association and administered by the U.S. Conference of Mayors. They were recently awarded the United Way "Century Award" for their long-standing corporate giving program.

How should a company get started on this road? Emrick suggests, "Become informed about the world situation. Look for mentors. Don't give up." Smith adds, "Be holistic, be clear and be confident." If you are dealing with a grassroots initiative, "start small, be successful, and communicate how you know you are successful, and replicate and demand replication because you are successful."

Victor Innovatex[18]

Started as a small woolen mill in 1947, Victor Innovatex is now an industry-leading fabric design and manufacturing company serving the contract furniture industry throughout North America and internationally from its headquarters in Saint-Georges, Quebec. The company's mission is "developing, manufacturing and marketing the best commercial fabric solutions for manufacturers and distributors in North America and in all growing markets worldwide."

The company has invested significant time and money in the development of what they call "Eco intelligence initiatives." They are focusing on sustainability improvements in both the products they offer and their manufacturing processes. Victor Innovatex has formed several vital partnerships with industry and sustainability leaders. Prominent among these is McDonough Braungart Design Chemistry (MBDC),[19] which is currently reviewing their manufacturing processes (including chemicals, dyes and energy use) to help develop more sustainability-oriented products to maximize the preservation and protection of the natural environment.

Through a partnership with MBDC and DesignTex,[20] Victor Innovatex is designing and producing the first truly technical nutrient textile optimized for material safety and continual recycling. In partnership with Rohner Textiles,[21] they have licensed Climatex LifeguardFR, biological nutrient textiles produced without toxins and heavy metals and using optimized dye stuffs. They are completely compostable and recyclable.

> *Our goal is to continue building a strong knowledge of sustainable design and manufacturing practices within our industry so that we can be both a resource for and an inspiration to companies who share the same commitment to preserving the health of the planet we share. This is the legacy we intend to leave to future generations.*
>
> — Victor Innovatex, Eco Intelligence Initiatives, website: http://www.victor-innovatex.com/en/eco/our.htm

Through a partnership with Carnegie,[22] Victor Innovatex has created a new high-performance textile called XorelPoly using the environmentally sustainable Xorel tape yarns with polyester yarns. The company is developing new products using recycled fibers from post-consumer polyethylene terephtalate (PET) and post-industrial PET.

Victor Innovatex uses renewable hydroelectric sources for 79 percent of the energy required by its facilities. They focus on quality control standards intended to eliminate waste products and minimize the need for backings and coatings. They have developed a proprietary yarn spinning process that saves natural resources and eliminates the need for lubricants. In processes where oils are used, most are 100 percent biodegradable. They recycle all polyester waste and by-products, plastic wrap and containers, cardboard, and all paper products that cannot be reused in-house. Victor Innovatex has installed a state-of-the-art water pre-treatment system at their new dyeing and finishing facility. They have also assisted their local municipality with the construction of a wastewater plant that returns water to a local river in better condition than when it was removed.

To genuinely integrate sustainability thinking into business practice, Victor Innovatex is providing education in sustainability, based on The Natural Step framework, for their employees in order to involve everyone in moving toward more sustainable practices.

Rejuvenation, Inc.[23]

Rejuvenation, Inc. consists of two organizations: Rejuvenation House Parts, a Portland, Oregon, retail store, and Rejuvenation Lamp and Fixture Co., a mail-order retail business that manufactures and sells period reproduction lighting to consumers. Currently the company employs 200 people, about two-thirds of them in the company's northwest Portland factory. The company has experienced 25 years of steady annual growth, netting $18.5 million in sales in 1999.

Rejuvenation has a long history of involvement in corporate responsibility programs based on the business philosophy of the owner, Jim Kelly. This involvement includes founding membership in the Oregon chapter of Business for Social Responsibility and employee "days of service" in the community. Three days are scheduled per year when employees can leave work to do a service project of their choice. Rejuvenation has also been an environmental leader in the construction and remodeling industry, addressing opportunities to reuse and recycle materials from house demolition. Because Rejuvenation is known for beyond-compliance environmental performance, the

Oregon Department of Environmental Quality invited it to participate in a project that offered consulting services for small to medium-sized companies. The consulting services allowed Rejuvenation to initiate an environmental management system based on the ISO standard and centered on The Natural Step framework. It established an environmental policy, an analysis of material inputs and outputs for the production process, and environmental metrics.

Some of the steps that Rejuvenation, Inc. has taken:

Aspects Analysis. The Natural Step System Conditions provided the basis for Rejuvenation's analysis of its environmental impacts. The Aspects Analysis, conducted as part of the ISO 14001 process, lists 42 activities and gives each a score in six categories: Extraction, Persistency, Toxicity, Biodiversity, Efficiency, and Social Equity. Scores for each category and frequency of activity are then totaled to derive an Aspect Score which helps allow the company to prioritize its activities.

The company took the eight highest-rated activities and set targets for improvement by analyzing legal, technological, financial, business, and customer considerations. Based on these targets, Rejuvenation defined indicators of progress, designing an improvement program for each that identifies staffing resources and timelines.

Manufacturing Processes. The Natural Step System Conditions provide the rationale for several changes that have been adopted or planned. These include more environmentally benign processes for metal cleaning, lacquering, antiquing, polishing, plating, and painting. For example, when metal lighting fixtures are buffed, toxic dust is produced. State environmental regulations prescribe that the company handle this waste stream in a safe and environmentally responsible manner, but the System Conditions call for a higher standard. Thus, Rejuvenation is investing over $10,000 in new buffing technologies that will reduce the generation of lead-bearing dust.

An investment of $110,000 in a water-based ultrasonic cleaning system has resulted in cleaner parts and potential ability to switch to water-based, clear-coating processes.

The company is developing new chemical processes for metal antiquing. The quality and consistency of finishes is especially critical to the company's competitive position. The current process is water-based but can leave contaminants in discharge water and residue from the discharge water that must be disposed. It is investigating process improvements to reduce water flows and technology improvements to purify discharge water more completely.

Packaging. Most Rejuvenation products are manufactured on a made-to-order basis and require considerable packaging, critical for protecting the product. Currently the company uses primarily roll paper as dunnage, along with considerable amounts of plastic materials, especially polyethylene tubes and bubble wrap. Alternative packaging materials and methods are being explored with the hope of lowering labor costs and damage rates while improving environmental performance. Managers performed a life-cycle analysis comparing expandable plastic foam to current packaging. The economic benefit of the foam would be considerable — $200,000 per year primarily due to lower labor costs and better product protection. However, the foam is persistent, and there are no good options for end-of-life management so most of the packaging would end up in the landfill. Because that alternative couldn't meet TNS System Condition two, it wasn't implemented. The company made the decision that the long-term environmental costs outweighed the short-term financial gains.

Energy. From a product life-cycle perspective, energy used by the product is one of the greatest environmental impacts. For eight years Rejuvenation has been designing period lighting that incorporates compact fluorescent bulbs, and it continues to develop new designs. It is now investigating Environmental Protection Agency funding to conduct a more thorough product life-cycle analysis. Managers believe such an analysis would make it possible for them to work with ballast manufacturers to promote compact fluorescent lighting that is more energy efficient.

Product take-back. Years ago ideas were formed to implement a product take-back program. Brass lighting is inherently re-workable, so it is possible to offer discounts either for trade or restoration. As time allows, more effort will be put into the development of a take-back program.

The Oregon Natural Step Network[24]

The Oregon Natural Step Network (ONSN), a project of the non-profit Northwest Earth Institute, supports organizations interested in using The Natural Step framework for sustainability in Oregon, with a focus in the Portland area. The ONSN provides a clear example of how a group of committed individuals can advance sustainability thinking and practice. In June of 1997, the Northwest Earth Institute, in collaboration with Nike and three other firms, hosted a sustainability conference. Nike provided conference space on their campus and donated the in-kind costs. A brochure announcing the event included a letter from Oregon Governor John Kitzhaber noting, "The Natural Step [framework] is an innovative approach for motivating private and governmental organizations to become leaders in the new era of sustainable practices."

After the conference, Dick and Jeanne Roy, founders of the Northwest Earth Institute, brought together about a dozen people who were interested in The Natural Step framework and began to meet regularly to explore how to take the concepts out to a wider public. They planned a series of workshops for the following summer. At each workshop, the organizers circulated a questionnaire that explored whether and how people wanted to move forward toward sustainability. One of the questions asked whether people wanted an organization to facilitate that process. Those who checked "yes" constituted the early initiators of the Oregon Natural Step Network. Other questions assessed levels of interest, engagement and needs that the ONSN might meet in the community. A small ONSN team contacted workshop participants to determine what the community needed and to provide coaching and encouragement for those who were planning to embark on a journey to sustainability.

Based on the information they gained, the team developed a business plan and a toolkit that contained background information on The Natural Step, helpful case studies, and early tools. People asked for more education, so the ONSN conducted more workshops. Interested people wanted to get together, so the ONSN organized breakfast meetings every other month, mainly under the leadership of Clem Laufenberg, one of the original group in Portland committed to implementing The Natural Step framework.

> *The passions that this evokes are incredible. I constantly get phone calls from people saying, 'I want to make my life's work sustainability. Help me figure out how to do that.' I tell them one way is to start by being a volunteer. We get a lot of volunteers. The challenge is managing that judiciously.*
>
> — Duke Castle, Oregon Natural Step Network

Duke Castle, also one of that group, comments, "We laid out a three-step process: first, build awareness about The Natural Step framework; second, educate people; and third, build an infrastructure of people who could network. One idea that emerged was the concept of peer learning groups: people who have a common interest, such as architects, who want to figure out how to use the TNS four System Conditions in their business." Today the ONSN has ten volunteer coaches who are available to follow up with organizations interested in learning more about sustainability. Through the coaching process, the ONSN identifies sectors where interest in sustainable practices is emerging, such as construction, human resources, education, and the public sector. The network of volunteers do the majority of the ONSN work. Empowered by their vision and driven by their passion, the remarkable sustainability learning community created in Portland by the Oregon Natural Step Network is yet another example of ordinary folks accomplishing extraordinary results.

Final Reflections

The themes, dynamics, stories and steps outlined in this chapter are captured most dramatically by a quote generally attributed to Margaret Mead, "Never doubt that a small group of thoughtful, committed people can change the world. Indeed it is the only thing that ever has."[25] Like Wendell Berry, the thoughtful, committed people we feature in this chapter understand that the old story is no longer functioning properly. So they are writing the new story in their day-to-day decisions and actions, starting with those things over which they have some control — what they purchase, how they renovate, how they use energy, how they design processes and products, how they handle their material flows, how they treat their own people, and how they transport goods and people — and by sharing their stories, try to influence others. They are individuals and groups who believe that they can, indeed, make a difference; that they can help move society in a more sustainable, and ultimately, more vibrant direction. What enables them to believe this?

Betty Sue Flowers, award-winning English professor at the University of Texas at Austin, proposes that the future is created, not simply by the facts we know, but, more importantly, by the stories we tell about who we are and who we might become. We cannot change the facts, but we can change the story. For example, we can't change the facts about where and when we were born, but we can tell the story of our lives from a variety of perspectives: as a hero story, victim story, seeker story, inventor story, and others. By changing the story, we also change how we experience the facts that surround us, and how we act upon them. Flowers also proposes that it is not only what we do that creates the future, it is also who we are and how we perceive our relationship to the world. Those things, in turn, influence, and are influenced, by the story we tell ourselves about ourselves. Flowers comments, "There is no handbook for what we are embarked on in this quest for sustainability. There *is* a way of being in relation to the world which allows us to see what's there and how we are all interconnected."[26]

In their book, *The Art of Possibility, Transforming Professional and Personal Life,* Rosamund Stone Zander, family therapist and landscape painter, and Benjamin Zander, conductor of the Boston Philharmonic Orchestra and professor at the New England Conservatory of Music, remind us that although we perceive the world through the evolved structure of our brains, it is our minds that construct meaning from what we perceive. Relying on evidence from neuroscience experiments, the Zanders comment, "We *perceive* only the sensations we are programmed to receive, and our awareness is further restricted by the fact that we *recognize* only those for which we have mental maps or categories."[27] In other words, *we invent our interpretations of reality.* The Zanders recount that "Einstein himself in 1926 told Heisenberg that it was nonsense to found a theory on observable facts alone: 'In reality, the very opposite happens. It is theory which decides what we can observe.'"[28] The Zanders suggest that since it's all invented anyway, "we might as well invent a story or a framework of meaning that enhances our quality of life and the life of those around us."[29] This is essentially what our featured groups are doing.

The Zanders tell a wonderful tale that illustrates how the stories we tell can make all the difference in the world we create:

The Monk's Story

A MONASTERY HAD FALLEN ON HARD TIMES. It was once part of a great order, which, as a result of religious persecution in the 17th and 18th centuries, lost all its branches. It was decimated to the extent that there were only five monks left in the motherhouse: the Abbot and four others, all who were over seventy. Clearly it was a dying order. There was a little hut in the woods surrounding the monastery that the Rabbi from a nearby town occasionally used as a hermitage. One day, it occurred to the Abbot to visit the hermitage to see if the Rabbi could offer any advice that might save the monastery. The two commiserated about how things had changed.

The time came when the Abbot had to leave. Feeling he had failed in his purpose, the Abbot asked the Rabbi once again for any advice that might save the monastery. 'No, I am sorry,' the Rabbi responded, 'I have no advice to give. The only thing I can tell you is that the Messiah is one of you.'

When the other monks heard the Rabbi's words, they wondered what possible significance they might have. Each wondered. 'The Messiah is one of us, here at the monastery? Could it be the Abbot? He has been our leader for so long. Could it be Brother Thomas? He is certainly a holy man; or Brother Elrod who, although crotchety, is very wise; or Brother Phillip who, although passive, is always magically there when he is needed? 'He couldn't mean me! But what if he did?' As each contemplated in this manner, the old monks began to treat each other with extraordinary respect, on the off-chance that one of them might be the Messiah. And on the off-off-chance that each monk himself might be the Messiah, they began to treat themselves with extraordinary respect.

Because the forest in which it was situated was beautiful, people occasionally came to visit the monastery, as most paths led to the dilapidated chapel. They sensed the aura of extraordinary respect that surrounded the five old monks, permeating the atmosphere. They began to come more frequently, bringing their friends. Some of the younger men who came to visit began to engage in conversation with the monks. After a while, one asked if he might join, then another, and another. Within a few years, the monastery became once again a thriving order, and — thanks to the Rabbi's gift — a vibrant, authentic community of light and love for the whole realm.[30]

※ ※ ※

What is the story that you tell yourself about yourself? What is the story that you tell about the future? What are the stories that the organizations we write about tell about themselves, and about the future? Are they moving quickly enough out of the story of a world that is unsustainable, like the dying monastery, to one that is vibrant and thriving? Are they doing the right things, the things that will matter? Do they even know what to do? Will their actions, large and small, make the difference and spread the idea and practice of sustainability fast enough and far enough? Will the things they do really change the world? We don't know, nor do they. We all are learners and teachers, writing a new story, creating a new dance, and making up the dancing lessons as we go.

CHAPTER 9

THE EVOLUTIONARY DANCE

*The truth is, if you asked me to choose between winning
the Tour de France and cancer, I would choose cancer.
Odd as it sounds, I would rather have the title of
cancer survivor than winner of the Tour, because
of what it has done for me as a human being,
a man, a husband, a son, and a father.*[1]

*The one thing the illness has convinced me of beyond
all doubt — more than any experience I've had as an
athlete — is that we are much better than we know.
We have unrealized capacities that sometimes only
emerge in crisis. So if there is a purpose to the suffering
that is cancer, I think it must be this: it's meant to
improve us.*[2]

— Lance Armstrong

WHEN LANCE ARMSTRONG DISCOVERED he had cancer, he made a choice. In retrospect, Armstrong says, "When you think about it, what other choice is there but to hope? We have two options, medically and emotionally: give up or fight like hell."[3] He only found out after his health returned that the odds that had been placed on his survival from cancer were as low as three percent. He ponders — what if he had lost his battle — and concludes, "I still believe I would have gained something in the struggle, because in what time I had left I would have been a more complete, compassionate, and intelligent man, and therefore more alive."[4]

It may well be that, as a civilization, we are already fighting against the odds but none of us knows enough to put a number to it. We don't know what we don't know. We are operating in a state of unconscious incompetence around how to create a world that works, one with human systems that thrive in healthy balance with the other systems in nature. With six billion people on this planet, and apparently more billions on the way, the totality of our activities, the consequences of our human engineering, amount to an evolutionary force on this planet. We are altering the very chemical composition of the air we breathe. We are changing the climate in unpredictable ways. We are endangering the health of the ecosystems in which we live, in many cases destroying them. Like the tiger, we may well be an endangered species without knowing it. We are conducting an uncontrolled and unconscious experiment on the life-supporting systems on which our species and countless other species depend. We are not doing this intentionally. It is an unintended consequence of innumerable decisions and actions taken by billions of people around the world: decisions and actions that make perfect sense to us on an individual or organizational level within the bounds of the stories we tell ourselves about how the world works.

Our hope, and our challenge, is to become conscious of the connection between these individual and organizational decisions and actions, on the one hand, and the health of our global systems, on the other. We can define "health" as the general condition of a system in terms of its soundness, vitality and proper functioning. Sustainability is a state of good health on a global systems level. We can define "disease" as a disorder with recognizable signs: a condition that causes medically or socially significant symptoms. As we pointed out in chapter 2, the symptoms that signal that the health of our global body is in danger are becoming abundantly clear. We do not have to look very far to find them: widespread poverty, pollution, ecosystem destruction, terrorism, and a host of others. Our evolutionary challenge is to face the fact that we are suffering from this disease. This is not an easy thing to do. Armstrong observes:

> We each cope differently with the specter of our deaths. Some people deny it. Some pray. Some numb themselves with tequila. I was tempted to do a little of each of those things. But I think we are supposed to try to face it straightforwardly, armed with nothing but courage. The definition of courage is: the quality of spirit that enables one to encounter danger with firmness and without fear.[5]

At the outset, we said this book is about ordinary people doing the extraordinary. What are they doing that is extraordinary? The same thing that makes Lance Armstrong extraordinary. They are trying to shift the state of health from one of disease to one of soundness, vitality and proper functioning — except in this case, it is the health of our world. They are paying attention to the symptoms and making a choice. Why? Because, as Darcy Winslow of Nike explains it, "Once you know what is going on, you can't un-know it."

Once you see and understand global society and its relationship with the rest of nature, once you understand the interconnectedness of everything in that system, you know that with every decision and action you take personally and professionally, you are either contributing to the health or to the disease of the whole. We each live our life within that whole. With that realization, your life shifts.

As Bob Warren, then Assistant Chief of Staff for Environmental Management of MCB Camp Lejeune commented after hearing Ray Anderson: "My conception of life and our role in the destiny of Planet Earth was changed forever." Donella Meadows reminds us that a shift in paradigm can occur in a millisecond, with an instantaneous realization. Every day, in every organization or group that we work in, or make presentations to, we encounter more and more people who have experienced this paradigm shift. For them, continuing to do things in the same old way is no longer acceptable. This brings us to why what they are doing is extraordinary.

The stories we tell in this book are about people acting with courage and passion. They are acting with and from their hearts. The word "courage," derived from the French word *coeur,* for heart, means "mental or moral strength to venture, persevere, and withstand danger, fear, or difficulty."[6] Why does it take mental or moral strength to make the choice to act on behalf of a healthy global system? Why does it take courage to dance with a tiger?

First of all, when we face the fact that humanity is on an unsustainable trajectory we move from a state of not knowing what we don't know to one of knowing that there is still much that we don't know. We enter a state of conscious incompetence. It is not a comfortable place, especially for people whose professional lives are built upon having achieved and demonstrated a high degree of competence. We don't know whether we have already crossed critical and irreversible ecological thresholds. We don't know what the effect is of all the persistent organic pollutants that we have been pouring into our air and water. We don't know what the implications are of climate change. We don't know whether our odds of survival or success are 3 percent, 50 percent or 90 percent. We don't know if the "treatment" we choose to deal with this disease is the right one, or at least an effective one, or even if it will eventually make things worse. We don't know what the right things are to do. We don't know what is in our power to control or to influence. We don't have the answers. We don't know whether by asking others to come to a similar realization, a similar straightforward facing of the facts, and admitting that we don't have the answers that this realization generates, we may be placing ourselves in danger of losing our credibility, our client, or even our jobs. It takes courage to act in the face of such uncertainty.

Secondly, it takes courage of the sort Armstrong refers to: the ability to encounter danger with firmness and without fear, the courage to believe that you *can* make a difference. We see this determination in the members of the skunk works group in CH2M HILL who, on their own time, and at their own expense, sought each other out in order to build their knowledge and capabilities around sustainable development. We see this resolve in Sarah Severn, Darcy Winslow, Heidi Holt McCloskey, Dave Newman, Dusty Kidd and numerous others in Nike as they forge ahead within a corporate environment that, like most corporate environments, believes that financial statements, revenue figures and the next "cool" product are the primary indicators of system health. We see this courage in John and Jane Emrick of Norm Thompson Outfitters as they break the mold of the business they have devoted years to build on the belief that business can and must lead the way to a healthy future, and that the only way to be successful as a company in the long-term is to contribute to the well-being of society as a whole.

In our view, humanity is at a crossroads of evolutionary importance. These individuals of whom we write, and the organizations in which they can thrive, are evolutionary pioneers, the forerunners who are exploring and drawing the maps of previously uncharted territory making it easier for others to follow with more certainty.

One of the common characteristics of these evolutionary pioneers is their expanded sense of responsibility. They have widened their sphere of concern to embrace not only the future of human society on a global level, but also the future of other species, or as the senior management team of Tourism Whistler said, "We will change the face of tourism so that it restores and protects the natural world for all the children of all the species." So their sphere of concern embraces life across borders, cultures, species and generations. Although they are operating on the level of the subsystem, they are taking responsibility for the health of the whole system because they see the connections between the two. At each off-site training during the nine-month program of sustainability education and integration at Nike, a common theme emerged and was reinforced: you *can* make a difference. Although Starbucks Coffee Company purchases only approximately one percent of the coffee produced in the world, external stakeholders and internal evolutionary pioneers believe that the company *can* make a major difference in the way the complex and entrenched coffee industry operates.

> *Things take place, there is a confluence of events and circumstances, and we can't always know their purpose, or even if there is one. But we can take responsibility for ourselves and be brave.*[7]
>
> — Lance Armstrong

Responsibility comes with this territory, and the understanding that the decisions and actions we take on a sub-systemic level affect the health of the global system. Responsibility comes with the belief that *you* can make a difference. Responsibility begins when we choose to face straightforwardly the fact that the health of the global system is in danger, and yet, in the face of that, we dare to dream of, and consciously choose to create, a system that is globally vital, prosperous and secure, and that functions in balance with the rest of nature.

So it seems only fitting that "corporate responsibility" is a growing trend. If sustainability is a word we use to mean the good health — the vitality and proper functioning — of the global system, then responsibility is the state of being or attitude required to move toward, and hopefully achieve, that condition. When we are responsible, we admit that our actions matter. We accept that we are either part of the problem or we are part of the solution. When we are responsible, we are accountable for the decisions and actions we take that contribute to a sustainable or unsustainable outcome for global society. When we are responsible, we are the ones with the authority to act. When we are truly responsible, others can count on us and trust us to make decisions and to act in ways that benefit the whole over the long-term and not just our own piece of the whole over the short-term. We are at an evolutionary crossroads. We are each responsible for the direction we choose — individually and collectively. That makes us accountable, personally and organizationally, for the world that we create and the legacy that we leave to future generations.

What gives us hope?

- The undeniable courage, intelligence, passion, persistence, humor, patience, determination, and sense of responsibility of the people whose stories you have read. They are evolutionary pioneers. They are role models. They are ordinary people and they are our heroes.

- The demonstration that an individual or a small group of committed people can make a difference. Such individuals and groups of individuals are making a difference in their organizations and their communities by acting responsibly in the areas that are in their spheres of control and by pushing the boundaries in their spheres of influence. In time, we expect that these organizations and communities will, in turn, be able to make a difference in even wider spheres of control and influence. You *can* make a difference. In a system, each thing is ultimately connected to everything else. The power to choose resides in each one of us.

- The fact that sustainability, a relatively new concept on the idea landscape, is finding its way into corporate core values, policies and business plans. It is showing up in the design of products, the way businesses are building, renovating and operating their facilities. It is showing up in how individuals, corporations and communities are beginning to look at the materials, energy and waste that flows through their systems and taking responsibility for how these flows are connected to the planetary systems that connect us all. It is being integrated into school curricula and prime time television. It is becoming part of legislation, community development plans, and the way that communities view themselves.

- The fact that these evolutionary pioneers are finding a voice and a platform for action in mainstream, prominent institutions, which have become influential icons in our culture.

Lance Armstrong's story about himself changed the day that he learned he had cancer. Yet he danced with that tiger and came out a better person for having done so. The story we have been telling ourselves, at least in western, industrialized culture, is that we are somehow separate from nature, that we can export our wastes and our problems to some other place forever, and they have somehow gone away; that we are not responsible for what happens to other parts of the world as a result of the lifestyle decisions and wasteful consumption that we personally choose in our own lives; that others — governments, non-profit organizations, other cultures — are accountable for solving the social and environmental problems we create, and that we are somehow immune from the disease that is infecting our global system. That is the old story. A new one is emerging. The evolutionary pioneers you have met in this book are beginning to tell that new story, and they are making it up as they go along. This takes courage; it is a huge responsibility. But, like Lance Armstrong, we believe that we are much better than we know. We have unrealized capacities. This evolutionary dance, like Ianu's dance, will emerge out of the way we each dance with our tigers and with each other, and, in turn, how these tigers learn to perform a new dance with us.

Appendix

THE NATURAL STEP FRAMEWORK

HOW *DOES* THE PROACTIVE ORGANIZATION or community design the future? The Natural Step provides a simple, yet elegant, framework to integrate environmental issues into the frame of business reality and to move the company toward sustainable development. The framework provides a whole-systems perspective, first articulated by Dr. Karl-Henrik Robèrt and Dr. John Holmberg, that explains systems in the simplest way so an organization can deal with complexity without either getting lost in it or denying that it exists.

The Natural Step framework provides a common language to talk about sustainability and facilitates the creation of shared goals that move the organization or community in a more sustainable direction. These attributes allow scientists, strategists, experts, non-experts, technicians, production line personnel, marketing and sales staff, and accountants, at all levels within an organization, to learn together effectively and to implement actions that lead to a more robust *and* sustainable future.

Despite the complex nature of today's environmental realities, the primary components of the global situation that we confront can be visualized simply. Imagine the walls of a giant funnel where societal demand for resources that are converted into goods and services (clothes, shelter, food, and transportation) and ecosystem services (clean water, clean air, and healthy soil) is increasing while resource availability and the ability of the ecosystem to continue to provide services are decreasing. As aggregate societal demand increases and the capacity to meet those demands decreases, society as a whole, metaphorically, moves into a narrower portion of the funnel. As the funnel narrows, there is less room to maneuver and there are fewer options available. The strategic organization first seeks to understand the larger environmental and social realities that are creating the funnel effect and then assesses its current reality with respect to this broader systemic perspective.

With this perspective firmly in mind, the organization creates scenarios based on how it would look and operate in a sustainable society — one that meets the four System Conditions. To build these scenarios, the organization assumes that, to be successful in this sustainable future, it will also meet all four System Conditions insofar as possible. Once this future desired state is envisioned, the organization "back-casts" from it to determine the steps required to reach it. Each step is planned as a platform for future steps. In contrast to forecasting, by which present methods are extrapolated into the future, back-casting encourages more innovative thinking. Our vision of the future state is less constrained by present, unsustainable practices, so we are able to define new conditions and set new goals.

THE FOUR SYSTEM CONDITIONS FOR SUSTAINABILITY

The four System Conditions were developed to articulate a framework for understanding sustainable human activities through a set of non-overlapping first-order principles. Ironically the very concept of sustainability did not become meaningful until we began to imagine that human activities could create a condition of socioeconomic-ecological unsustainability. For that reason, to derive the first-order principles, we begin by asking through what mechanisms, or activities, can we possibly deteriorate or destroy the complex ecological system on which we all depend. We then indicate that these activities would not occur in a sustainable society. Although we can easily imagine what an unsustainable society would look like, it is harder to define, in detail, how *the* sustainable society will look because there are infinite ways in which such a society could evolve. What we can describe are the principles upon which that evolution must be based, and from there develop a framework for planning in this complex system.

The mechanisms through which human activities can deteriorate, or otherwise negatively affect, nature are then translated into statements concerning the minimum environmental criteria a society must meet to be sustainable. These statements are then articulated as the four System Conditions:

> In the sustainable society, nature is not subject to systematically increasing...
>
> 1. ...concentrations of substances extracted from the Earth's crust,
>
> 2. ...concentrations of substances produced by society,
>
> or

3. ...degradation by physical means;

and in that society . . .

4. ...human needs are met worldwide.

The System Conditions provide a framework for sustainability that makes societal metabolism congruent with the overall conditions of the underlying natural resource base of the Earth. Any sustainable society will meet these principles as a minimum requirement. The first three System Conditions describe the mechanisms through which human activities can deteriorate, disrupt, or destroy the natural cycles on which life on Earth depends. The fourth System Condition signals that society cannot hope to meet the first three System Conditions if the ability of human communities to meet their basic needs is systematically undermined. This is because immediate survival needs will take precedence over long-term sustainability needs and will sabotage the process of aligning with the first three System Conditions.

To understand why these four System Conditions describe the minimum conditions for socioeconomic-ecological sustainability, we need only refer to some very basic scientific understanding of how our complex Earth system works.

SCIENTIFIC BACKGROUND TO THE NATURAL STEP FRAMEWORK

The Natural Step framework begins with two fundamental assumptions. The first is an ethical assumption that destroying the future capacity of the earth to support life is fundamentally wrong. The second is a biophysical and societal assumption that humanity cannot tolerate continual degradation of the environment. We may argue about what levels of degradation and loss of living systems we can survive within, but no one argues that we can survive with continuous loss or degradation. The rules of the biophysical world cannot be amended, changed or negotiated; the laws of nature ultimately supersede man-made laws.

The scientific background upon which The Natural Step framework is built is not new. It derives its force from the most basic laws of science. Nonetheless, at a societal level, we operate as if these scientific laws do not set the context for sustainable development.

Dr. Robèrt approached his inquiry into what is needed for society to be sustainable from the perspective of cellular biology, the area of his expertise and daily work as a cancer researcher. Humans share a common evolution with other animals and plants. All life forms are made of cells that consume resources, create waste, and depend on each other for their biological evolution.

To understand what is required to create a sustainable society, we need to begin with the physical laws that support and constrain life; the evolutionary context of biological life on this planet; and the cyclical principle that governs the metabolism of cells, organisms and societies. This basic scientific background is well known to scientists. However, its relevance to sustainability and to the day-to-day life decisions of individuals and business decisions of companies and other organizations is not as commonly understood.

Basic scientific principles

The following basic scientific principles serve as the foundation for The Natural Step framework:

1. Matter and energy cannot be created or destroyed. (According to the first law of thermodynamics and the principle of matter conservation.)

2. Matter and energy tend to disperse. (According to the second law of thermodynamics.) This means that sooner or later matter that is introduced into society will be released into natural systems.

3. Material quality can be characterized by the concentration and structure of matter. We never consume energy or matter because it is neither created nor destroyed. What we consume is the structure or quality of energy or matter.

4. The net increase in material *quality* on Earth is produced primarily by sun-driven processes. Photo-synthesis is the only large-scale producer of material quality.

Matter and energy cannot be created or destroyed.

Among the most important of the laws that govern energy and material transformations in all physical systems are three important conservation laws upon which physicists agree. The first law deals with energy. Energy exists in a number of different forms including gravitational energy, chemical energy, electrical energy, heat, light and motion, all measured in the same energy units called joules. These different forms of energy are constantly being transformed from one type to another. According to the law of conservation of energy, also known as the first law of thermodynamics, energy is neither destroyed nor created during these transformations. The total energy input always matches the total energy output.

The second conservation law deals with matter: the conservation of mass during material transformations. According to this law, the total mass of the material inputs to a transformation process equals the total mass of the material outputs. This means that to produce certain material products, we must find the equivalent material resources to create those products. It also means that all material resources we exploit and transform through human activities must end up some-where — if not in products, then in the environment.

The third conservation law governs the total quantity of each indi-vidual atomic element during (non-nuclear) material transformations. For example, gasoline doesn't disappear as it is used in a car; it sim-ple changes to a different form, much of it as molecular garbage, that although invisible, exists nonetheless. The total amount of carbon that is released during the combustion of a carbon-based fossil fuel must be the same as the total amount of carbon originally contained in the fuel.

In summary, the Earth is a closed system with respect to matter. This means that the overall mass of the Earth remains constant; we have the same volume of matter now as we did 4.5 billion years ago. In other words, nothing disappears; it just takes a different form.

Matter and energy tend to disperse.

The first law of thermodynamics refers to the quantity of energy dur-ing transformation. The second law of thermodynamics refers to the availability of energy to perform useful work. The first law indicates that the total quantity of energy remains the same before and after transformation. The second law indicates that the quantity of energy becomes less and less available to perform useful work as it passes through successive transformations. Energy becomes more dissipated and less useful. This is referred to as the entropy of a system. States with greater entropy are those where less energy is available to per-form useful work. States with low entropy have more available energy. The second law of thermodynamics suggests that energy and material transformations operate to reduce the available energy in the system and increase the dissipation of matter throughout the system.

Material quality can be characterized by the concentration and structure of matter: that which gives it value.

The laws stating that nothing is created or disappears apply to everything — matter and energy. Every industrial process and every economic activity involves the transformation of materials and energy from one form to another, and these laws provide very specific rules and limits that govern those transformations. The only thing that can disappear is the quality or value of matter. The spontaneous tendency of energy and matter to dissipate, as described in the second law of thermodynamics, is what changes or diminishes material quality. Because nothing disappears and everything tends to disperse, a carpet turns to dust and a car turns to rust, and not the reverse. Dust does not reassemble into carpet or rust into a car. As matter disperses it loses its concentration and structure, in other words it loses its order. Both biological and economic values come from concentration and structure. A bottle of pure ink has economic and functional value, as does a bathtub filled with pure water. As the ink is dripped into the water it disperses and both lose their economic and functional value. The contaminated water, in fact develops a negative economic and functional value, becoming a disposal problem.

The net increase in material quality on Earth is produced primarily by sun-driven processes.

The very existence of continued life on Earth seems to contradict the second law of thermodynamics. Instead of declining into a greater entropic state, the Earth abounds with more and more complex biological organization made possible by the continuous flow of available energy from the sun. The increase in entropy resulting from energy and material transformations is exported from the system in the form of low-grade heat energy. Input energy is needed to counteract the tendency of materials to dissipate. Through the slow process of evolution, the global ecosystem has developed a complex interactive network of material cycles to accomplish this. One example is the carbon cycle through which dissipated (high-entropy) carbon is transformed into fixed (low-entropy) carbon through photosynthesis, the process by which green cells transform solar energy into chemical energy. Solar input provides the supply of high-quality energy, which maintains the ecological balance. The global material cycles provide the process through which degraded materials are returned naturally to available states using this solar input.

To summarize, while the Earth is a closed system with regard to matter, it is an open system with respect to energy. This is the reason why the system hasn't already run down with all of its resources being converted to waste. The Earth receives light from the sun and emits heat into space. The difference between these two forms of energy creates the physical conditions for order in the biosphere — the thin surface layer which is in the path of the sun's energy flow, in which all of the necessary ingredients for life as we know it are mingled.

Green plant cells are the primary producers of this order through photosynthesis. They capture solar radiation in order to concentrate and structure dispersed matter. Green cells are the only ones that produce more order than they consume. Humans and other animals always consume more order than we create.

The evolutionary context

Life evolved on this planet within the possibilities and constraints of the physical laws described in the preceding section. Life continues as an evolving system of increasing complexity and organization. According to our current understanding of the birth and evolution of the universe, the abundance and variety of life and life forms on Earth arose from an evolutionary story dating back billions of years.

If we look back only 3.5 billion years, ignoring for now the billions of years it took for cosmic and stellar evolution, the Earth consisted primarily of a swirling stew of compounds, such as cyanides, carbon dioxide, methane, ammonia — an atmosphere certainly hostile to life as it exists now. Approximately 2.5 billion years ago the first plant cell appeared, most likely in the Earth's earliest oceans. Through their life processes, these primitive cells — over a very long time — contributed to the process of detoxifying the biosphere of compounds such as hydrogen sulfide, carbon monoxide and hydrogen cyanide. This alteration in the biosphere was critical to the evolution of life. This detoxification was accompanied by a gradual enrichment of the atmosphere with oxygen, a by-product of the production of organic molecules from the evolution of blue-green algae.

Additional quantities of oxygen were also released through the deposit of carbon, originating from CO_2, into sediments. This oxygen was first tied up in new chemical bonds, such as the oxidation of iron and other materials. Only after these oxygen sites had been saturated could the concentration of oxygen in the atmosphere increase. As the amount of oxygen increased, the ozone layer in the stratosphere was established. It protected the Earth's surface from ultraviolet radiation, and made it possible for new and progressively more complex life forms to survive. These early plant cells evolved so slowly that even after two or three billion years they were still primitive. The first green plants appeared about 1.5 billion years ago. Photosynthesis — initiated by the blue-green algae — was developed further by green plants. Plants' ability to capture energy from the sun and convert it into chemical energy is the foundation on which all life is built.

Between 0.7 and 1 billion years ago, the first animal cells appeared. The evolutionary process continued to be fueled by a constant supply of ordered energy from the sun as some of the energy captured by green plants was consumed by animal cells in increasingly complex food chains and webs. Both plant and animal life forms grew increasingly complex and diverse, and the giant cycles of which they are a part, and which they helped create, expanded.

In evolutionary terms, the arrival of *homo sapiens* is relatively recent, occurring only an estimated two million years ago. In the short time span since humans discovered how to use concentrated energy resources such as fossil fuels and nuclear power, rapid changes have occurred. Humans now have access to tremendous flows of matter, primarily driven by fossil fuels that result from billions of years of evolution. Unfortunately, the way that we are using these resources results in flooding the biosphere with waste, which puts us at risk of changing its delicate balance.

The scope of human impact on the environment has become an evolutionary force on a planetary scale. Unlike the evolution of the complex systems that make up the biosphere, however, the changes being created by our complex and growing human societies are taking place not over the course of billions or even millions of years, but over the course of decades. Natural resources are shrinking and plant and animal species are becoming extinct at a rate faster than ever before. Meanwhile, carbon dioxide and other pollutants in the atmosphere and oceans are reaching alarming levels. As a rapidly increasing human population strives to duplicate the consumption patterns of the industrialized nations, the scope of this impact is likely to increase while the time for life to adapt to these changes decreases.

The cyclic principle

Billions of years of evolution have resulted in highly complex systems and cycles that maintain biological life on Earth. Plant cells synthesize more structure than is broken down elsewhere in the biosphere. For this to continue, waste must be recycled. In modern industrial society, however, visible and invisible garbage (pollution) accumulates either because it is building up faster than nature can break it down or because it is in a form that nature does not recognize and therefore cannot break down readily.

Just as cells and organisms have metabolisms, so too does society. This metabolism is based on solar energy flows, cyclic material flows, and one-way flows of energy and materials from beneath the Earth's crust. Although industrialization has made it possible to support a large human population — currently more than six billion people worldwide, and growing — this growth has been characterized by a linear processing of energy and materials. However, for the socioeconomic-ecological system to remain in balance, we must process this matter and energy so it can be reintegrated into the sun-driven cycles of nature.

To avoid the systematic accumulation of waste in nature, we must understand the mechanisms through which waste can accumulate. If waste is systematically accumulating in the biosphere at the expense of resources, it is because:

- matter is systematically introduced to the biosphere from the Earth's crust at a faster rate than it is re-deposited,

- matter is produced by society at a faster rate than it can be deposited in the Earth's crust or be used as building blocks in nature, and

- nature is being turned into waste (such as greenhouse gases) while its sun-driven capacity to process waste into resources is diminished.

We process matter and energy to meet our needs, such as food, shelter, clothing, mobility, communication, and comfort. As we do this we create waste. The cyclic principle simply implies that we must either keep that waste out of nature, or nature must be able to use that waste as a building block for more life within a reasonable time scale.

SUMMARY

The System Conditions provide a model for sustainability that creates a framework for society's activities and makes societal metabolism compatible with the overall conditions of its underlying natural resource base. Any sustainable society would meet these principles as a minimum requirement.

In a sustainable society the flows are in balance and nature can reconstitute order at the same rate it is consumed. Society takes no more from the Earth's crust than can be returned to the crust by natural processes. Society does not produce persistent synthetic compounds that build up in nature. Society draws on renewable resources no faster than they can be regenerated, and does not reduce the productive capacity of nature by detrimental manipulation of green surfaces. Human society is efficient, population is stabilized, and basic human needs are met.

Notes

1. The Dance of Sustainability

1 *I Hope You Dance.* Music and lyrics by Mark D. Sanders and Tia Sillers, performed by Lee Ann Womack, Universal-MCA Music Publishing, Inc., 2000.

2 Armstrong, Lance, *It's Not About the Bike: My Journey Back to Life*, New York, G.P. Putnam's Sons, 2000.

3 Ibid, pp. 2-3.

4 Nattrass, Brian and Mary Altomare, *The Natural Step for Business: Wealth, Ecology and the Evolutionary Corporation*, Gabriola Island, B.C., New Society Publishers, 1999.

5 The Natural Step is an international non-profit, scientific research, educational and advisory organization with offices in nine countries focusing on issues of sustainable development. The Natural Step framework for sustainability is an effective science-based method for both conceptualizing and acting upon issues of sustainability. The Natural Step four System Conditions for a sustainable society are part of The Natural Step framework.

6 *I Hope You Dance,* op.cit.

2. A Complex Choreography

1 Berlin, Irving, *Let's Face the Music and Dance*, music and lyrics, 1936.

2 Gallopin, Gilberto, Al Hammond, Paul Raskin, and Rob Swart, *Branch Points: Global Scenarios and Human Choice*, A resource paper of the Global Scenario Group, Stockholm, Stockholm Environment Institute, 1997, p. 9.

3 Ibid.

4 World Commission on Environment and Development, *Our Common Future*, Oxford, Oxford University Press, 1987.

5 See Elkington, John, *Cannibals with Forks: The Triple Bottom Line of 21st Century Business*, Gabriola Island, B.C., New Society Publishers, 1998.

6 See "Message from the Director," Office of Sustainability and Environment website, City of Seattle, www.cityofseattle.net /environment/director.htm.

7 For a more detailed discussion of identifying first-order principles for sustainability,

see Nattrass, Brian and Mary Altomare, op.cit., pp. 21-22.

8 Robèrt, Karl Henrik, et al., "Strategic sustainable development, selection, design and synergies of applied tools." *Journal of Cleaner Production*, Elsevier Science, Ltd., February, 2002. Unpublished manuscript, The Natural Step, Stockholm.

9 Hawken, Paul, Amory Lovins, and L. Hunter Lovins, *Natural Capitalism*, New York, Little, Brown and Company, 1999, pg. 10.

10 Ibid.

11 Benyus, Janine M., *Biomimicry: Innovation Inspired by Nature*, New York, William Morrow, 1997.

12 Ecological footprinting is a concept developed by Bill Rees and Mathis Wackernagel in their book, *Our Ecological Footprint: Reducing Human Impact on the Earth*, Gabriola Island, B.C., New Society Publishers, 1996. The ecological footprint is a non-monetized indicator of human pressure on the biosphere. For any population, its ecological footprint represents the biologically productive area required to meet human needs by producing crops, wood, meat, and fish, to absorb the carbon dioxide emitted from burning fossil fuels, and to provide the space needed for the infrastructure used by that population.

13 World Wildlife Fund International, The UNEP World Conservation Monitoring Centre, Redefining Progress, and the Centre for Sustainability Studies, *Living Planet Report 2000,* London, Banson Production, 2000, p.1.

14 World Resources Institute, United Nations Development Programme, United Nations Environment Programme, and the World Bank, *World Resources 2000-2001*, Washington, D.C., World Resources Institute, 2000.

15 Ibid., pp. 44-47.

16 Ibid., pp. 44-52.

17 Worldwatch Institute, *Vital Signs 2001 The Trends that are Shaping Our Future,* New York, W. W. Norton Company, 2001.

18 North American Commission for Environmental Cooperation, *The North American Mosaic: A State of the Environment Report*, Montreal, 2002. The text of this document is available at: www.cec.org/soe/index.

19 United Nations Environment Programme, "Declaration Of The United Nations Conference On The Human Environment," *Report of the United Nations Conference on the Human Environment* 21st plenary meeting, June 16, 1972, Chapter 11. The text of the declaration can be found on the United Nations Development Programme (UNDP) website at: www.unep.org/Documents/Default.asp?DocumentID=97&ArticleID=1503

20 World Commission on Environment and Development (Brundtland Commission), op.cit.

21 For more information on the Rio Declaration on Environment and Development (Agenda 21) and related documents and conferences, see: the United Nations, Sustainable Development website: www.un.org/esa/sustdev/index.html.

22 Strong, Maurice, *Where on Earth Are We Going?*, Toronto, Alfred A. Knopf, 2000, p. 4.

23 Macy, Joanna, "The Great Turning," *Resurgence Magazine*, Devon, England, Resurgence, issue 186, Jan-Feb, 1998. The text for this article can be found on the Resurgence website: www.gn.apc.org/resurgence/186/macy186.htm

24 Macy, Joanna, "The Great Turning: Reflections on Our Moment in History," *Earth Light Magazine*, Oakland, California. The text of the article can be found on the EarthLight website at: www.earthlight.org/jmacyessay.html

25 Haines, Stephen G., *The Complete Guide to Systems Thinking and Learning*, Amherst, Mass., HRD Press, Inc., 2000, p. 39.

26 The World Business Council for Sustainable Development (WBCSD) is a coalition of 150 international companies united by a shared commitment to sustainable development via the three pillars of economic growth, ecological balance and social progress. Members are drawn from more than 30 countries and 20 major industrial sectors. For more information on the WBCSD, see their website: www.wbcsd.org.

27 The International Forum on Globalization (IFG) is an alliance of sixty leading activists, scholars, economists, researchers and writers formed to stimulate new thinking, joint activity, and public education in response to economic globalization. For more information, see their website: www.ifg.org./

28 United Nations Development Programme, *Human Development Report 1999*, Oxford, Oxford University Press, 1999. The text of this document is available on the UNDP website: www.undp.org/hdro/99.htm

3. Stories We Tell, The World We Create

1 McKee, Robert, *Story: Substance, Structure, Style, and the Principles of Screenwriting*, New York, Harper Collins, 1997, p. 2.

2 Berry, Wendell, "The New Story," *In Context*, no. 12, (winter 1985/86), p 1. The text of this article is available on the In Context website at: www.context.org/ICLIB/IC12/TOC12.htm.

3 Fairley, Julie Reder "Ianu's Dance," www.limetech.com/links/Superintendents/1_Leadership/1_Leadership_Fables/1_Audio_Stories/3_Ianus_Dance.

4 Bateson, Mary Catherine, *Overlapping Lives*, New York, Random House, 2000, p. 5.

5 Burke, Kenneth, "Literature as Equipment for Living," *The Critical Tradition: Classic Texts and Contemporary Trends*, ed. David H. Richter, New York, St. Martin's Press, 1989, pp. 512-17.

6 Bateson, op. cit., p.5.

7 Bateson, Gregory, *Mind and Nature: A Necessary Unity*, New York, Bantam Books, 1988, p. 13.

8 Ibid. p. 15.

9 Mazza, Patrick, "To make our lives a better story: From fragmentation to the unity of mind and nature," *Cascadia Planet Webzine*, Feb. 19, 1997, www.tnews.com/text/unity.html.

10 Quinn, Daniel, *Ishmael*, New York, Bantam Books, 1993.

11 Korzybski, Alfred, *Science and Sanity*,

5th edition. Lakeville, Conn.: The International Non-Aristotelian Library Publishing Company, 1958.

12 Bateson, Gregory, "Form, Substance and Difference," a speech delivered in 1970 at The Paintings of F. Michael Wells Library and posted on the rawpaint.com website: www.rawpaint.com/library/bateson/formsubstancedifference.html.

13 Rogers, op. cit., p. 11.

14 For more information on Innovation Diffusion, see particularly Rogers, Everett M., *Diffusion of Innovations,* 4th edition, New York, The Free Press, 1995; AtKisson, Alan, *Believing Cassandra: An Optimist Looks at a Pessimist's World,* Vermont, Chelsea Green Publishing Company, 1999; and Gladwell, Malcolm, *The Tipping Point: How Little Things Can Make a Big Difference,* Boston, Little, Brown and Company, 2000.

15 Gladwell, op. cit.

16 Rogers, op. cit., p. 163.

17 Gladwell, op. cit., See chapters 4 and 5, pp. 133-192.

18 Capra, Fritjof, *Uncommon Wisdom: Conversations with Remarkable People,* New York, Bantam Books, 1989, p. 78.

19 Zawinski, Andrena, "Profile of Muriel Rukeyser," *Poetry Magazine,* found on PoetryMagazine.com at www.poetry-magazine.com/archives/1999/oct-nov99/rukeyser.htm.

20 Atlee, Tom, "The power of story – the story of paradigm," The Co-Intelligence Institute, Eugene, Oregon, " www.co-intelligence.org/I-powerofstory.html, 2001.

21 Bateson, Mary Catherine, op.cit., p. 12.

4. Nike

1 This quote is accredited to Albert Einstein. See http:charon.sfsu.edu/dance/DanceAphorisms.htm.

2 All figures throughout are in U.S. dollars unless noted otherwise.

3 United Nations, *Human Development Report 2000,* New York, United Nations Publications, 2000, pp. 36-38, www.undp.org/hdr2001/.

4 Ibid. pp.36-38.

5 Srinivasan, T.N., "Living Wage in Poor Countries.," This paper is available electronically on Academic Consortium on International Trade website: www.spp.umich.edu/rsie/acit/ACITViews.htmlhttp://www.unc.edu/depts/livwage/clwa/srinivasan.pdf.

6 Information on Nike's history is taken from the following sources: Katz, Donald, *Just Do It: The Nike Spirit in the Corporate World,* Holbrook, Massachusetts, Adams Publishing, 1994, interviews, and the Nike website: www.nikebiz.com/story/hist_our.shtml

7 More detailed information on Reuse-A-Shoe can be found in the Nike Corporate Responsibility Report www.nikebiz.com/reporting/index.shtml and on the Nike website: www.nikebiz.com.

8 Hawken, Paul, *The Ecology of Commerce: A Declaration of Sustainability,* New York, Harper Business, 1993.

9 McDonough Braungart Design Chemistry, LLC (MBDC), is a product and process design firm dedicated to revolutionizing the design of products and services worldwide. William McDonough and Dr. Michael Braungart founded MBDC in 1995 to promote and shape what they call the "Next Industrial Revolution" through the implementation of eco-effective design principles. For more information see their website: www.mbdc.com.

10 Phil Knight's letter can be found on the inside cover of the Nike Corporate Sustainability Report. The text of the report is available on-line as well as a downloadable format on Nike's website: www.nikebiz.com/reporting/index.shtml.

11 www.nikebiz.com/reporting/index.shtml.

12 Some of this material is adapted from Nike's Corporate Responsibility Report, available on line at www.nikebiz.com/reporting/index.shtml. We strongly recommend, that if you are interested in what Nike is doing and how they are communicating what they are doing to stakeholders, that you take the time to read this report.

13 For more information on The Global Alliance, see their website: www.theglobalalliance.org/.

14 For more information on CERES, see their website: www.ceres.org/.

15 For more information on the Global Compact, see their website: www.unglobalcompact.org/.

16 For more information on the Fair Labor Association, see their website: www.fairlabor.org/.

17 For more information on the World Wildlife Fund, Climate Savers, and the Center for Energy and Climate Change, see their websites: www.worldwildlife.org/climate and www.energyandclimate.org.

18 VOC is the term used to refer to volatile organic compounds, substances containing carbon and different proportions of other elements such as hydrogen, oxygen, fluorine, chlorine, bromine, sulfur, or nitrogen; these substances easily become vapors or gases. VOCs are commonly used as solvents (paint thinners, lacquer thinner, degreasers, and dry cleaning fluids). VOCs have been associated with eye, nose, and throat irritation; headaches, loss of coordination, nausea; damage to liver, kidney, and central nervous system. Some organics can cause cancer in animals; some are suspected or known to cause cancer in humans. For more information see the U.S. Environmental Protection Agency indoor air quality website: www.epa.gov/iaq/voc.html.

19 World Vision is an international relief and development organization, established in 1950. It promotes the well-being of all people, especially children, working on six continents. For more information on World Vision, see their website: www.wvi.org.

20 The International Program on the Elimination of Child Labor (IPEC) works towards the progressive elimination of child labor by strengthening national capacities to address child labor problems, and by creating a worldwide movement to combat it. IPEC's priority target groups are bonded child laborers, children in hazardous working conditions and occupations, and children who are particularly vulnerable, i.e. very young working children (below 12 years of age), and working girls. For more information on IPEC, see their website: www.ilo.org/public/english/standards/ipec.

21 Save the Children was founded in the United States in 1932 as a non-profit child-assistance organization to make lasting, positive change in the lives of children in need. Save the Children currently works in 19 states across the United States as well as in 47 other countries in the developing world to help children and families improve their health, education and economic opportunities. Save the Children is a member of the International Save the Children Alliance, an association of 26 independent organizations that provide child-oriented emergency response, development assistance and advocacy for children's rights in more than 100 countries. For more information on Save the Children, see their website: www.savethechildren.org.

22 The United Nations Children's Fund (UNICEF) was established in 1946 by the United Nations to meet the emergency needs of children in post-war Europe and China. Its full name was the United Nations International Children's Emergency Fund. In 1950, its mandate was broadened to address the long-term needs of children and women in developing countries everywhere. UNICEF became a permanent part of the United Nations system in 1953, when its name was shortened to the United Nations Children's Fund. Headquartered in New York, UNICEF maintains programs in 162 countries and territories. For more information on UNICEF, see their website: www.unicef.org.

23 The Population and Community Development Association (PDA) is a non-governmental, non-profit organization committed to serving Thailand's rural poor. It operates a wide variety of programs covering diverse activities including free vasectomies, income generation programs in villages, forest replanting schemes, vegetable banks, industry relocation into rural areas, mobile health clinics, environmental education, and a democracy project. For more information on the PDA, see their website: www.pda.or.th.

24 The Nike Corporate Responsibility Report is available on-line at www.nikebiz.com/reporting/index.shtml.

25 From Nike's history found on their website at: www.nikebiz.com/story/

hist_our.shtml.

26 See the Phil Knight letter in the inside cover of the Nike Corporate Responsibility Report, op. cit.

5. Starbucks

1 Dicum, Gregory and Nina Luttinger, *The Coffee Book: Anatomy of an Industry from Crop to Last Drop,* New York: The New Press, 1999.

2 Good, Jonathon, "Coffee," an article found on the University of Minnesota, Twin Cities University Libraries, James Ford Bell Library on-line library resources: www.bell.lib. umn.edu/Products/coffee.html, 2001.

3 Dicum, Gregory, and Nina Luttinger, op.cit.

4 Lloyd, Marion and Leila Fadel, "The shadow of globalization, the coffee connection," *Boston Globe,* May 29, 2001, sec. A, p.1. The text of this article is on the Boston Globe Newspaper website: www.boston.com/globe/nation/packages/globalization/ stories/the_coffee_connection.htm.

5 Oxfam America, "Oxfam and Cambridge City Council honor fair trade coffee" (press release), May, 2001. The text of the press release is available on the Oxfam America website: www.oxfamamerica.org/news/prel_fairtradeday.html

6 Lloyd, Marion and Leila Fadel, op. cit.

7 Collier, Robert, "Mourning Coffee," *San Francisco Chronicle,* 20 May, 2001.

8 The background and history of The Starbucks Coffee Company in this section is drawn from: Schultz, Howard, *Pour Your Heart Into It,* New York, Hyperion, 1997, interviews, and the Starbucks website: www.starbucks.com.

9 Melville, Herman, *Moby Dick,* New York, Bantam Books, 1981.

10 Schultz, Howard, op. cit., p. 36.

11 Ibid., p. 62.

12 Ibid., pp. 202-03.

13 Ibid., p. 4.

14 Ibid.

15 Excerpts taken from Schultz, Howard, ibid., pp. 101-02.

16 Ibid., p. 291.

17 For more information on UCO, see the Starbucks website: www.starbucks.com.

18 See the Corporate Responsibility section of the Starbucks website: www.starbucks.com.

19 CARE is one of the world's largest private international relief and development organizations. Founded in the aftermath of World War II, CARE enabled Americans to send more than 100 million CARE Packages to survivors of the conflict in Europe and Asia. CARE has become a leader in sustainable development and emergency aid, reaching tens of millions of people each year in more than 60 countries in Africa, Asia, Europe and Latin America. For more information on CARE, see their website: www.care.org.

20 Conservation International (CI) is a non-profit organization that applies innovations in science, economics, policy and community participation to protect the Earth's richest regions of plant and animal diversity in the hotspots, major tropical wilderness areas and key marine ecosystems. With headquarters in Washington, DC, CI works in more than 30 countries on four continents. For more information about CI's programs, see their website: www.conservation.org.

21 The Calvert Social Investment Foundation (Calvert Foundation) is a non-profit organization, associated with the Calvert Group mutual fund company, that was established to help end poverty through investment. It serves as a facility for individuals and institutions, seeking to place capital on softer terms to finance affordable homes, fund small and micro businesses and to make available essential community services. For more information see their website: www.CalvertFoundation.org.

22 TransFair USA is the only non-profit certification organization for Fair Trade products in the U.S. Their mission is to increase the availability of Fair Trade Certified products throughout the U.S. by creating partnerships with industry, and to increase consumer awareness about the importance of Fair Trade, thereby building consumer demand for Fair Trade Certified products. Currently more than 85 coffee roasters and tea companies offer a Fair Trade option. And consumers can find Fair Trade Certified products in over 7,000 retail

locations across the country. For more information on TransFair USA, see their website: www.transfairusa.org.

23 EnterpriseWorks Worldwide is a non-profit organization that fights poverty through self-help economic development programs for the poor in Africa, Asia, and Latin America. For more information, see their website: www.enterprise-works.org/.

24 A division of Conservation International, The Center for Environmental Leadership in Business provides a forum for collaboration between the private sector and the environmental community. It promotes business practices that reduce industry's ecological footprint, contribute to conservation, and create value for the companies that adopt them. For more information, see their website: www.celb.org/aboutus.html.

25 Founded in 1997, the Consumer's Choice Council is a non-profit association of 66 environmental, consumer, and human rights organizations from 25 different countries, dedicated to protecting the environment and promoting human rights and basic labor standards through eco-labeling. For more information see their website: www.consumerscouncil.org.

26 The Rainforest Alliance is an international non-profit organization dedicated to the conservation of tropical forests for the benefit of the global community. Their mission is to develop and promote economically viable and socially desirable alternatives to the destruction of this endangered, biologically diverse natural resource. For more information see their website: www.rainforest-alliance.org/about/index.html.

27 The Smithsonian Migratory Bird Center focuses on clarifying the causes for declines in migratory bird populations before the situation becomes desperate. For more information on the Center's work on shade grown coffee, see their website: natzoo.si.edu/smbc/Research/Coffee/coffee.htm.

28 The LEED Green Building Rating System is a program of the U.S. Green Building Council. It is a voluntary, consensus-based, market-driven building rating system based on existing proven technology. It evaluates environmental performance from a "whole building" perspective over a building's life cycle, providing a definitive standard for what constitutes a "green building." The LEED rating system is based on accepted energy and environmental principles and strikes a balance between known effective practices and emerging concepts. The LEED rating system has four levels based on the number of points received in the certification process: LEED certified, 26-32 points; silver level, 33-38 points; gold level, 39-51 points, and platinum level, 52+ points. For more information on the LEED system or the U.S. Green Building Council, see the USGBC website: www.usgbc.org.

6. Whistler

1 Resort Municipality of Whistler, *"Whistler Environmental Strategy,"* p. 9. The text of the executive summary of the Whistler Environmental Strategy is available on the website of the Resort Municipality of Whistler, reading room: www.whistler.net/rmow/reading.

2 According to the *World of Education* section on the history and people of British Columbia, evidence points to Drake's 1597 visit to the territory that is now B.C., making him the first European to "discover" this region. For more details see website: library.educationworld.net/canadafacts/bc_history.html.

3 "The Legend of Wountie," Native Lore Index, 2001. The text of this legend is available on the Native Lore Index website: www.ilhawaii.net/~stony/lore15.html.

4 Mountain Agenda, *Mountains of the World: Tourism and Sustainable Mountain Development*, Price, M., Wachs, T., and Byers, E. (editors), prepared for the United Nations Commission on Sustainable Development, Institute of Geography, University of Berne (Centre for Development and Environment) and Swiss Agency for Development and Cooperation. Paul Haupt AG, Berne, 1999. The text for this document is available on the Mountain Forum website: www.mtnforum.org/resources/library/magen99a.htm.

5 World Tourism Organization, *Tourism: 2020 Vision, a New Forecast,* World

Tourism Organization, Madrid, Spain, 1999.

6 Ibid.

7 Mountain Agenda, op. cit.

8 This section on Whistler's history was derived from many sources including: "A brief history of Whistler," Whistler/Blackcomb website: www.whistler-blackcomb.com/company/media/history.asp, "Whistler History," Whistler Museum website: www.whistlermuseum.org/, Squamish History, Squamish Nation website: www.squamish.net/about/salish.htm, and interviews.

9 Resort Municipality of Whistler, *Whistler 2002*, Whistler, B.C., 2000. A copy of this document is available on the RMOW website: (go to www.whistler.net/rmow/reading/ to download a copy of the document).

10 Ibid., p. 17.

11 For the proceedings of the Whistler Sustainability Symposium, held December 2000, please see www.awarewhistler.org/sustainability/seminarproceedings.pdf.

12 For more information on the "Whistler. It's Our Nature" initiative and associated documents see: www.whistleritsournature.ca.

13 Background information on Intrawest Corporation was adapted from their website: www.intrawest.com.

14 Special thanks to Esther Speck for sharing insights from work on her master's thesis on the Fairmont Chateau Whistler and providing detailed information and analysis of their programs.

7. CH2M HILL

1 Allenby, Brad, "Earth Systems Engineering: The World As Human Artifact," *The Bridge*, National Academy of Engineering, vol. 30, no. 1 (spring 2000). The text of this article is available on the American Society of Civil Engineers Professional Community, Sustainable Development website: www.asce.org/sustainabledev/nae_esewha.cfm.

2 Medem Sanjuán, José, "The Role of Engineers in Sustainable Development," speech delivered at the FIDIC 2000 Conference: Sustainability, the challenge of the new millennium, Honolulu, Hawaii, September. Text of the speech can be found on the FIDIC website at: www.fidic.org/conference/2000/talks/monday/medem/default.asp.

3 Ibid.

4 Ibid.

5 *Encarta World English Dictionary*, Microsoft Word Corporation, 1999.

6 Agenda 21 is a comprehensive plan of action to be taken globally, nationally and locally by organizations of the United Nations System, Governments, and Major Groups in every area in which humanity impacts on the environment. Agenda 21, the Rio Declaration on Environment and Development, and the Statement of Principles for the Sustainable Management of Forests were adopted by more than 178 Governments at the United Nations Conference on Environment and Development (UNCED) held in Rio de Janerio, Brazil, June 1992. For more information on Agenda 21 and the UNCED conference, see the United Nations Sustainable Development website: www.un.org/esa/sustdev/agenda21.htm.

7 For more information on CH2M HILL's professional capabilities toward implementing sustainable development solutions, see their websites: CH2M HILL in the U.S.: www.ch2m.com; CH2M HILL in Canada: www.ch2mhillcanada.com.

8 Adaptive management is a system of managing long-term development projects with an appreciation of the uncertainties and potential adaptations that may influence the directions and implementation of the project over time. Adaptive management balances long-term sustainable use of natural resources with protection of those resources to reduce the risk of irreversible biodiversity extinctions. The adaptive management cycle has four steps: set project objectives; conduct resource assessment and monitoring programs, using standard protocols and working with teams of national and international experts; evaluate the biological and ecological findings from the ecosystem under study; and use assessment findings to implement long-term monitoring and to make needed changes in the project plan.

For more information on adaptive management, see: C.S. Holling, (ed.), *Adaptive Environmental Assessment and Management*, vol.3, International Series on Applied Systems Analysis, Toronto, John Wiley & Sons, 1980.

8. Dancing Lessons

1 Jacques d'Amboise is recognized as one of the finest classical dancers of modern times. In 1976, while a principal dancer with the New York City Ballet, d'Amboise founded the not-for-profit National Dance Institute in the belief that the arts have a unique power to engage and motivate individuals towards excellence. For this particular quote, see The Dance Page website, quotes: www.panix.com/~twp/dance/d_quotes.htm.

2 Agnes de Mille was an innovative and influential American dancer and choreographer who was born in Harlem, New York in 1905 and died in 1993. She choreographed many musicals, arranged dances for the films, directed plays, and choreographed television programs. For more information on de Mille, see "Women in American History," *Encyclopedia Britannica* on-line: www.britannica.com/women/articles/de_Mille_Agnes_George.html; for this quote, see the Dancer's Domain website: www.angelfire.com/oh2/chezsarah/bquotes.html.

3 Nattrass, Brian and Mary Altomare, *The Natural Step for Business: Wealth, Ecology and the Evolutionary Corporation*, Gabriola Island, New Society Publishers, 1999, op. cit., Chapter 8.

4 Meadows, Donella, "Places to Intervene in a System." *Whole Earth Magazine*, (winter, 1997). The text of this article is on the Whole Earth website: www.wholeearthmag.com/ArticleBin/109.html.

5 Ibid.

6 Ibid.

7 Anderson, Ray, *Mid-Course Correction: Toward a Sustainable Enterprise, The Interface Model*, Atlanta, Georgia, Peregrinzilla Press, 1999.

8 The Interface model can be found on the Interface website at: www.interfaceinc.com

9 We include a chapter on environmental and sustainability management systems in *The Natural Step for Business*, op. cit., Chapter 9. Also see Dixon Thompson, *Tools for Environmental Management, A Practical Introduction and Guide*, Gabriola Island, B.C., New Society Publishers, 2002.

10 Nike: www.nikebiz.com; Starbucks: www.starbucks.com; Interface: www.interfaceinc.com

11 For more information on BCBC, see their website: www.bcbc.bc.ca/

12 The British Columbia Climate Change Business Plan was adopted in October 2000. It is a three-year plan of specific actions to reduce greenhouse gas emissions, improve air quality, and manage energy costs. The text of the business plan can be downloaded in pdf-format on the government website: http://wlapwww.gov.bc.ca/air/climate/ccbuspln.pdf.

13 For more information on Norm Thompson Outfitters, see their website: www.normthompson.com.

14 A bioswale is a drainage canal that diverts runoff water into a natural area where native wetland plants help absorb and recycle it.

15 The Environmental Defense Fund (EDF) is a leading national non-profit organization based in New York, representing more than 300,000 members. EDF links science, economics, and law to create innovative, equitable, and cost-effective solutions to the most urgent environmental problems. For more information on EDF, see their website: www.environmentaldefense.org.

16 The Pew Charitable Trusts is a philanthropic organization that supports non-profit activities in the areas of culture, education, the environment, health and human services, public policy and religion. Based in Philadelphia, the Trusts make strategic investments that encourage and support citizen participation in addressing critical issues and effecting social change. For more information on the Pew Charitable Trusts, see their website: www.pewtrusts.com.

17 The Certified Forest Products Council is an independent, not-for-profit, voluntary initiative committedto promoting

responsible forest products buying practices throughout North America in an effort to improve forest management practices worldwide. The Certified Forest Products Council actively promotes and facilitates the increased purchase, use and sale of third-party independently certified forest products and promotes the transition away from forest products originating in forests that have been identified as endangered through a scientifically credible, land-based assessment process. For more information on the Certified Forest Products Council, see their website: www.certifiedwood.org/general/who-is-cfpc.htm

18 Victor Innovatex is an industry-leading fabric design and manufacturing company serving the contract furniture industry. To learn more about them, see their website: www.victor-innovatex.com.

19 McDonough Braungart Design Chemistry, LLC (MBDC), is a product and process design firm dedicated to revolutionizing the design of products and services worldwide. William McDonough and Dr. Michael Braungart founded MBDC in 1995 to promote and shape what they call the "Next Industrial Revolution" through the implementation of eco-effective design principles. For more information see their website: www.mbdc.com/.

20 DesignTex is a design, marketing and distribution company that was acquired by Steelcase in 1988 and is now a member of Steelcase Surfaces Partnership. For more information on DesignTex, see their website: www.dtex.com/about/abt_cohist.htm

21 Rohner Textiles AG is a Swiss textile manufacturer. For more information see: www.climatex.com/en/story/manufacturer/manufacturer_rohner.html

22 Carnegie is a designer and manufacturer of contract textiles for commercial interiors. For more information see: www.carnegiefabrics.com/company/index.htm.

23 Information on Rejuvenation Inc. was provided through a case study prepared by Wayne Rifer in April 2000 for the Oregon Natural Step Network. For more information, contact Duke Castle, Oregon Natural Step Network, 506 SW Sixth Avenue, Suite 1100, Portland, OR 97204 (503) 241-1140. For more information on Rejuvenation, Inc., see their website: www.rejuvenation.com.

24 The Oregon Natural Step Network (ONSN), a project of the Northwest Earth Institute, was formed to support Oregon business, governmental, and educational organizations interested in using The Natural Step (TNS) framework for sustainability. The Network is a membership organization open to interested organizations and individuals. For more information on the ONSN, see their website: www.ortns.org.

25 This quote is attributed to Margaret Mead, noted anthropologist. For more information see Margaret Mead's biography on www.mead2001.org/Biography.htm.

26 From a talk given at The Natural Step national conference in Atlanta, Georgia, in October 2000, by Dr. Betty Sue Flowers. Dr. Flowers is a poet, an editor, a consultant to international corporations, and an author who has collaborated with Bill Moyers to produce four books emerging from several of Moyers' PBS television series. Flowers is one of 41 academics recognized for their personal commitment to motivating students and their outstanding contributions to the teaching profession. Her talk is available on video and CD and can be ordered through The Natural Step office in San Francisco. Their website is: www.naturalstep.org.

27 Zander, Rosamund Stone and Benjamin Zander, *The Art of Possibility, Transforming Professional and Personal Life*, Boston, Massachusettes, Harvard Business School Press, 2001, pp. 10-11.

28 Ibid., p. 10.

29 Ibid., p. 13.

30 Ibid., pp. 52-53. Adaptation.

9. The Evolutionary Dance

1 Armstrong, Lance, op. cit., p. 265.

2 Ibid., p. 273.

3 Ibid.

4 Ibid.

5 Ibid., p. 272.

6 Merriam-Webster Online Dictionary: www.m-w.com/cgi-bin/dictionary

7 Armstrong, Lance, op. cit., p. 271.

References

Allenby, B. "Earth Systems Engineering: The World As Human Artifact," *The Bridge*, National Academy of Engineering, vol. 30, no. 1, (spring 2000). The text of this article is available on the American Society of Civil Engineers Professional Community, Sustainable Development, website www.asce.org/sustainabledev/nae_esewha.cfm.

Anderson, R. *Mid-Course Correction: Toward a Sustainable Enterprise, The Interface Model*. Atlanta, Georgia: Peregrinzilla Press, 1999.

Armstrong, L. (with S. Jenkins). *It's Not About the Bike: My Journey Back to Life*. New York: G.P. Putnam's Sons, 2000.

AtKisson, A. *Believing Cassandra: An Optimist Looks at a Pessimist's World*. Vermont: Chelsea Green Publishing Company, 1999.

Atlee, T. "The Power of Story — the Story of Paradigm," The Co-Intelligence Institute. www.co-intelligence.org/I-powerofstory.html, 2001.

Bateson, G. *Mind and Nature: A Necessary Unity*. New York: Bantam Books, 1988.

Bateson, G. "Form, Substance and Difference." A speech delivered in 1970 at The Paintings of F. Michael Wells library and posted on the rawpaint.com website: www.rawpaint.com/library/bateson/formsubstancedifference.html.

Bateson, M. C. *Overlapping Lives*. New York: Random House, 2000.

Benyus, J. M. *Biomimicry: Innovation Inspired by Nature*. New York: William Morrow, 1997.

Berlin, I. *Let's Face the Music and Dance*, music and lyrics, 1936.

Berry, W. "The New Story." *In Context*, no.12, (winter 1985/86). The text of this article is available on the *In Context* web-site at: www.context.org/ICLIB/IC12/TOC12.htm.

British Columbia, Government of, "The British Columbia Climate Change Business Plan." The text of the business plan can be down-loaded in pdf format on the government website: http://wlap-www.gov.bc.ca/air/climate/ccbuspln.pdf.

Burke, K. "Literature as Equipment for Living." *The Critical Tradition: Classic Texts and Contemporary Trends*, ed. David H. Richter. New York: St. Martin's Press, 1989.

Capra, F. *Uncommon Wisdom: Conversations with Remarkable People*. New York: Bantam Books, 1989.

Collier, R. "Mourning Coffee," *San Francisco Chronicle*. 20 May, 2001.

Dicum, G. and N. Luttinger, *The Coffee Book: Anatomy of an Industry from Crop to Last Drop*. New York: The New Press, 1999.

Elkington, J. *Cannibals with Forks: The Triple Bottom Line of 21st Century Business*. Gabriola Island, B.C.: New Society Publishers, 1998.

Encarta World English Dictionary. New York: St. Martin's Press, 1999.

Fairley, J. R. "Ianu's Dance." *Leadership Fables*. The text of this story is available on the Links Learning website: http://www.limetech.com/links/Superintendents/1_Leadership/ 1_Leadership_Fables/1_Audio_Stories/3_Ianus_Dance, 2001.

Gallopin, G., A. Hammond, P. Raskin, and R. Swart. *Branch Points: Global Scenarios and Human Choice*. A resource paper of the Global Scenario Group, Stockholm, Sweden, Stockholm Environment Institute,1997.

Gladwell, M. *The Tipping Point: How Little Things Can Make a Big Difference*. Boston, Mass.: Little, Brown and Company, 2000.

Good, J. "Coffee." University of Minnesota, Twin Cities University Libraries, James Ford Bell Library on-line library resources: www.bell.lib.umn.edu/Products/coffee.html, 2001.

Haines, S. G. *The Complete Guide to Systems Thinking and Learning*. Amherst, Mass.: HRD Press, Inc., 2000.

Hawken, P. *The Ecology of Commerce: A Declaration of Sustainability*. New York: Harper Business, 1993.

Hawken, P., A. Lovins, and L. H. Lovins. *Natural Capitalism*. New York: Little,

Brown and Company, 1999.

Holling, C.S. (ed.). *Adaptive Environmental Assessment and Management*, vol.3. International Series, on Applied Systems Analysis. Toronto: John Wiley & Sons, 1980.

Katz, D. *Just Do It: The Nike Spirit in the Corporate World*. Holbrook, Mass.: Adams Publishing, 1994.

Korzybski, A. *Science and Sanity*, 5th edition. Lakeville, Conn.: The International Non-Aristotelian Library Publishing Company, 1958.

"The Legend of Wountie." Native Lore Index, 2001. The text of this legend is available on the Native Lore Index website: www.ilhawaii.net/~stony/lore15.html.

Lloyd, M. and L. Fadel. "The Shadow of Globalization, the Coffee Connection." *Boston Globe*, 29 May 2001.

Macy, J. "The Great Turning." *Resurgence Magazine*, Devon, England, Resurgence 186, Jan-Feb, 1998. The text for this article can be found on the Resurgence website: www.gn.apc.org/resugence/186/macy186.htm.

Macy, J. "The Great Turning: Reflections on Our Moment in History." *Earth Light Magazine*. Oakland, California. (The text of the article can be found on the EarthLight website at: www.earthlight.org/jmacyessay.html.)

Mazza, P. "To Make Our Lives a Better Story: From Fragmentation to the Unity of Mind and Nature." *Cascadia Planet Webzine:* Feb. 19, 1997. www.tnews.com/text/unity.html.

McKee, R. *Story: Substance, Structure, Style, and the Principles of Screenwriting.* New York: Harper Collins, 1997.

Meadows, D. "Places to Intervene in a System." *Whole Earth Magazine*, (winter, 1997). The text of this article can be found on the Whole Earth website: www.wholeearthmag.com/ArticleBin/109.html.

Medem Sanjuán, J. "The Role of Engineers in Sustainable Development." A speech delivered at the FIDIC 2000 Conference: Sustainability, the challenge of the new millennium, Honolulu, Hawaii, September 2000. Text of the speech can be found on the FIDIC website at: www.fidic.org/conference/ 2000/talks/monday/medem/default.asp.

Melville, H. *Moby Dick*. New York: Bantam Books, 1981.

Mountain Agenda. *Mountains of the World: Tourism and Sustainable Mountain Development*. Price, M., Wachs, T., and Byers, E. (editors). Prepared for the United Nations Commission on Sustainable Development, Institute of Geography, University of Berne (Centre for Development and Environment) and Swiss Agency for Development and Cooperation. Paul Haupt AG Berne, 1999. The text for this document is available on the Mountain Forum website: www.mtnforum.org/resources/library/magen99a.htm.

Nattrass, B. and M. Altomare. *The Natural Step for Business: Wealth, Ecology and the Evolutionary Corporation*. Gabriola Island, B.C.: New Society Publishers, 1999.

Nike, Inc. *Corporate Responsibility Report*. Beaverton, Oregon, 2001. The text of this report can be viewed on line and be downloaded from: www.nikebiz. com/reporting/index.shtml.

North American Commission for Environmental Cooperation. *The North American Mosaic: A State of the Environment Report*, Montreal, 2002. The text of this document is available at: www.cec.org/soe/index.

Oxfam America. "Oxfam and Cambridge City Council honor fair trade coffee" (press release), May, 2001. The text of the press release is available on the Oxfam America website: www.oxfamamerica.org/ news/prel_fairtradeday.html.

Quinn, D. *Ishmael*. New York: Bantam Books, 1993.

Rees, W., and M. Wackernagel. *Our Ecological Footprint: Reducing Human Impact on the Earth*. Gabriola Island, B.C.: New Society Publishers, 1996.

Resort Municipality of Whistler. *Whistler 2002*. Whistler, B.C., 2000. A copy of this document is available on the RMOW website: www.whistler.net/rmow/reading.

Resort Municipality of Whistler. "Whistler Environmental Strategy." The text of the executive summary of the Whistler Environmental Strategy is available on the website of the Resort Municipality of

Whistler, reading room: www.whistler.net/rmow/reading.

Resort Municipality of Whistler. "Whistler Sustainability Symposium proceedings." Whistler, B.C., December 2000. A copy of this document is available on the RMOW website at: www.awarewhistler.org/sustainability/seminarproceedings.pdf.

Robèrt, K. H., Schmidt-Bleek, B., Aloisi de Larderel, J., Basile, G., Jansen, J. L., Kuehr, R., Price-Thomas, P., Suzuki, M., Hawken, P., and Wackernagel, M. "Strategic Sustainable Development: Selection, Design and Synergies of Applied Tools." *Journal of Cleaner Production:* Elsevier Science, Ltd., June 10, 2002, 197-214.

Rogers, E. M. *Diffusion of Innovations,* 4th edition. New York: The Free Press, 1995.

Sanders, M.D. and S. Sillers. *I Hope You Dance,* performed by Lee Ann Womack, Universal-MCA Music Publishing, Inc., compact disk, 2000.

Schultz, H. *Pour Your Heart Into It.* New York: Hyperion, 1997.

Srinivasan, T.N. "Living Wage in Poor Countries." This paper is available electronically on Academic Consortium on International Trade website: www.spp.umich.edu/rsie/ acit/ ACITViews.html.

Strong, M. *Where on Earth Are We Going?,* Toronto: Alfred A. Knopf, 2000.

Thompson, D. *Tools for Environmental Management: A Practical Introduction and Guide,* Gabriola Island, BC: New Society Publishers, 2002.

United Nations Development Programme. *Human Development Report 1999.* Oxford: Oxford University Press, 1999. The text of this document is available on the UNDP website: www.undp.org/hdro/99.htm.

United Nations Development Programme. *Human Development Report 2000.* New York: United Nations Publications, 2000, pp.36-38. The text of this document is available on the UNDP website: www.undp.org/hdr2001.

United Nations Environment Programme. "Declaration Of The United Nations Conference On The Human Environment." *Report of the United Nations Conference on the Human Environment,* 21st plenary meeting, Stockholm, June 16, 1972. The text of the declaration can be found on the United Nations Development Programme (UNDP) website at: www.unep.org/ Documents/Default.asp?DocumentID=97&ArticleID=1503.

World Commission on Environment and Development. *Our Common Future.* Oxford: Oxford University Press, 1987.

World Resources Institute, United Nations Development Programme, United Nations Environment Programme, and the World Bank. *World Resources 2000-2001.* Washington, DC: World Resources Institute, 2000.

World Tourism Organization. *Tourism: 2020 Vision, a New Forecast.* World Tourism Organization: Madrid, Spain, 1999.

Worldwatch Institute. *Vital Signs 2001: The Trends that are Shaping Our Future.* New York: W. W. Norton Company, 2001.

World Wildlife Fund International, The UNEP World Conservation Monitoring Centre, Redefining Progress, and the Centre for Sustainability Studies. *Living Planet Report 2000.* London:Banson Production, 2000.

Zander, Rosamund Stone and Benjamin Zander. *The Art of Possibility: Transforming Professional and Personal Life.* Boston, Mass.: Harvard Business School Press, 2001.

Zawinski, Andrena, "Profile of Muriel Rukeyser." *Poetry Magazine.* found on PoetryMagazine.com at www.poetry-magazine.com/archives/1999/oct-nov99/ rukeyser.htm.

Websites:

Academic Consortium on International Trade, www.spp.umich.edu/rsie/acit/ ACITViews.html.

American Society of Civil Engineers Professional Community, Sustainable Development, www.asce.org/sustainabledev.

British Columbia Buildings Corporation, www.bcbc.bc.ca.

British Columbia Climate Change Business Plan, http://wlapwww.gov.bc.ca/air/climate/ccbuspln.pdf.

The Calvert Social Investment Foundation, www.CalvertFoundation.org

Cascadia Planet Webzine, www.tnews.com.

CARE (Cooperative for Assistance and Relief Everywhere), www.care.org.

Carnegie Fabrics, www.carnegiefabrics.com.

Center for Energy and Climate Change, www.energyandclimate.org.

Certified Forest Products Council, www.certifiedwood.org.

CH2M HILL, www.ch2m.com.

CH2M HILL in Canada, www.ch2mhill-canada.com.

Coalition for Environmentally Responsibility Economies (CERES), www.ceres.org.

Conservation International, www.conservation.org.

Dancer's Domain, www.angelfire.com/oh2/chezsarah/bquotes.html.

Dance Page, www.panix.com/~twp/dance.

DesignTex, www.dtex.com/about/abt_cohist.htm.

Encyclopedia Britannica on-line, www.britannica.com.

Environmental Defense Fund, www.environmentaldefense.org.

Ford Foundation, www.fordfound.org.

Global Alliance, www.theglobalalliance.org.

Global Compact, www.unglobalcompact.org.

"Ianu's Dance" www.limetech.com/links/Superintendents/1_Leadership/1_Leadership_Fables/1_Audio_Stories/3_Ianus_Dance.

In Context Journal, www.context.org.

Interface, Inc., www.interfaceinc.com.

International Federation of Consulting Engineers (FIDIC), www.fidic.org.

International Forum on Globalization, www.ifg.org.

International Institute for Sustainable Development, www.iisd.org.

International Program on the Elimination of Child Labor (IPEC), www.ilo.org/public/english/standards/ipec.

Intrawest Corporation, www.intrawest.com.

James Ford Bell Library, University of Minnesota, www.bell.lib.umn.edu.

Resurgence Magazine, www.gn.apc.org/resurgence.

McDonough Braungart Design Chemistry, LLC, www.mbdc.com.

Mountain Forum, www.mtnforum.org.

Native Lore Index, www.ilhawaii.net/~stony/lore15.html.

Nike, www.nike.com

Oxfam America: www.oxfamamerica.org.

Norm Thompson Outfitters, www.normthompson.com.

North American Commission for Environmental Cooperation: www.cec.org/soe/index.

Pew Charitable Trusts, www.pewtrusts.com.

Poetry Magazine.com, www.poetry-magazine.com/archives/1999/oct-nov99/rukeyser.htm.

Population and Community Development Association (PDA), www.pda.or.th.

Rejuvenation Inc., www.rejuvenation.com.

Resort Municipality of Whistler, www.whistler.net/rmow.

Rohner Textiles AG, www.climatex.com/en/story/manufacturer/manufacturer_rohner.html.

Save the Children, www.savethechildren.org.

Squamish Nation, www.squamish.net.

Starbucks Coffee Company, www.starbucks.com.

Stockholm Environment Institute, www.sei.se.

The Natural Step Australia, www.ozemail.com.au/~natstep

The Natural Step Canada, www.naturalstep.ca.

The Natural Step Israel, contact: ecorrect@netvision.net.il

The Natural Step Japan, www.tnsj.org

The Natural Step New Zealand, www.naturalstep.org.nz

The Natural Step South Africa, contact: natstep@iafrica.com

The Natural Step Sweden, www.detnaturligasteget.se/

The Natural Step UK, www.naturalstep.org.uk

The Natural Step US, www.naturalstep.org

TransFair USA, www.transfairusa.org.

United Nations Children's Fund (UNICEF), www.unicef.org.

United Nations Development Programme, www.undp.org.

United Nations Sustainable Development, www.un.org/esa/sustdev/index.html.

U.S. Environmental Protection Agency, Air Quality, website, www.epa.gov.

Victor Innovatex, www.victor-innovatex.com.

Whistler/Blackcomb, www.whistler-black-comb.com.

Whistler It's Our Nature, www.whistlerits-ournature.ca.

Whistler Museum, www.whistlermuseum.org.

Whole Earth Magazine, www.wholeearth-mag.com.

World Business Council for Sustainable Development, www.wbscd.org.

World Resources Institute, www.wri.org.

World Vision, www.wvi.org.

World Wildlife Fund, Climate Savers, www.worldwildlife.org/climate.

Index

Numbers following the letter "n" refer to endnotes, with chapter numbers in superscript where needed. Numbers in italics refer to figures.

Index of authors and company representatives

About the Authors

D R. BRIAN NATTRASS AND MARY ALTOMARE are internationally recognized authorities on the strategy, learning, and implementation of sustainable business practices and corporate responsibility. They alternate as board members of The Natural Step International (TNSi) in Stockholm, and are co-founders of the Western Institute for Sustainable Development & Management (WISDM) in collaboration with Simon Fraser University in Vancouver. Nattrass and Altomare are the authors of one of the leading books on business and sustainability, *THE NATURAL STEP FOR BUSINESS: Wealth, Ecology and the Evolutionary Corporation*. They advise Fortune 500 companies, municipalities, and various levels of government across the United States and Canada on their paths to sustainability.

Prior to dedicating himself to corporate responsibility and sustainable development, **Dr. Nattrass** had a twenty-year career in corporate law and finance. He practised commercial law for over a decade, was CEO of a high-tech public company for five years, and is the principle author of Canada's first book on corporate finance for the entrepreneur, *Raising Money: The Canadian Guide to Successful Business Finance*. He is a member of the Law Societies of Alberta and British Columbia.

Mary Altomare has been instrumental in helping to define the strategic vision for dozens of organizations throughout North America, Central America, and Europe, and coaching them through successful change initiatives. Her recognized skills in program and project design, curriculum development and delivery, and personal and strategic coaching have helped dozens of organizations accelerate their progress towards sustainability. She has held senior administrative positions at Yale and Duke universities.

Both live in Sea-to-Sky country on the west coast of British Columbia where they enjoy being close to nature in one of the most beautiful places on Earth.

To further the dialogue about sustainable business practices and corporate responsibility, you can contact Dr. Brian Nattrass and Mary Altomare via e-mail at: innostrat@aol.com.

If you have enjoyed *Dancing with the Tiger*, you might enjoy other

BOOKS TO BUILD A NEW SOCIETY

Our books provide positive solutions for people who want
to make a difference. We specialize in:

• Conscientious Commerce • Progressive Leadership
• Sustainable Living • Ecological Design and Planning
• Natural Building & Appropriate Technology • New Forestry
• Educational and Parenting Resources • Environment and Justice
• Resistance and Community • Nonviolence

New Society Publishers

ENVIRONMENTAL BENEFITS STATEMENT

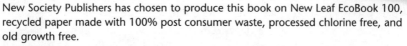

New Society Publishers has chosen to produce this book on New Leaf EcoBook 100,
recycled paper made with 100% post consumer waste, processed chlorine free, and
old growth free.

For every 5,000 books printed, New Society saves the following resources:[1]

38	Trees
3,424	Pounds of Solid Waste
3,767	Gallons of Water
4,914	Kilowatt Hours of Electricity
6,224	Pounds of Greenhouse Gases
27	Pounds of HAPs, VOCs, and AOX Combined
9	Cubic Yards of Landfill Space

---

[1]Environmental benefits are calculated based on research done by the Environmental Defense Fund and
other members of the Paper Task Force who study the environmental impacts of the paper industry.

For more information on this environmental benefits statement, or to inquire about environmentally
friendly papers, please contact New Leaf Paper – info@newleafpaper.com Tel: 888 • 989 • 5323.

For a full list of NSP's titles, please call **1-800-567-6772** *or check out our web site at:*

www.newsociety.com

NEW SOCIETY PUBLISHERS